A DREAMSPEAKER CR
VOLUME

# The Broughtons

## AND VANCOUVER ISLAND— KELSEY BAY TO PORT HARDY

### NEW, REVISED SECOND EDITION

ANNE & LAURENCE YEADON-JONES

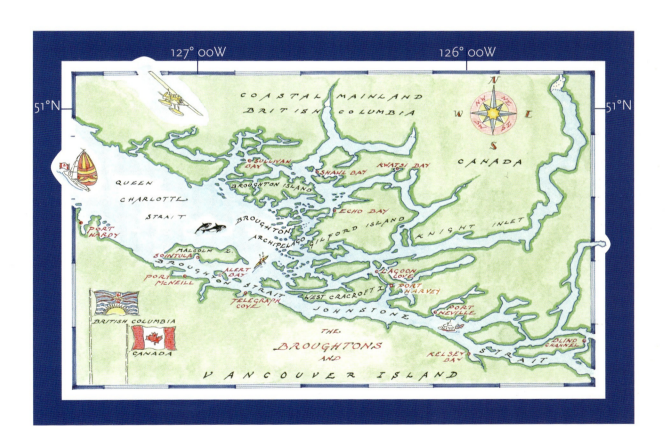

**HARBOUR PUBLISHING**
*www.harbourpublishing.com*

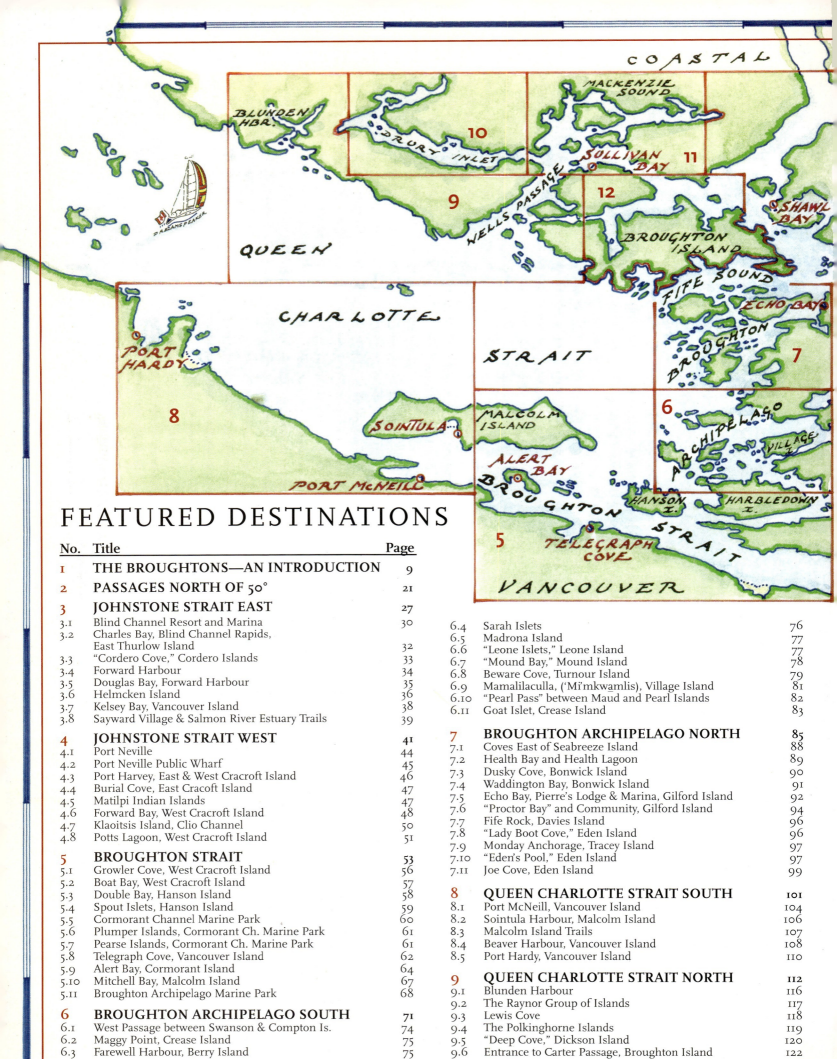

# FEATURED DESTINATIONS

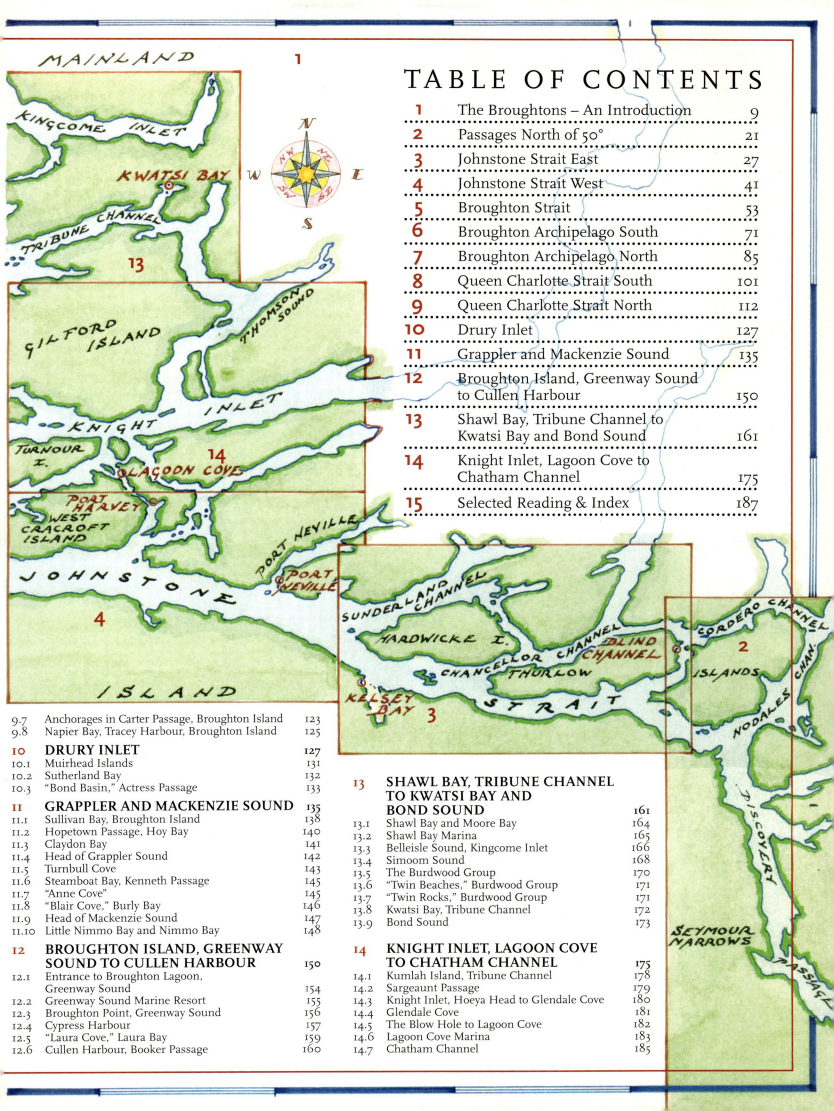

# TABLE OF CONTENTS

Cover: Dreamspeaker *in front of "Lacy Falls,"*
*Tribune Channel*

Second edition, copyright © 2016 Anne and Laurence Yeadon-Jones. First edition
  copyright the authors © 2006.
Photographs and illustrations copyright © 2006 and 2016 by Laurence Yeadon-
  Jones, except as noted.

1 2 3 4 5 — 20 19 18 17 16

Harbour Publishing Co. Ltd.
P.O. Box 219
Madeira Park, BC
V0N 2H0
www.harbourpublishing.com

Edited by Ariel Brewster
Proofread by Patricia Wolfe
Composition by Mary White
Printed and bound in China

## WE WOULD LIKE TO HEAR FROM YOU!

We hope you enjoyed using Volume 5 of *A Dreamspeaker Cruising Guide.*

We welcome your comments, suggestions, corrections and any ideas about what you would like to see in future editions of the guide(s). Please drop us a line at Harbour (address at right; c/o *Dreamspeaker*), send an email to info@harbourpublishing.com or email the authors at info@dreamspeakerguides.com.

Harbour Publishing acknowledges financial support from the Government of Canada
through the Book Publishing Industry Development Program and the Canada
Council for the Arts, and from the Province of British Columbia through the British
Columbia Arts Council and the Book Publisher's Tax Credit through the Ministry of
Provincial Revenue.

Cataloguing data available from Library and Archives Canada
ISBN 978-1-55017-713-8

*Caution:* This book is meant to provide experienced boaters with cruising information about the waters covered. The suggestions offered are not all-inclusive and, due to the possibility of differences of interpretation, oversights and factual errors, none of the information contained in this book is warranted to be accurate or appropriate for any purpose other than the pursuit of great adventuring and memorable voyages. *A Dreamspeaker Cruising Guide* should be viewed as a guide only and not as a substitute for official government charts, tide and current tables, coast pilots, sailing directions and local notices to boaters. Excerpts from charts are for passage planning only and are not to be used for navigation. Shoreline plans are not to scale and are not to be used for navigation. The publisher and authors cannot accept any responsibility for misadventure resulting from the use of this guide and can accept no liability for damages incurred.

# FOREWORD

## *Dreaming of the Broughtons*

The Broughton Islands comprise the vast cruising area of British Columbia that lies between the east coast of Vancouver Island and the mainland inlets. It stretches north from about Kelsey Bay to the top end of Queen Charlotte Strait. Except for the narrow, well-travelled thoroughfare of Johnstone Strait and Queen Charlotte Strait – part of the famed Inside Passage route – it is a remote section of the coast. Due to its distance from the major economic and population centres, it remains little touched by industry or settlement. It is an area of pristine beauty where cruising boats can have an anchorage all to themselves for as long as they like. It is an area so jam-packed with winding waterways and places to explore that one could spend a lifetime simply poking about. It's also home to some of BC's more interesting destination marinas peopled by some of the province's true characters who will provide plenty of down-home hospitality and make your stay unforgettable. There is also a strong First Nations heritage, evidenced by the area's ancient pictographs, old and new villages and totems.

In this, the fifth *A Dreamspeaker Cruising Guide,* authors Anne and Laurence Yeadon-Jones have done an admirable job of trying to sort out this amazingly complex area and have done so in a way that makes it clear and accessible. This is no easy mission, and few other cruising guide authors have attempted such a daunting project. Not only have they tackled the Broughton Islands, they've also included cruising information to the east coast of Vancouver Island and the adjacent mainland inlets – a task that is almost as complex as the Broughtons.

As with their previous guides, the Yeadon-Joneses have a passion for the areas they write about and their text captures their enthusiasm and inspires the reader. The large format of the *Dreamspeaker* guides allows for numerous photos, plenty of text and Laurence's delightful and detailed hand-drawn maps. Together, the elements combine in a beautiful package that has a warm and inviting feel, but is also full of with important cruising information.

Peter A. Robson
Former Editor, *Pacific Yachting* magazine

*The Authors,* Dreamspeaker *and* Tink *in Sullivan Bay*

### SPECIAL THANKS TO:

**Corilair**, for their efficient floatplane service between Vancouver Island and the Broughtons, www.corilair.com

### GRATEFUL APPRECIATION TO OUR INDUSTRY SUPPORT:

HUB International Insurance Brokers, Specialist Marine Insurance — www.HUBmarine.ca

C-Tow, Marine Assistance Network — www.c-tow.ca

Beta Marine Canada, powering *Dreamspeaker*'s explorations — www.betamarinecanada.com

Helly Hansen, Lifestyle and sailing gear to the Dreamspeaker Team — www.hellyhansen.com

### ACKNOWLEDGEMENTS

Rob Hare at Canadian Hydrographic Service (CHS), for his assistance.

Bruce Jackman, North Island Marina, for his friendly assistance in locating aerial information.

The island and coastal people for their time and encouragement while researching this guide.

Peter Robson for his insightful foreword.

Dorene Gould and John Lopez, for technical assistance and friendship.

Our family and friends, for their conviction that we are still sailing in the right direction.

*DREAMSPEAKER* type SHE 36

| | |
|---|---|
| Length overall | 37' |
| Length on water | 27' |
| Beam | 10.6' |
| Draft | 6.6' |
| Height above water | 50.0' |

### AUTHORS' SAILBOAT

*Dreamspeaker* is a 36-foot SHE, a fibreglass sloop designed by Sparkman and Stephens and built by South Hants Engineering, UK, in 1979. She has a fin keel, draws 6.5 feet and sails like a dream. *Tink*, our faithful dinghy, is a 10-foot Tinker RIB, designed and hand-built by Henshaw Inflatables, UK. The oarlocks and wooden oars make for smooth, easy rowing. Sadly, the design has now been discontinued.

FOR THE BOUNDLESS SPLENDOUR OF THE BROUGHTONS

EXPLORE ITS DELICATE BEAUTY WITH RESPECT AND CARE

*"More boats are going north now, and I am hoping that an increased awareness of the beauty of our coast will bring concern for our environment everywhere."*

—*John Chappell,* Cruising Beyond Desolation Sound, *1987.*

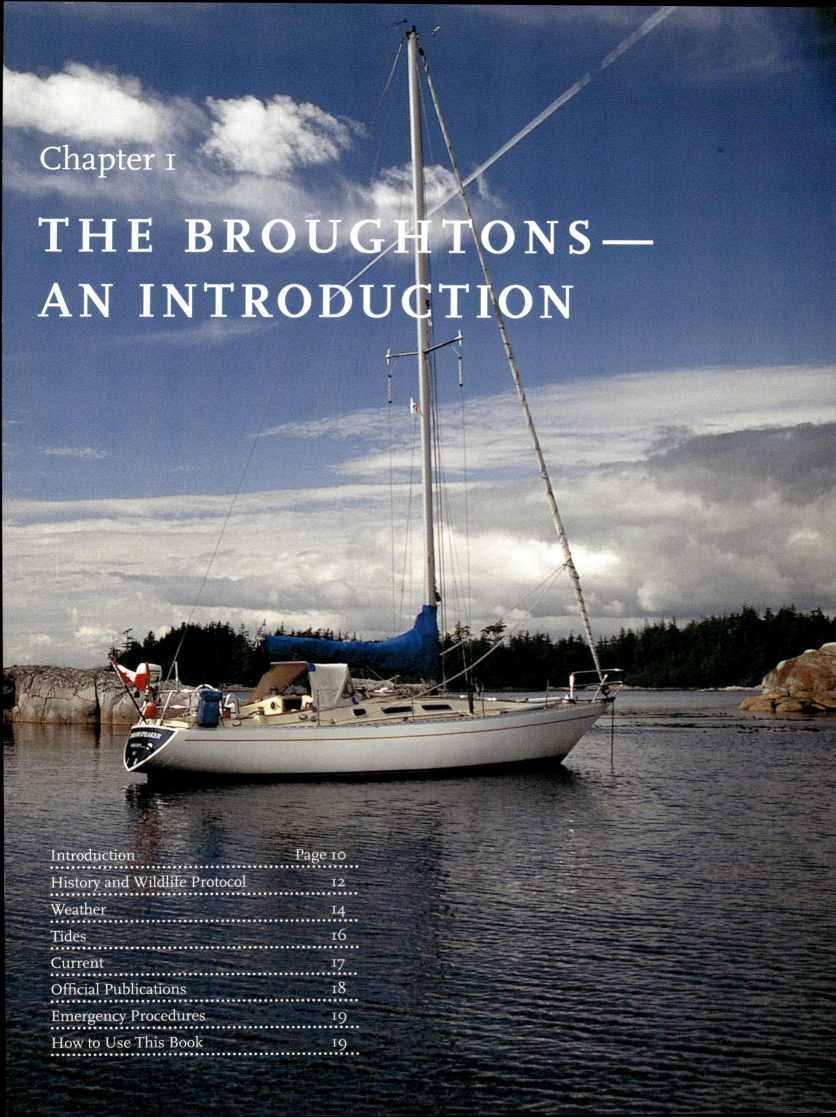

# Chapter 1

# THE BROUGHTONS— AN INTRODUCTION

# Chapter 1
# THE BROUGHTONS — AN INTRODUCTION

### CUSTOMS

Call 1-888-226-7277 (8:30 a.m.–4:30 p.m.) seven days a week. The ports of entry covered by this guide for recreational boaters entering Canadian waters are located in Campbell River at the Coast Marina (250-287-7455) and Discovery Harbour Marina (250-287-2614). Prince Rupert, on the mainland, is the next customs port of entry.

### HOLDING TANKS AND PUMP-OUT STATIONS

No sewage may be discharged in BC waters where there is a pump-out station available. Where there is no facility, strict regulations govern where and when sewage may be discharged into coastal waters. To be compliant, see the Pleasure Craft Sewage Prevention Regulation of the Canada Shipping Act.

*A memorial totem pole in Alert Bay*

NOTE: *All numbers on borders are distances in nautical miles. All depths indicated on illustrated charts are in metres.*

In Canada's Pacific Northwest, mid-coast on British Columbia's vast and intricate coastline, lies a region known simply as the Broughtons. The area hosts British Columbian and Washington State recreational boaters and is fast becoming internationally renowned for its spectacular beauty and abundant wildlife.

On a chart, the Broughtons resemble a complex jigsaw puzzle, the pieces joined by navigable water. This puzzle is really quite simple and comprises three main components:

The coastal mainland anchors the region at 51° north and its backdrop of snow-capped mountains is deeply indented by sounds, channels and sinuous inlets.

"The Village of Islands" – the Broughton Archipelago – is a maze of islands and islets with a plethora of anchorages and one-boat hideaways. Family-run marinas offer fuelling, moorage and provisioning facilities, allowing boaters to intersperse their quiet explorations with a night or two of socializing with friends or new acquaintances. Enjoy the local trails, happy-hour gatherings, communal potluck suppers and the convenience of hot showers and laundry facilities.

Northern Vancouver Island's mountainous backbone forms a rain shadow and natural breakwater from the Pacific Ocean, shielding the Broughtons and creating a gentle and temperate raincoast paradise.

Cruising boaters will find that it's as much an adventure getting there as it is exploring the area's unspoiled wilderness and rich diversity of birds and wildlife. Take your time while cruising through the Broughtons to uncover the coast's 12,000 years of history, from the ancient white-shell midden beaches and clam gardens of the Kwakiutl First Nations to the first European settlers.

# KEY DESTINATIONS—EAST TO WEST

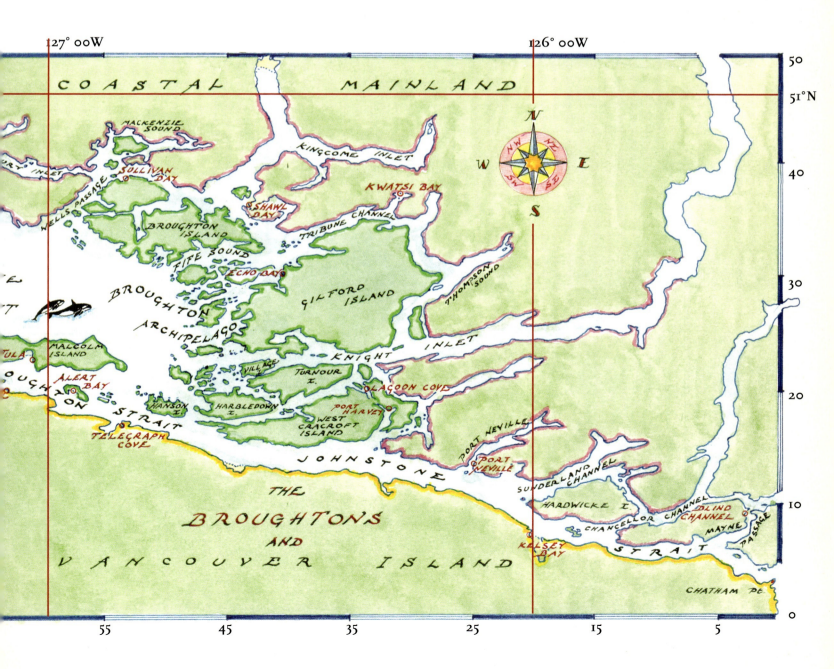

# HISTORY AND WILDLIFE PROTOCOL

Canoe Shaped Serving Dish by
Sam Charlie, given to Bill

The proliferation of white-shell midden beaches in the Broughton Archipelago give evidence to the large population of First Nations (Kwakiutl) people that lived in the area over 10,000 years ago. About 4,000 years ago, more than 20,000 indigenous people lived in the region between Blunden Harbour and Broken Islands.

Local fisherman and environmentalist Bill Proctor, who has called the Broughton neighbourhood home for over 70 years, knows of over 200 village sites where larger villages were populated by as many as 400 people. Daily activities for the men included fishing, hunting, building canoes, carving totem poles from cedar tree trunks, and constructing homes and ceremonial houses using cedar planks and split cedar boards. Women took care of gathering food, smoking fish and game, managing family and home activities and producing clothing from soft cedar bark.

British explorer Capt. James Cook, along with Spanish explorers Dionisio Alcala Galiano and Cayetano Valdes, were the first European explorers to discover and investigate the Inside Passage of the Pacific Northwest in the late 1770s. A follow-up British expedition to claim the Pacific Northwest for the Crown was led by Capt. George Vancouver; while surveying the region in HMS *Chatham* during the early 1790s, he named Broughton Strait and Broughton Archipelago for Lt. Commander William Robert Broughton, who was responsible for conducting the survey.

During the early to mid-1800s, trade with First Nation communities was significant (especially the trade of otter furs), although after the devastating 1870s smallpox epidemic the coastal indigenous population declined by more than 60 percent. During the late 1800s and early 1900s, a large number of European settlers moved to the area and introduced farming, logging, fishing and mining; we see evidence of these occupations today in the remains of homesteads and farms, ruins of logging operations and canning factories, and abandoned mines.

## PETROGLYPHS AND PICTOGRAPHS

Petroglyphs, or ancient First Nations rock carvings, are pictures carved into rocks and cliffs, while pictographs are rock paintings using natural dyes made from roots and berries. According to Beth Hill's *Rock Carvings of the Pacific Northwest*, both include a variety of images from "mythological animals made with flowing, curving lines, to flat fish and birds and little human stick figures in a brittle dance," which give us an insight into the prehistoric world of the indigenous people in the Pacific Northwest. Please respect these ancient sites, which are often found on private property and require prior permission to visit. In this volume, the accessible, recorded sites can be found in Forward Harbour, Port Neville Narrows, Robber's Knob, Port Neville, Fort Rupert and Lizard Point, Malcolm Island. (See Selected Readings, Beth Hill's *Rock Carvings of the Pacific Northwest* and Judith Williams' *Two Wolves at the Dawn of Time*.)

*The delightful pen-and-ink drawings on these pages have been kindly provided by artist Yvonne Maximchuk, and appear in* Full Moon, Flood Tide *by Bill Proctor and Yvonne Maximchuk.*

*Yvonne is a working artist and teacher, proficient in watercolour and acrylic media as well as drawing and pottery techniques. She is also a naturalist and avid gardener and offers art retreats at SeaRose Studio on Gilford Island, her seaside home with an abundant coastal garden and fabulous view. Visit her website at: www.yvonnemaximchuk.com.*

### ANCIENT SHELL MIDDENS AND CLAM GARDENS OR TERRACES

**M**ost Native villages were built above large clam beaches, in good, sunny spots, and shell middens were formed over thousands of years as clams were harvested and the shells were deposited on the beaches. Clam gardens or terraces, however, were well-tended clam beaches protected by a ring of rocks piled along the low-tide perimeter, often with a clear space left for landing canoes. These gardens often served a dual purpose during herring season, when hemlock boughs were used to trap quantities of these nutritious fish between the rocks. There are over 300 recorded sites in the Broughton Archipelago, and numerous other sites – from Orcas Island in Washington State to as far north as Sitka, Alaska – have also been documented. Evidence shows that these clam gardens may be totally unique in the world. (See Selected Reading, Bill Proctor, *Full Moon, Flood Tide* and Judith Williams' *Clam Gardens: Aboriginal Mariculture on Canada's West Coast*.)

### CULTURALLY MODIFIED TREES

**C**ulturally Modified Trees (CMTs) are large, old red cedar trees that the First Nations people flattened off on one side to split off boards usually three feet wide and about four inches thick to use in the construction of their villages. – Bill Proctor, *Full Moon, Flood Tide*.

### WILDLIFE PROTOCOL: GRIZZLY AND BLACK BEARS

"**B**ears are most active before 10 a.m. and after 4 p.m., and they tend to bed down during the middle of the day. When walking in bear country, always be alert and look out for bear signs, and always make a bit of noise so as not to startle a bear. Bears have very poor eyesight but they have a good nose. If the wind is at your back, most bears will smell you and be gone before you ever see them. Don't ever think that you can outrun a bear, don't try to feed one and don't ever get between a mother and her cub," (Bill Proctor, *Full Moon, Flood Tide*). The owners of Kwatsi Bay Marina advise visitors to take along a fog- or air horn when hiking in the area. They have found that this is one of the most effective ways to let bears know that you are around. For more detailed information on bear safety visit the WSPA (World Society for the Protection of Animals) at www.wspa.ca.

CMT– Burdwood Group

### WILDLIFE PROTOCOL: WHALES, PORPOISES, DOLPHINS, SEALS, SEA LIONS AND BIRDS ON LAND

**A**s the number of visiting boats increases, the need to minimize our impact on marine animals and birdlife is imperative, and regulations in Canada and the US prohibit any harassment or disturbance. This includes the interference with an animal's ability to hunt, feed, communicate, socialize, rest, breed and care for its young. Try to stay at least 100 metres away from any marine mammals or birds.

Reduce speed to less than 7 knots when within 400 metres of whales. Avoid abrupt course changes, and limit your viewing time to a maximum of 30 minutes. If possible, do not approach whales from the front or behind – always approach or leave from the side, moving in a direction parallel to their direction. Stay on the offshore side of any whales when they are travelling close to shore, and remain at least 200 metres offshore at all times. For more detailed information, visit www.nmfs.noaa.gov/pr/education/viewing.htm.

# WEATHER

*A weather front passes over Forward Harbour at dawn*

There are only two marine forecast areas that cover the Broughton region east to west: Johnstone Strait and Queen Charlotte Strait.

Marine forecasts and warnings are available in the Broughton region as continuous marine broadcasts on the following VHF Channel frequencies – WX1: 162.55 Weather Channel 1, Alert Bay.

Call the following continuous marine weather recordings:
Vancouver – 604-666-3655
Comox – 250-339-9861
Campbell River – 250-286-3575
Port Hardy – 250-949-7148

For further information on weather products and services visit Environment Canada at www.weatheroffice.ec.gc.ca.

Environment Canada West Coast Weather Publications
*Mariners Guide: West Coast Marine Weather Services.*
*Marine Weather Hazards Manual – West Coast: A Guide to Local Forecasts and Conditions.*
*The Wind Came All Ways*, by Owen Lange.

*Note: at the start of each chapter, the relevant forecast area and observation sites are listed.*

S ummer weather from mid-June to mid-September begins with the Pacific High anchoring itself off the northern tip of Vancouver Island. This high-pressure system, which brings clear skies, sunshine and westerly winds, could arrive mid-May; however, it could also arrive in late July.

Bad weather is associated with low pressure, rain, overcast skies and easterly winds. Depending on the strength of the high, the good weather and bad weather are cyclical.

**MARINE FORECAST ISSUE TIMES:**

0400. 1030. 1600 & 2130. Issue times remain the same throughout the year.

**MARINE WARNINGS:**

| | |
|---|---|
| Small Craft Warning | 20–33 knots |
| Gale Warning | 34–47 knots |
| Storm Warning | 48–63 knots |
| Hurricane Force Wind Warning | 64 knots or more |

*Note: The "Small-Craft Warning" means just that – winds forecast at between 20 and 30 knots can be hazardous to small craft.*

**WIND:** The prevailing summer winds are westerly – anywhere from SW to WNW. These westerly winds are strongest as the high-pressure ridge approaches, and can blow continuously for weeks at a time in the early summer, tapering off in July and August.

Westerly winds that begin as a sea breeze at around noon in Queen Charlotte Strait will often increase in force to 15–20 knots until early evening, dying off completely near sundown. This afternoon breeze increases as it moves into Johnstone Strait, accelerated by the topography of the strait. These winds will often reach 25–30 knots off Chatham Point by late evening. Westerly winds usually become light during the early morning hours.

Easterly winds are not as predictable when accompanied by a low-pressure front or cyclonic disturbance. This is hunkering-down weather with overcast skies, rain and unstable winds ending in gale-force gusts.

**WAVES:** Ocean swells from the open Pacific Ocean may be encountered in Queen Charlotte Strait. These swells are usually from the northwest and generally are not a hazard in themselves. Hazardous wave action in this region develops as a result of the wind interacting with the tidal current. It's best to travel when the winds are in the same direction as the current. (See Current, page 17.)

Summer weather in the Broughtons can be glorious, and locals will wax lyrically about "another beautiful day in paradise." However, it is good to remember that daytime conditions are generally five degrees cooler than in Desolation Sound. Water temperatures are also much colder, and usually not conducive to a leisurely swim!

Following is a list of average summer air temperatures recorded at Alert Bay:

| May | 10.4°C (50.6°F) |
|-----|-----------------|
| June | 12.5°C (54.5°F) |
| July | 14.1°C (57.1°F) |
| August | 14.4°C (58°F) |

*The sunset after-glow reflects on the mirror-calm waters of Tracey Harbour*

**FOG:** Fog is a common occurrence in the summer months. The relatively warm, moist westerly wind over the cool water creates fog, which forms in Queen Charlotte Strait and is then funnelled eastward into the sounds, channels, passages and inlets. On most days, this fog will burn off and clear around noon. Fog can become a navigational hazard, especially in busy Johnstone Strait. Refrain from venturing into poor visibility if fog is forecast or you see it silently moving in; it's best to seek refuge before it envelops your boat and threatens visibility.

**RAIN:** The Broughton region is known as the raincoast for good reason, and the area receives its fair share of rainfall during the fall, winter and spring months. Although summer is the driest season with glorious days of sunshine and blue skies, precipitation is still part of the weather package, so be prepared.

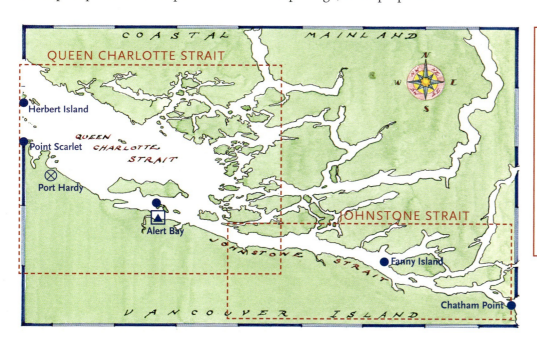

West Coast Marine Weather Forecast Areas and Observation Sites

KEY:

- - - - Marine Forecast Areas

● Marine Weather Reporting Station

▲ WeatherRadio 1
WX1 162.59 MHz

⊗ WeatherRadio Canada
103.70 MHz

# TIDES
## *(The Vertical Movement of Water)*

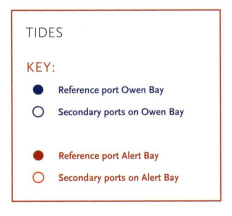

Low water exposes the rock in "Pearl Passage," Broughton Archipelago

Refer to *Canadian Tide and Current Tables, Volume 6.* Published annually.

*Note:* At the start of each chapter we list the reference and secondary ports that are within – or influence – the area covered. The chart below indicates the approximate position of the reference and secondary ports.

Tide tables contain essential navigational information and must be acquired prior to venturing into these waters. A working knowledge of the tides and currents, and their interplay with the wind, is fundamental to safe navigation in this region.

Tides and current, although interlinked, are two quite different variables to be considered in passage planning and navigation.

Tide, the vertical movement of water, will rise (flood) or fall (ebb). Their height on Canadian charts is calculated upon chart datum. Current, the horizontal movement of water, is directionally defined and its speed calculated in knots.

The tidal range (low, low water to high, high water) in the Broughton region is significant. A 4.5-m (15-ft) range is common on a large or spring tide, with the highest tides occurring near full moon. These tidal ranges gradually become less on the monthly cycle, then build again. Tides are semidiurnal, having two highs and two lows each day. The ability to calculate the depth under your boat's keel accurately is important for safe passages and when anchoring overnight.

In general the flooding tide creates an easterly current and the ebbing tide a westerly current; however, be aware that due to the maze of channels, the current may flow in quite different directions locally.

### TIDES

KEY:

● Reference port Owen Bay

○ Secondary ports on Owen Bay

● Reference port Alert Bay

○ Secondary ports on Alert Bay

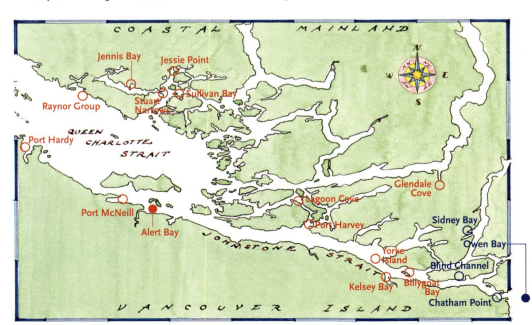

# CURRENT
## (The Horizontal Movement of Water)

Refer to *Canadian Tide and Current Tables, Volume 6*. Published annually.

*Note: At the start of each chapter we list the reference current stations and secondary current stations that are within – or influence – the area covered. The chart below indicates the approximate positions of the reference and secondary current stations.*

It is essential to be able to calculate the time of slack water, the direction and strength of the current and to be aware of the locations where current may pose a hazard to navigation.

*A whirlpool in Current Passage off Helmcken Island*

**D**ue to the large tidal range, the currents in the Broughton region are generally strong. From 2–3 knots in Queen Charlotte Strait, the current increases eastward as water is funnelled into Broughton Strait and Johnstone Strait. In the inlets, passages, sounds and channels, 4–5 knots is not uncommon. Rapid water of 5–7 knots can be found in the restricted passages and narrows and turbulent water may be present. Very swift currents of 6–10 knots (or more) will be found in charted rapids, and turbulent water will be present in the form of upwellings, eddies and whirlpools. It is always best to time transiting rapids at slack water.

Strong currents and rapid turbulent water present hazards in and of themselves, but when they are combined with moderate to strong opposing wind, this creates steep, choppy waves – extremely hazardous to small craft. Johnstone Strait is infamous for what's known locally as the "devil's cauldron" – when westerly winds of 20–30 knots (or more) oppose an ebbing current.

**CAUTIONARY NOTE:** *Times of slack water (turns) at the rapids may differ significantly from the times of shore-side high and low water. For the safety of boat and crew, it is of paramount importance to be able to read and interpolate the tide and current tables accurately.*

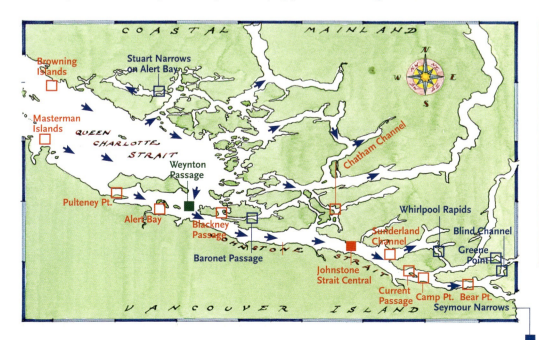

### West Coast Marine Current

**KEY:**

- ■ Reference Station Seymour Narrows
- □ Secondary Station on Seymour Narrows
- ■ Reference Station Johnstone Strait Central
- □ Secondary Station on Johnstone Strait Central
- ■ Reference Station Weynton Passage
- → Current Direction on a Flood Tide

# OFFICIAL PUBLICATIONS

## CHARTS AND NAUTICAL PUBLICATIONS

We have carefully designed this cruising guide to work in conjunction with the publications, and above each destination we have referenced the appropriate charts required.

For their safety, all operators of ships and boats are required to have official, up-to-date charts and publications on board that cover the area they are navigating. These charts can be referenced from *Pacific Coast Catalogue, Nautical Charts and Related Publications* – Canadian Hydrographic Service (CHS), and are available at any chart dealer, free of charge. Visit www.charts.gc.ca.

Individual charts are the primary tools used by professional mariners and boaters, and those referenced below will cover the entire area included in this volume (Volume 5):

## ELECTRONIC CHARTS

Electronic charts are either raster (a simple electronic image of the paper charts) or vector (with additional information not available in paper or raster charts). Most manufacturers of charting software are licensed to use CHS chart data in their digital products. While CHS does not sell charts directly to the public, they distribute through a very large dealer network. Monthly updates to the charts are included with a licence. For more information, visit www.charts.gc.ca.

*Note: In almost all cases, up-to-date paper charts and tide tables are still a legal, on-board requirement for all craft in Canadian waters. For the few exceptions, see the chart carriage requirements in the Charts and Nautical Publications Regulations, 1995 of the Canada Shipping Act.*

## APPROACH WAYPOINTS

Approach waypoints are latitude and longitude positions based on NAD 83 and shown in degrees, minutes and decimals of a minute. They are located in deep water from a position where the illustrated features will be readily discernible in daylight.

## PUBLICATIONS

We recommend the following publications to accompany your copy of *A Dreamspeaker Cruising Guide, Volume 5*. For further reading, consult the Selected Reading list on p. 188.

## NAUTICAL PUBLICATIONS

*Canadian Tide and Current Tables, Volume 6: Discovery Passage and West Coast of Vancouver Island* (updated annually)
*Symbols and Abbreviations, Terms – Chart 1*, as used on Canadian Charts
*Pacific Coast List of Lights, Buoys and Fog Signals*
*Sailing Directions – British Columbia Coast* (South Portion)
*Boating Safety Publications*, Canadian Coast Guard
*The Canadian Aids to Navigation System: Marine Navigation Services Directorate*
*Protecting British Columbia's Aquatic Environment: A Boater's Guide*

*Pulteney Point Light on the west tip of Malcolm Island*

## CHARTS FOR VOLUME 5, THE BROUGHTONS

3515 – Knight Inlet 80 000
Simoom Sound 20 000

3539 – Discovery Passage 40 000
Seymour Narrows 20 000

3543 – Cordero Channel 40 000
Greene Point Rapids 20 000
Dent and Yuculta Rapids 20 000

3544 – Johnstone Strait, Race and
Current Passage 25 000

3545 – Johnstone Strait, Port Neville to
Robson Bight 40 000

3546 – Broughton Strait 40 000
Port McNeill 20 000
Alert Bay 20 000

3547 – Queen Charlotte Strait,
Eastern Portion 40 000
Stuart Narrows 20 000
Kenneth Passage 20 000

3548 – Queen Charlotte Strait, Central
Portion 40 000
Blunden Harbour 15 000
Port Hardy 15 000

3564 – Johnstone Strait
Port Neville 20,000
Havannah Channel and Chatham Channel 20,000
Chatham Channel 10,000

# EMERGENCY PROCEDURES

**THE CANADIAN COAST GUARD** is a multitask organization whose primary role of search and rescue is supported by the following roles: maintaining the Aids to Navigation, operating the Office of Safe Boating and, in association with Environment Canada, the Marine Weather Forecast. For a copy of the *Safe Boating Guide*, call 1-800-267-6687. For search and rescue call:

TELEPHONE:    1-800-567-5111
CELLULAR:        *311
VHF CHANNEL:    16

## EMERGENCY RADIO PROCEDURES

MAYDAY: For immediate danger to life or vessel.

PAN-PAN: For urgency but no immediate danger to life or vessel.

For MAYDAY or PAN-PAN transmit the following on VHF Channel 16 or 2182 kHz.

1. MAYDAY, MAYDAY, MAYDAY (or PAN-PAN, PAN-PAN, PAN-PAN), this is (vessel name and radio call sign).

2. State your position and the nature of the distress.

3. State the number of people on board, and describe the vessel (length, make/type, colour, power or sail and registration number).

NOTE: *If the distress is not life-threatening, the Coast Guard will put out a general call to boaters in your area for assistance. A tow at sea by a commercial operator can be expensive. Check whether your insurance policy adequately covers a marine tow.*

# HOW TO USE THIS BOOK

This sample layout identifies the various features of this cruising guide to give you plenty of information and help you reach your destination safely.

Chapter & featured destination reference
Chapter legend
Destination locator
Approach waypoint latitude & longitude
Tips on best approach & anchorages
Cautionary note

Depth contour (approximate position). Depths reduced to lowest normal tide (zero tide)
Sepia area indicates shoreline that covers & uncovers with the tide
Solid black line indicates HW mark
Green area indicates land above HW mark
Blue area indicates shallower water
White area indicates deeper water that is safe for navigation
Red broken line indicates a safe approach course
✱Asterisk indicates approximate position of approach waypoint
Aerial approach or ambient photograph

*HW: high water*
*LW: low water*

All depths as indicated are in metres.

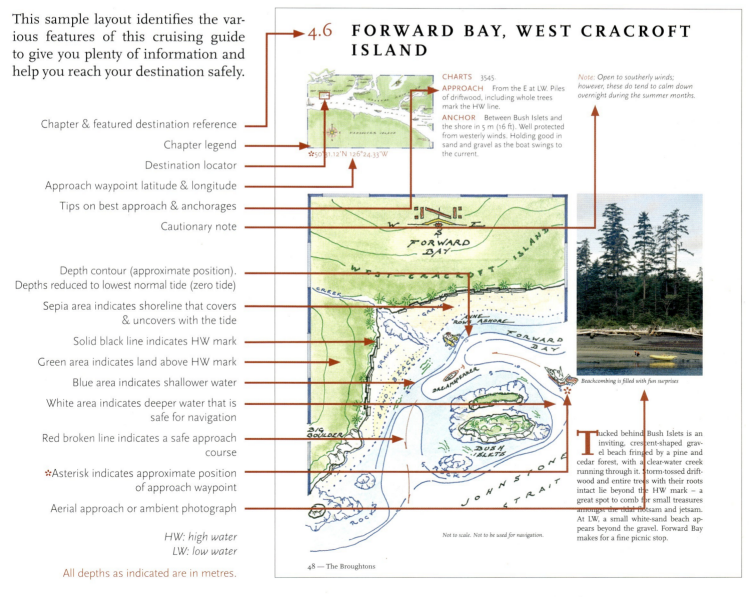

### 4.6  FORWARD BAY, WEST CRACROFT ISLAND

**CHARTS**  3545.
**APPROACH**   From the E at LW. Piles of driftwood, including whole trees mark the HW line.
**ANCHOR**   Between Bush Islets and the shore in 5 m (16 ft). Well protected from westerly winds. Holding good in sand and gravel as the boat swings to the current.

Note: *Open to southerly winds; however, these do tend to calm down overnight during the summer months.*

✱50°31.12'N 126°24.33'W

*Beachcombing is filled with fun surprises*

Tucked behind Bush Islets is an inviting, crescent-shaped gravel beach fringed by a pine and cedar forest, with a clear-water creek running through it. Storm-tossed driftwood and entire trees with their roots intact lie beyond the HW mark – a great spot to comb for small treasures amongst the tidal flotsam and jetsam. At LW, a small white-sand beach appears beyond the gravel. Forward Bay makes for a fine picnic stop.

*Not to scale. Not to be used for navigation.*

48 — The Broughtons

WELCOME to PORT HARDY

FISHING · LOGGING · MINING

*Port Hardy is the westerly limit of this guide*

Chapter 2

# PASSAGES NORTH OF 50°

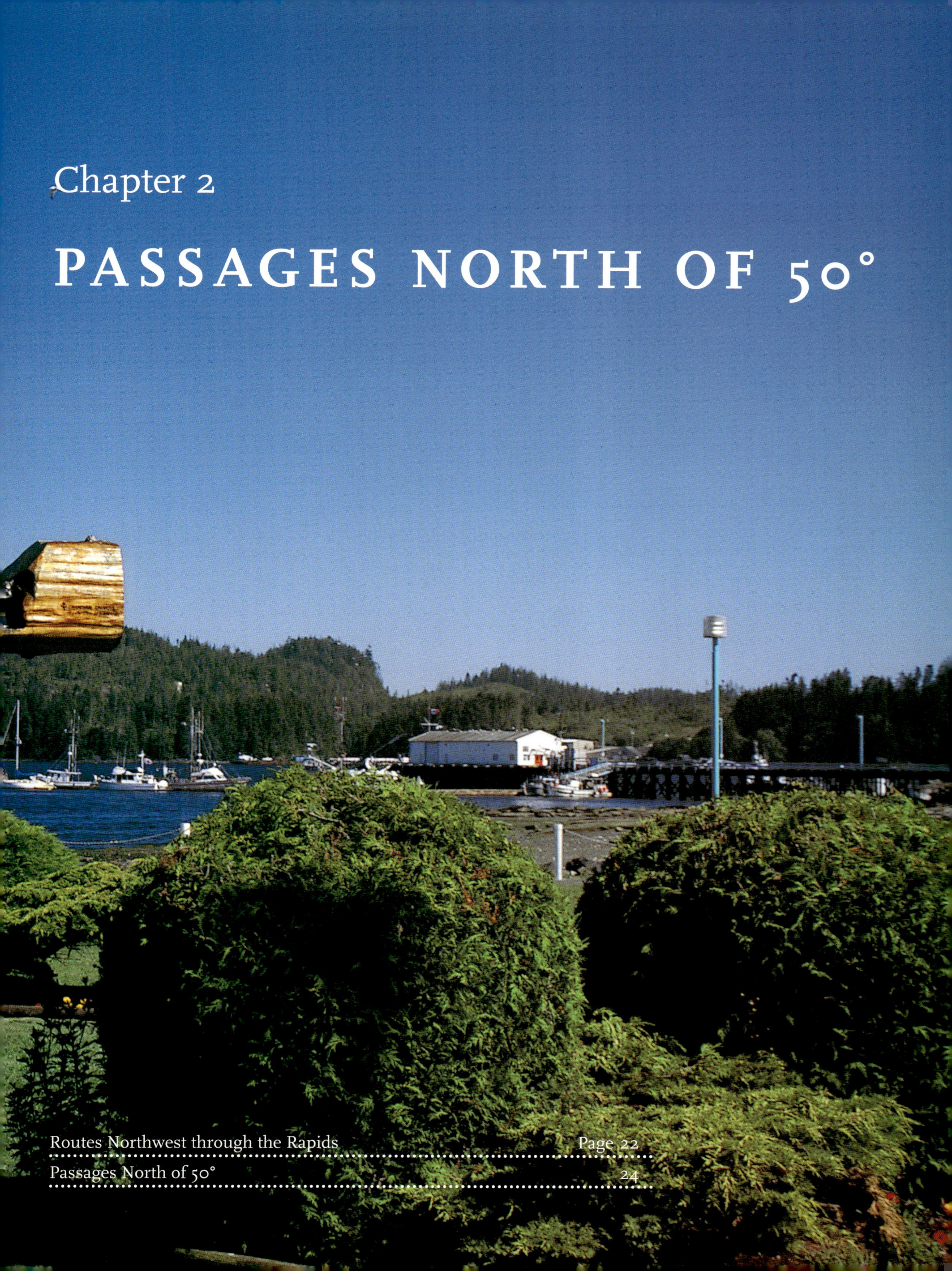

The Pacific Northwest greets all nations

# Chapter 2
# ROUTES NORTHWEST THROUGH THE RAPIDS

The following *Dreamspeaker* titles will guide you north:

Volume 4    *The San Juan Islands*

Volume 1    *The Gulf Islands & Vancouver Island –*
*Victoria & Sooke to Nanaimo*

Volume 3    *Vancouver, Howe Sound & the Sunshine Coast –*
*Princess Louisa Inlet and Jedediah Island*

Volume 2    *Desolation Sound & the Discovery Islands*

Volume 2–Desolation Sound & the Discovery Islands

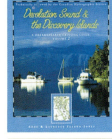

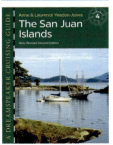

The following text and chart opposite are intended as a synopsis for passage planning. Passage planning is a serious component of safe navigation. Take time to consider the conditions you will be encountering, and take precautions accordingly.

The region north of 50°, as depicted in the chart, is comprehensively covered in *A Dreamspeaker Cruising Guide Volume 2 – Desolation Sound and the Discovery Islands*.

For the recreational boater travelling from home ports in southern British Columbia and Washington State to the Broughtons, the journey is a challenge and commitment in itself. With a distance of some 90 nautical miles to Lund from Vancouver, BC, and twice that from Seattle, WA, this trip takes a good deal of planning. South of 50°, fuel, moorage, provisioning and marine services are relatively numerous and comprehensively covered by *A Dreamspeaker Cruising Guide Volumes 1, 3* and *4*.

North of 50°, *A Dreamspeaker Cruising Guide Volume 2 – Desolation Sound and the Discovery Islands* will serve for planning the passages through the initial channels and rapids. Fuel, moorage, provisions and marine services are not as numerous, and Campbell River is the last real urban centre with well-developed marine services and a regional airport with feeder floatplane services to the outlying communities and resorts.

There are two passages north – the western and eastern routes, with a central diversion through the Okisollo Channel. All have tidal gates in the form of rapids and swift currents in the channels, a limited choice of fuel, moorage and provisioning options, and an excellent selection of anchorages.

*Dreamspeaker*'s route was north to Lund from Vancouver, then northwest to Campbell River before embarking on a passage via Seymour Narrows and Discovery Passage to begin the cruise to the Broughtons. This is a good shakedown for any vessel, usually the first big one of the season, and Campbell River is the perfect location to obtain boat parts and fix any mechanical problems prior to your cruise further north.

# KEY DESTINATIONS

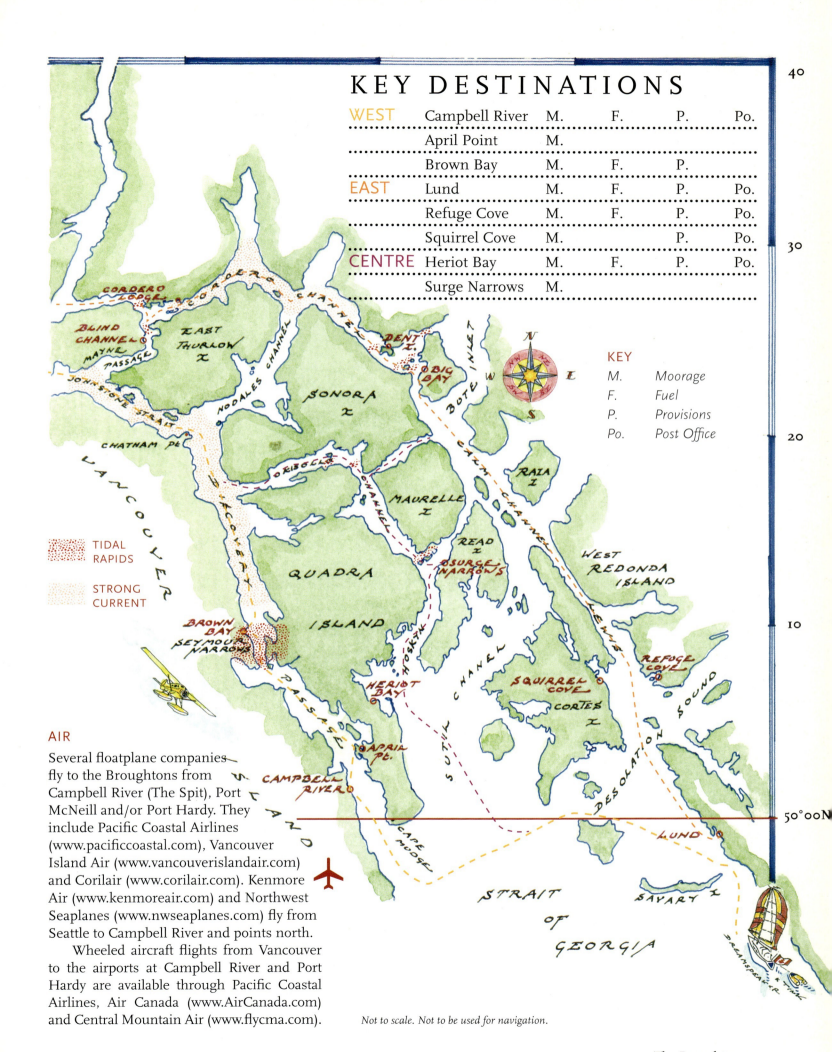

| | | | | | |
|---|---|---|---|---|---|
| **WEST** | Campbell River | M. | F. | P. | Po. |
| | April Point | M. | | | |
| | Brown Bay | M. | F. | P. | |
| **EAST** | Lund | M. | F. | P. | Po. |
| | Refuge Cove | M. | F. | P. | Po. |
| | Squirrel Cove | M. | | P. | Po. |
| **CENTRE** | Heriot Bay | M. | F. | P. | Po. |
| | Surge Narrows | M. | | | |

**KEY**

| | |
|---|---|
| M. | *Moorage* |
| F. | *Fuel* |
| P. | *Provisions* |
| Po. | *Post Office* |

CORDERO LODGE

BLIND CHANNEL

MAYNE PASSAGE

EAST THURLOW x

CORDERO CHANNEL

NODALES CHANNEL

JOHNSTONE STRAIT

CHATHAM PT.

DENT I.

BIG BAY

BUTE INLET

CALM CHANNEL

SONORA x

OKISOLLO CHANNEL

DISCOVERY CHANNEL

VANCOUVER

MAURELLE I.

RAZA I.

READ I.

SURGE NARROWS

WEST REDONDA ISLAND

**TIDAL RAPIDS**

**STRONG CURRENT**

QUADRA ISLAND

HOSKYN CHANNEL

SUTIL CHANNEL

LEWIS CHANNEL

SQUIRREL COVE

REFUGE COVE

BROWN BAY
SEYMOUR NARROWS

HERIOT BAY

CORTES I.

DESOLATION SOUND

## AIR

Several floatplane companies fly to the Broughtons from Campbell River (The Spit), Port McNeill and/or Port Hardy. They include Pacific Coastal Airlines (www.pacificcoastal.com), Vancouver Island Air (www.vancouverislandair.com) and Corilair (www.corilair.com). Kenmore Air (www.kenmoreair.com) and Northwest Seaplanes (www.nwseaplanes.com) fly from Seattle to Campbell River and points north.

Wheeled aircraft flights from Vancouver to the airports at Campbell River and Port Hardy are available through Pacific Coastal Airlines, Air Canada (www.AirCanada.com) and Central Mountain Air (www.flycma.com).

PASSAGE

APRIL PT.

CAMPBELL RIVER

CAPE MUDGE

50°00N

SAVARY I.

LUND

STRAIT OF GEORGIA

DREAMSPEAKER & TINK

*Not to scale. Not to be used for navigation.*

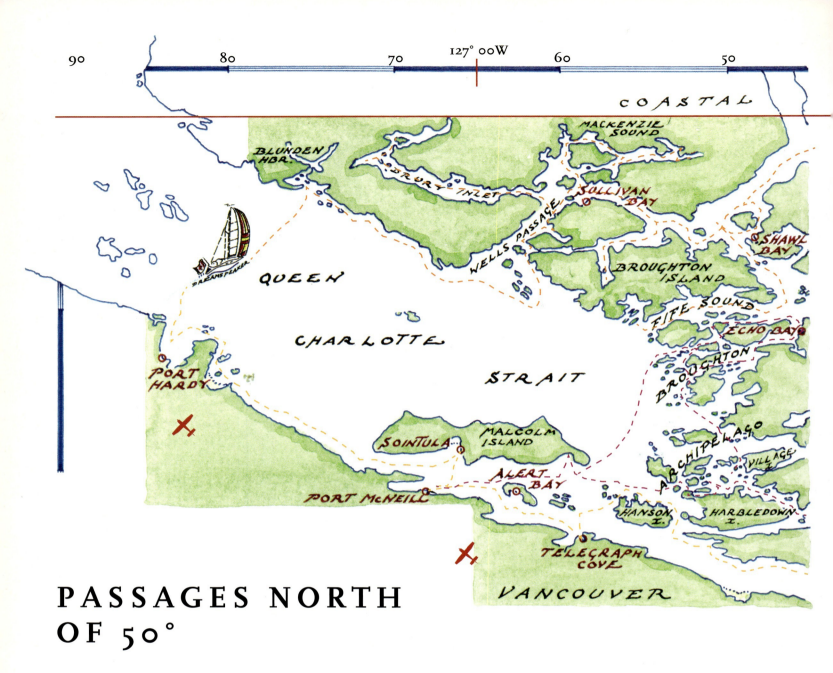

# PASSAGES NORTH OF 50°

*There are regional airports at Port McNeill and Port Hardy with fixed-wheel, floatplane, and helicopter charter services to all the destinations in the Broughton region.*

The Volume 5 chapters follow the route taken by *Dreamspeaker* and her crew while researching this guide.

Taking up where *A Dreamspeaker Cruising Guide Volume 2 – Desolation Sound and the Discovery Islands* left off, Volume 5 begins in the waters of Maybe Passage and travels west from Blind Channel via Johnstone and Broughton straits and the friendly communities of Vancouver Island.

After an immersion in First Nations culture in Alert Bay, Cormorant Island, Volume 5 travels north into the "Village of Islands" in the Broughton Archipelago – two chapters of remote anchorages, First Nations villages and fun family-run resorts.

Returning south to refuel and provision in Port McNeill, the adventure continues after a visit to the community of Sointula on Malcolm Island. *Dreamspeaker* travels west to Port Hardy and across Queen Charlotte Strait to Blunden Harbour, then east to explore the labyrinthine waters of the coastal mainland, visiting the floating community and marina at Sullivan Bay and then venturing into the fjord-like splendor of Kingcome and Knight Inlets. Finally, there's a lovely layover at LAGOON COVE MARINA and, in Port Harvey, a shelter from a westerly gale.

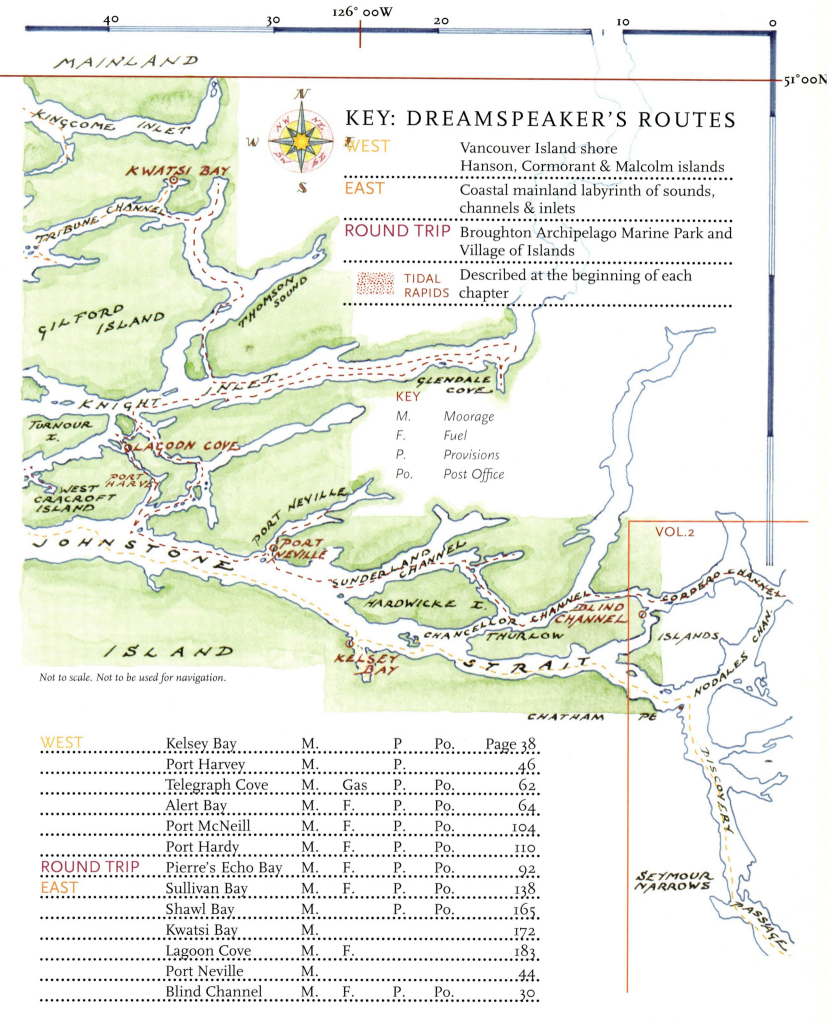

MAINLAND

## KEY: DREAMSPEAKER'S ROUTES

**WEST** — Vancouver Island shore
Hanson, Cormorant & Malcolm islands

**EAST** — Coastal mainland labyrinth of sounds, channels & inlets

**ROUND TRIP** — Broughton Archipelago Marine Park and Village of Islands

**TIDAL RAPIDS** — Described at the beginning of each chapter

### KEY

| | |
|---|---|
| M. | Moorage |
| F. | Fuel |
| P. | Provisions |
| Po. | Post Office |

*Not to scale. Not to be used for navigation.*

VOL.2

*Chancellor Channel from Billygoat Bay, Helmcken Island*

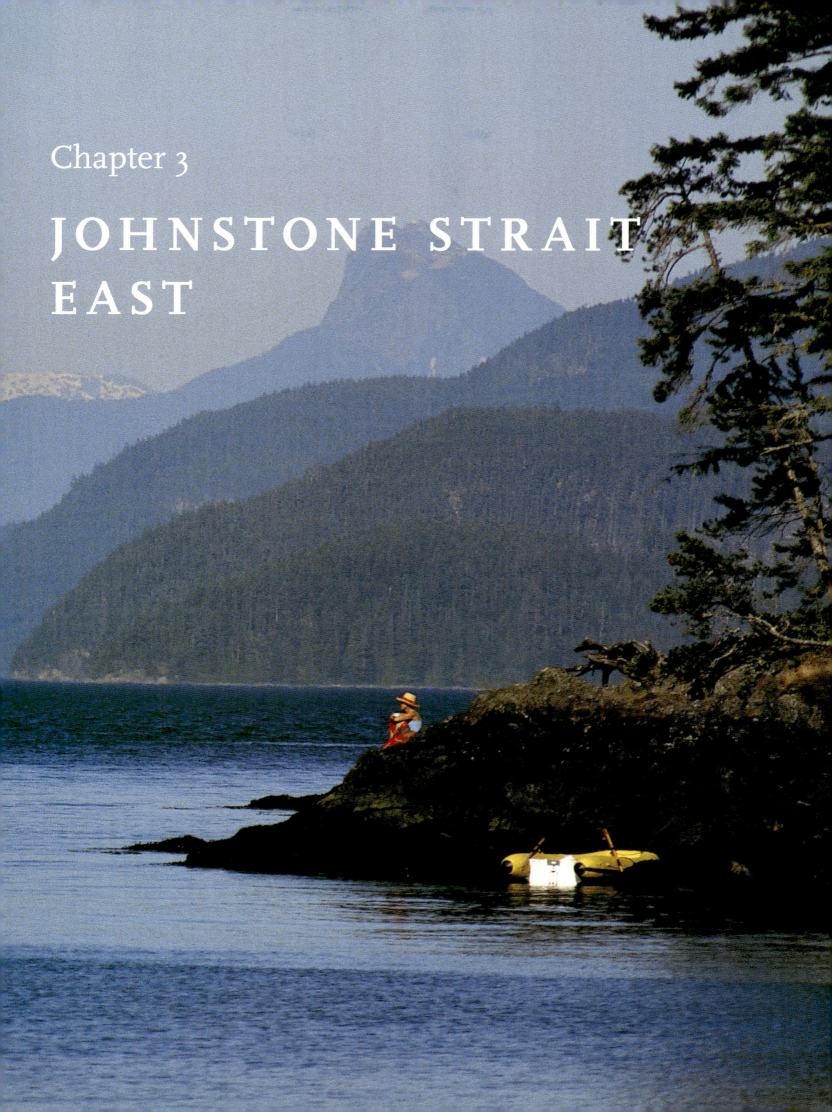

Chapter 3

# JOHNSTONE STRAIT EAST

# Chapter 3
# JOHNSTONE STRAIT EAST

**TIDES** – *Volume 6,*
*Canadian Tide and Current Tables*
Reference Port – Owen Bay
Secondary Ports – Blind Channel,
Cordero Island
Reference Port – Alert Bay
Secondary Ports – Billygoat Bay, Kelsey
Bay

**CURRENTS**

Reference Station – Seymour Narrows
Secondary Stations – Blind Channel,
Greene Point Rapids, Whirlpool Rapids
Reference Station – Johnstone Strait
Central
Secondary Station – Current Passage

**WEATHER**

Weather Station – WX1 162.55 MHZ
Area – Johnstone Strait
Reporting Stations – Fanny Island, Chatham Point

*The unique burger stand in Kelsey Bay*

**CAUTIONARY NOTES:** *Johnstone Strait is notorious for strong, summer westerly winds. The swift currents in East Johnstone Strait will create potentially dangerous seas when wind-against-current conditions prevail. On a large tide, East Johnstone Strait averages 5 knots of current on both the ebb and flood. Consult your chart for the Traffic Separation Scheme (TSS) and stay clear of the shipping lanes, as the strait is a busy commercial artery.*

*Currents can range from 5 to 7 knots on the northern route via Blind Channel and Greene Point Rapids through Chancellor and Wellbore Channels. The prudent navigator will run with the current and endeavour to transit rapids at slack water. Due to turbulence caused by the strong current, a dinghy or yacht tender should always be stowed on deck.*

This is a chapter on transiting, which needs to be well planned as it presents a potential challenge to the cruising boater. Johnstone Strait is famous for its strong westerly winds, while the rapids, channels and passages are noted for their strong currents and turbulent waters. The scenery, however, is dominated by snow-capped mountain ranges and stunning vistas.

Routes west are via Mayne Passage and Johnstone Strait, with potential shelter at Helmcken Island and Kelsey Bay. The alternative route is north via Blind Channel and Greene Point Rapids, and west via Chancellor and Wellbore Channels, through Whirlpool Rapids to the shelter of Douglas Bay in Forward Harbour.

BLIND CHANNEL RESORT AND MARINA is a major staging post for boaters planning their cruise to the Broughtons. We made an early morning start from Blind Channel to take advantage of light winds and the ebb current to Helmcken Island, where we investigated two small anchorages that provided protected overnight anchorage and a cozy spot to hide while waiting out the adverse tide in Current Passage.

Travelling with the current to Kelsey Bay the following morning, we found a safe haven for local fish boats and transient boaters. Its entrance might not look that inviting in a blow, but once inside there is good protection and a neighbourly community that welcomes visitors. Sayward Village is a pleasant 15-minute walk from the dock, and the lovely Salmon River Estuary Trails are teeming with birdlife.

*Note: On our return journey from the Broughtons, we enjoyed a thrilling downwind sail as the westerly wind and flood tide carried us through Sunderland Channel to a rendezvous with friends in Forward Harbour.*

# FEATURED DESTINATIONS

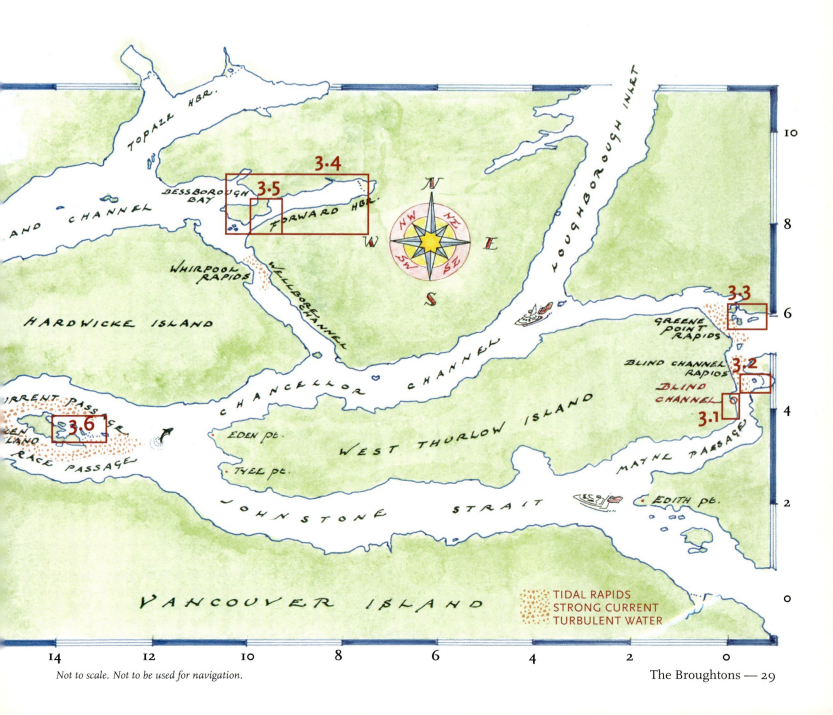

*Not to scale. Not to be used for navigation.*

# 3.1 BLIND CHANNEL RESORT AND MARINA

✳ 50°24.90'N 125°29.90'W

**CHARTS** 3543. 3312, p. 24.

**APPROACH** With caution, because a back eddy, running counter to the current in Mayne Passage, creates a strong current setting into the marina facility.

**MARINA** BLIND CHANNEL RESORT AND MARINA, toll-free 1-888-329-0475 or VHF Channel 66A, has extensive visitor moorage with Wi-Fi.

**FUEL** Open all year round, the fuel dock is operated by the resort. Gas, diesel and propane are available.

*Lovely Blind Channel Resort and Marina*

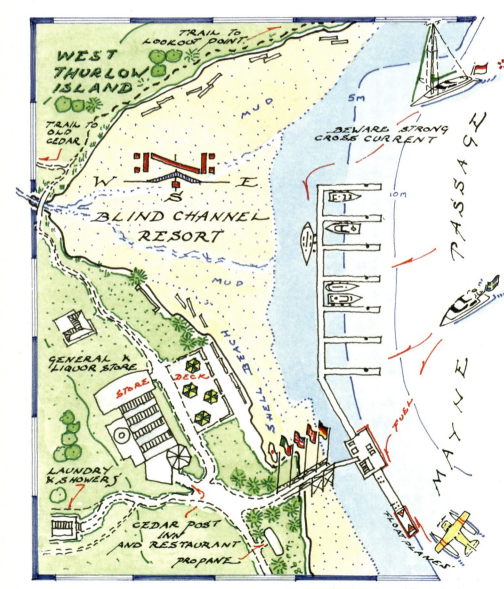

*Not to scale. Not to be used for navigation.*

Pristine docks, colourful artwork and terra cotta pots spilling over with flowers welcome you to BLIND CHANNEL RESORT AND MARINA, owned and operated by three generations of the Richter family. In business since 1970, this resort has a restaurant and patio, store, post office, liquor outlet and waterside cottages with full facilities. Moorage comes with 24-hour power and piped spring water. The marina offers free moorage of two to three hours to boaters while they shop or dine at the resort. There is garbage service with a commercial incinerator. Shower and laundry facilities are also available.

The well-stocked store offers delicious baked goods, picnic fare and fresh bread daily in high season. It also carries a variety of basic provisions, frozen meats and a selection of fresh produce. "Spring water ice" is produced on site, and fishing licences, charts, guides, books and unique gifts are also sold. Pick up a hiking trail map and visit the 800-year-old cedar in the forest behind the resort.

Edgar and the late Annemarie Richter's artistic talents can also be seen in the CEDAR POST RESTAURANT, where gourmet meals are served, along with a selection of wines. In summer, reservations are essential.

*BLIND CHANNEL RESORT is a major staging point for
boaters beginning their cruise west to the Broughtons
or for those at the end of their Desolation Sound cruise.
For Dreamspeaker it was the last stop at the end of a
Broughtons cruise before heading south.*

# 3.2 CHARLES BAY, BLIND CHANNEL RAPIDS, EAST THURLOW ISLAND

CHARTS   3543.

APPROACH   (A) Charles Bay, from Mayne Passage at LW slack. (B) From the N, off Shell Point. Transit Blind Channel Rapids, on or near slack water.

ANCHOR   Due N of Eclipse Islet. Swing in the back eddies in depths of 2–4 m (6–13 ft). Holding good in mud.

❀ (A) 50°25.02'N 125°29.70'W
❀ (B) 50°25.44'N 125°30.03'W

*At anchor off the shingle beach, Charles Bay*

Good crabbing and well-protected anchorage can be found across the way from BLIND CHANNEL RESORT in secluded Charles Bay. Sheltered from southeasterly and northwesterly winds and the effects of the Greene Point and Blind Channel Rapids, this small haven offers peace. Beautiful Eclipse Islet, encircled by clear water, provides an idyllic picnic spot. You can pick fresh sea asparagus, poke around the rocks or just laze on the colourful pebble beach, watching boat traffic in Mayne Passage challenge the Blind Channel Rapids. The bay, although open to Mayne Passage, lies in the wind shadow of W Thurlow Island and is, therefore, well protected from the prevailing summer westerly winds.

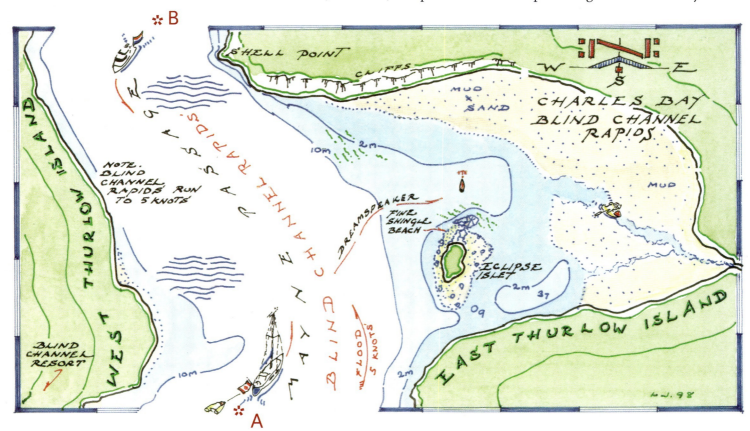

# "CORDERO COVE," CORDERO ISLANDS

✿50°26.40'N 125°20.60'W

CHARTS   3543. 3312, p. 24.

APPROACH   From the S, the channel between the S islands is fringed by kelp. A rock lies off the W tip of the easternmost island.

ANCHOR   Good sheltered anchorage, away form the turbulence and eddies in Cordero Channel, can be found in the cove. Depths of 6–12 m (19–39 ft), holding over a mud, sand and weed bottom.

*Sunset over West Thurlow Island*

Not to scale. Not to be used for navigation.

This surprisingly ideal anchorage is protected from northwesterly winds and the swift current in Cordero Channel by three charming islands. The SE basin also affords some protection in southeast winds.

With a pleasant view out to bustling Cordero Channel, the place we have christened "Cordero Cove" is a great spot for exploring, picnicking, shell collecting and just lazing in the cockpit. Many tranquil hours can be spent basking on the smooth-rock islet in the cove's NW corner.

You'll be lulled by the musical sound of water gushing through the narrow gap and tumbling over rocks at HW. The best spot to spread your picnic blanket is on the downy moss and grass patch on the westernmost island, with a great view over to the Greene Point Rapids.

# FORWARD HARBOUR

✿ (A) 50°28.65'N 125°47.05'W
✿ (B) 50°28.11'N 125°46.37'W

**CHARTS** 3544.

**APPROACH** The approaches to Forward Harbour lie (A) NW and (B) SE of Midgham Islets. The entrance channel between Louisa Point and Robson Point is wide and clear.

**ANCHOR** In Bessborough Bay only as an alternative in easterly winds. Open to the full westerly fetch of Cumberland Channel. Forward Harbour entrance channel has a small bight on the northern shore, which can accommodate 2 boats. Good all-round protection – a stern line ashore is recommended. For Douglas Bay see p. 35. In the head of the harbour, deep anchorage is available for larger boats and vessels, with plenty of swinging room.

**MARINA** FORWARD HARBOUR has moorage for transient boaters by reservation. Their docks have 20 m (65 ft) of water below at LW and can accommodate boats up to 24 m (80 ft). Water, washrooms, showers and wireless internet are available. There is power along the docks, but it isn't steady and consists of solar panels and a generator. There is no restaurant, but cooking facilities are available. Call ahead (250-230-1075 or 403-505-1190) or email fwdhbr@msn.com. They monitor VHF Channel 6.

*The entrance channel to Forward Harbour*

An ancient rock petroglyph site, good anchorage and transient moorage facilities at the fishing lodge can be found at the head of commodious Forward Harbour.

The lodge offers dinner in its restaurant by reservation and has shower, laundry and telephone facilities. Trips to view the local grizzlies and petroglyphs are offered to overnight moorage guests, and their fully guided ATV Adventure Wilderness Tours visit Heydon Lake and Topaze Harbour. See bears on the beach, canoe, take a refreshing swim before lunch and enjoy the selection of wildlife and birds that call this lovely area home.

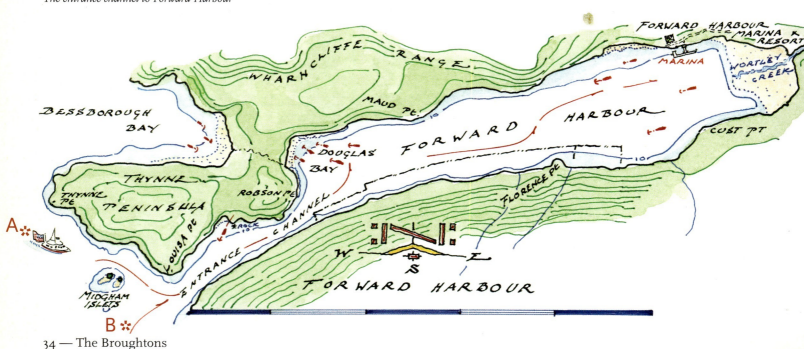

**CHARTS** 3543.

**APPROACH** The approach to Forward Harbour lies NE or SE of Midgham Islets; Douglas Bay is free of obstructions.

**ANCHOR** Off the sand and gravel beach in Douglas Bay, in 4–10 m (13–32 ft) with enough room for 8–10 boats to swing comfortably. The bay is protected from all but outflow winds, with holding good in sand and gravel.

**CAUTIONARY NOTE:** *Boats will tend to swing towards the northern shore when gale force westerly winds combine with the current.*

✱50°28.75'N 125°45.09'W

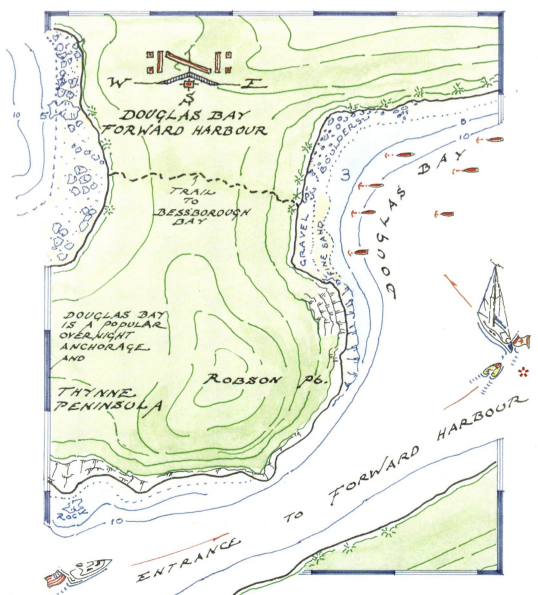

A popular overnight anchorage for boaters at the start or end of their Broughton cruise, Douglas Bay offers a fine-sand and gravel beach backed by pine and maple trees. From here, an interesting flotsam and jetsam trail zigzags through the forest to Bessborough Bay and its sandy swimming beach.

We visited in the aftermath of a westerly gale, and the white sand was covered with blobs of bracken-coloured jellyfish and mounds of kelp and seaweed, which the slim-legged sandpipers picked through delicately. The head of the bay was a beachcomber's paradise, with everything from huge reels of plastic piping to wayward fenders and lengths of blue rope. Only then did we realize that displaying beach finds along the trail had become a summer tradition.

*Note: After a recent, bad winter storm, the trail has since become far more challenging.*

## 3.6 HELMCKEN ISLAND

✿ (A) 50°24.14'N 125°51.19'W
✿ (B) 50°24.24'N 125°51.94'W

**CHARTS** 3544.

**APPROACH** (A) Billygoat Bay from the W between the 2 islets. The range mark is to starboard. Beware of the reef and a rock to the E. (B) "Deer Cove" is a clear run in from the NE.

**ANCHOR** (1) At the head of the bay in depths of 5–6 m (16–19 ft). Good protection from westerly winds with holding good in mud. (2) Beyond the old log dump, off the gravel beach (outside the eel grass) in depths of 7–8 m (22–26 ft). Holding is moderate in gravel and mud. Although this bay is more open than (A), it is well protected from westerly winds.

*Note: A good spot to hide while waiting out foul weather in Johnstone Strait.*

*Deer are a common shoreline sight*

These two cozy anchorages certainly came in handy after an unsuccessful attempt to navigate east beyond Current Passage on a flooding tide.

We tucked into the head of Billygoat Bay and shared the tranquil anchorage with jumping fish, kingfishers and plump seals sunning themselves on the rocks. The view NE to Chancellor Channel is lovely and the fresh seaweed picked from the shoreline's rocky outcrops was delicious.

"Deer Cove" (named by us, after the resident deer) is the more scenic of the two spots with views NE and SE down Johnstone Strait with mighty Mount Waddington in the distance. Stretch your legs and and take the dog along for a hike on the old logging roads.

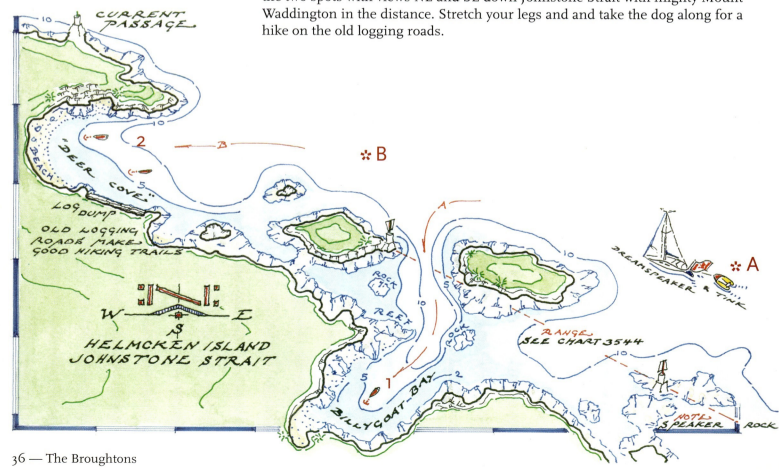

*Snug in Kelsey Bay while gale force winds blow in Johnstone Strait*

✿ 50°23.86'N 125°57.55'W

**CHARTS**   3544.

**APPROACH**   With extreme caution. A floating breakwater extends out from a stone breakwater. Enter between the starboard mark (red) and the rusting ship hulls that lie to the S.

**PUBLIC WHARF**   Three fingers extend SE behind the breakwater; during the summer months, rafting up is the norm. In a westerly blow, all boats rock and roll, although the outer portion of "C" dock is the most exposed. The wharf is managed by the Sayward Harbour Authority and space is based on a first-come, first-served basis. Maximum length for vessels is 65 ft (19.8 m).

There is no fuel available, but there is power and water.

**SAYWARD FUTURES WHARF**   Space is available at this wharf outside the breakwater. It is operated by the Sayward Futures Society. Reservations available by phoning 250-282-0018 or use their online contact form at www.kelseybaybc.com.

**BOAT LAUNCH**   Ramp is private.

**CAUTIONARY NOTE:** *On the ebb tide a strong back eddy runs across the entrance. This back eddy is less strong on a flood tide.*

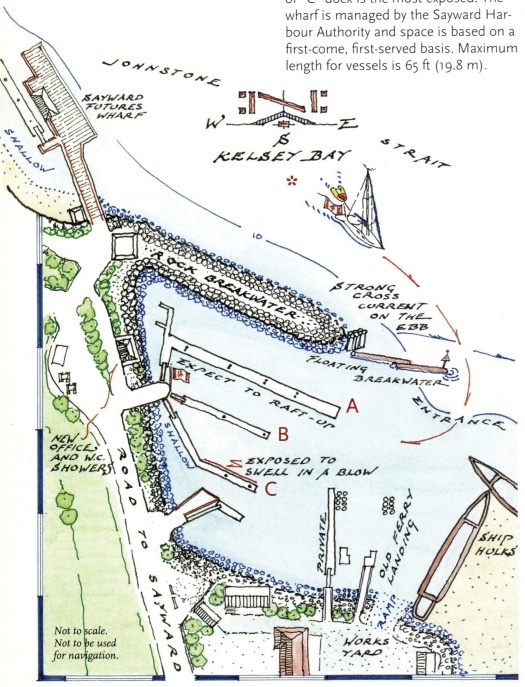

Not to scale.
Not to be used
for navigation.

A safe haven for local fish boats, Kelsey Bay and its entrance might not be that inviting in a blow, but once inside, there is protection from the winds in Johnstone Strait and a welcoming community. Washrooms and shower and laundry facilities are available at the head of the public wharf.

The Sayward Futures Society is working hard to make the Port of Kelsey Bay attractive to cruising boaters, and appreciates visitors to its office and tourist information centre located on the old government wharf north of the rock breakwater. The Society's building is also home to a gift store offering local products and information about whale-watching and wildlife tours; internet access is also available. The view across Johnstone Strait is spectacular, and the day we visited, a large pod of orcas at play in the strait thrilled a crowd of viewers on the dock.

# SAYWARD VILLAGE AND SALMON RIVER ESTUARY TRAILS

For chart approach and moorage information, see Kelsey Bay (opposite).

✿ 50°23.76'N 125°56.33'W

3.7 FOR DETAIL

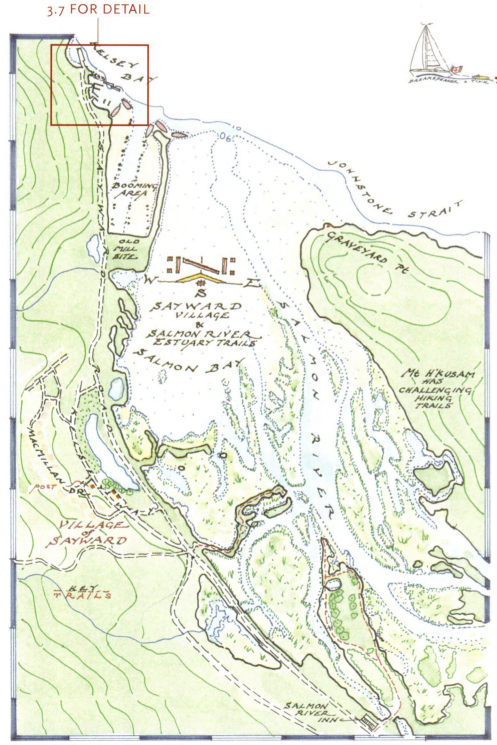

*Not to scale. Not to be used for navigation.*

**N**eat and tidy homes, manicured lawns and flower-filled hanging baskets greet visitors to the picturesque Village of Sayward, a pleasant 15-minute walk from Kelsey Bay. Picnic in the shaded, grassy park fronted by a lagoon filled with wildlife, or take a leisurely stroll along the lovely Salmon River Estuary Trails, with abundant birdlife. A solid, wooden lookout provides views over the Salmon River and its maze of tributaries out to Johnstone Strait.

*A windswept marsh fronts Sayward Village*

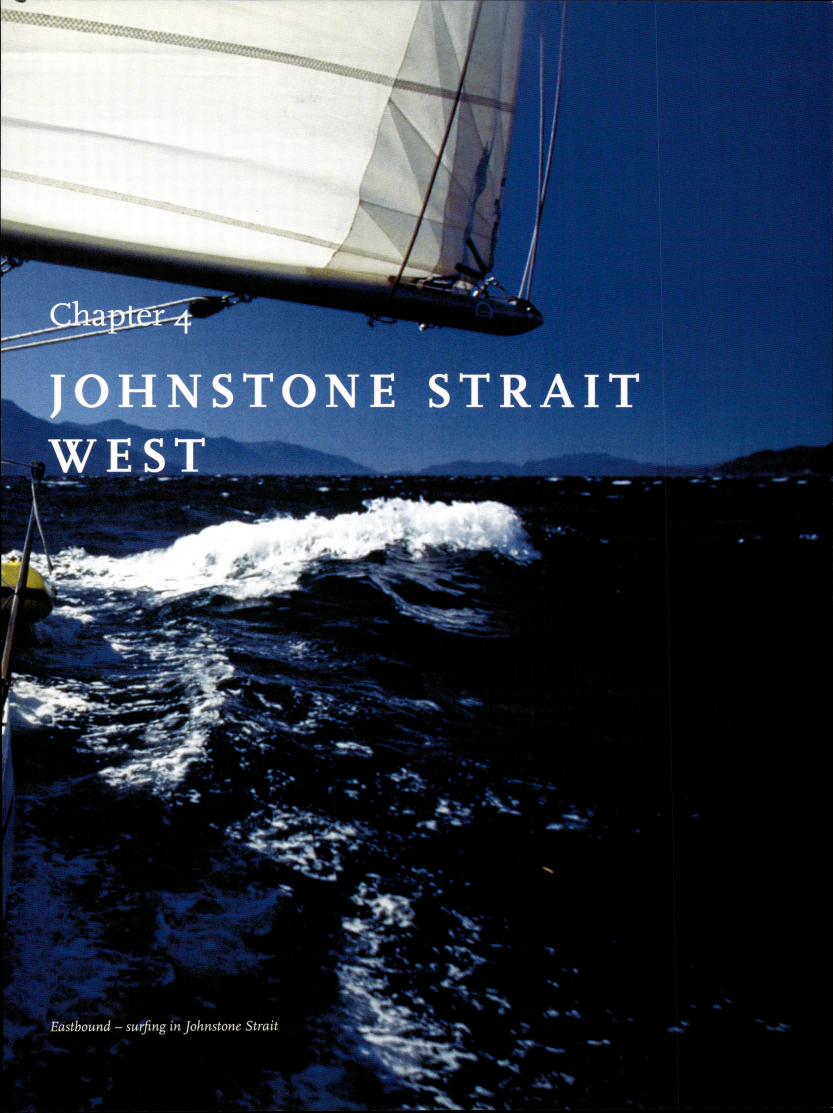

# Chapter 4

# JOHNSTONE STRAIT WEST

*Eastbound – surfing in Johnstone Strait*

# Chapter 4
# JOHNSTONE STRAIT WEST

**TIDES** – *Volume 6,*
*Canadian Tide and Current Tables*
Reference Port – Alert Bay
Secondary Ports – Port Neville, Port
Harvey

**CURRENTS**

Reference Station – Johnstone Strait
Central
Secondary Station – Forward Bay
*Note* – *Strong currents of up to 4 knots*
*occur at the entrance to Port Neville.*
*On a large tide, currents of up to 2 knots*
*occur in Havannah Channel.*

**WEATHER**

Weather Station – WX1 162.55 MHZ
Area – Johnstone Strait
Reporting Station – Fanny Island

*A salmon seiner at work in Johnstone Strait*

CAUTIONARY NOTES: *Strong westerly*
*winds forecast for Johnstone Strait equate*
*to similarly strong winds in Sunderland*
*and Havannah Channels. Although the*
*current runs a maximum of 1.5 knots in*
*West Johnstone Strait, in a wind-against-*
*current situation this section of the strait*
*is notorious for uncomfortable, short and*
*choppy seas. These can be potentially*
*hazardous for small craft.*

All craft travelling east or west between Hard-wicke and the Broken Islands have to transit the western portion of Johnstone Strait. It would be prudent to plan your journey on an ebb tide and before the westerly winds get up, as there is little shelter in Johnstone Strait or Sunderland Channel. If shelter is required, visit lovely Port Nev-ille. Unfortunately, its historic post office and store, which was also a museum and art gallery, is now closed. Stay overnight, keep an eye out for the deer population, or investigate the peaceful, upper reach-es of Port Neville.

Many boaters wishing to shorten their Johnstone Strait transit will head north via Havannah and Chatham Channel to LAGOON COVE MARINA (Chapter 14) or continue west to explore the anchorages and shell-midden beaches in Clio Channel and the wild-life-filled wetlands in Potts Lagoon.

We opted for the morning ebb to Forward Bay, West Cracroft Island, before heading west into Broughton Strait (see Chapter 5). Tucked be-hind Bush Islets, the bay offers a charming picnic stop and an inviting, crescent-shaped gravel beach fringed by storm-tossed driftwood.

It was not until our homeward-bound journey that we discovered Port Harvey, a quiet inlet be-tween East and West Cracroft Islands. Seeking shel-ter from a 45-knot westerly gale, we found protected and comfortable anchorage at the head of the inlet, and the very welcoming PORT HARVEY MARINE RESORT.

# FEATURED DESTINATIONS

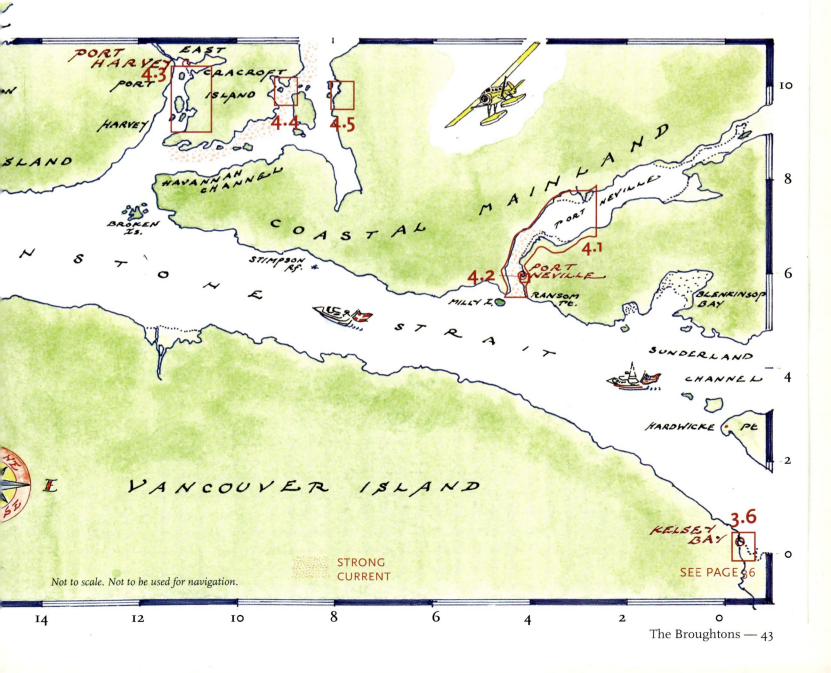

Not to scale. Not to be used for navigation.

STRONG CURRENT

SEE PAGE 36

# 4.1 PORT NEVILLE

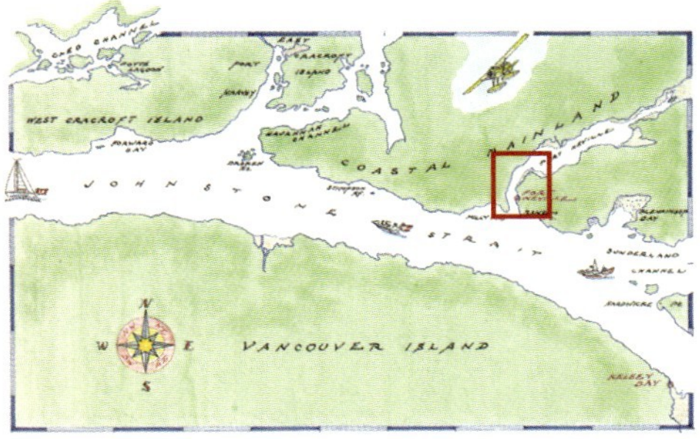

✲50°28.92'N 126°05.28'W

CHARTS 3545. For exploration beyond July Point consult chart 3564, which is more detailed.

APPROACH The entrance lies between Ransom Point and Neville Point. The public wharf is on the E shore of the entrance channel. SW of July Point, note rocks with less than 2 m (6 ft) at LW.

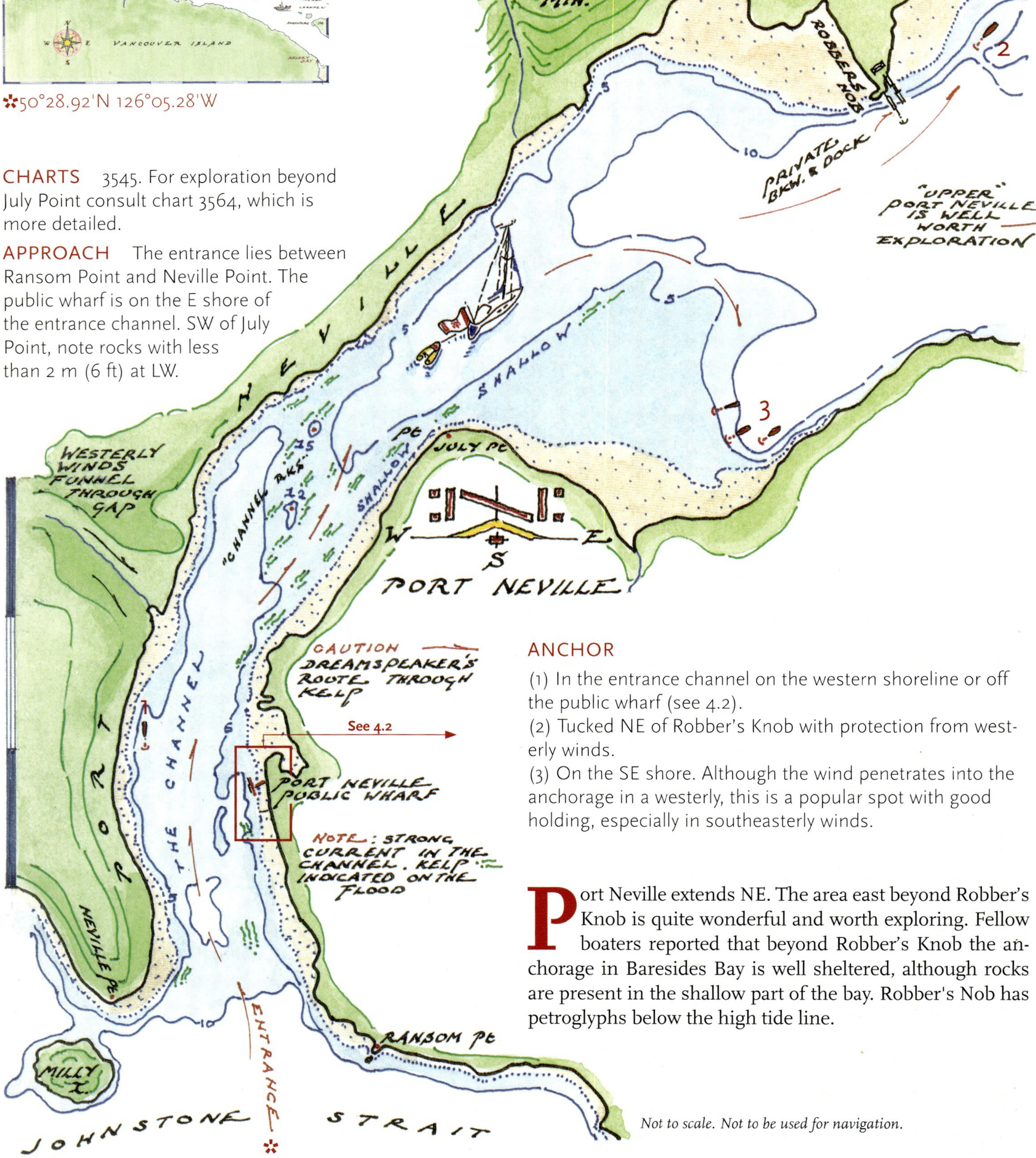

TERRAIN RISES DRAMATICALLY TO VICTORY MTN.
ROBBERS NOB
PRIVATE BKW. & DOCK
"UPPER" PORT NEVILLE IS WELL WORTH EXPLORATION
NEVILLE
SHALLOW
WESTERLY WINDS FUNNEL THROUGH GAP
"CHANNEL RKS"
JULY PT
PT
PORT NEVILLE
CAUTION
DREAMSPEAKER'S ROUTE THROUGH KELP
See 4.2
PORT NEVILLE PUBLIC WHARF
NOTE: STRONG CURRENT IN THE CHANNEL. KELP INDICATED ON THE FLOOD
PORT
THE CHANNEL
NEVILLE PT
ENTRANCE
RANSOM PT
MILLY I.
JOHNSTONE STRAIT


ANCHOR

(1) In the entrance channel on the western shoreline or off the public wharf (see 4.2).

(2) Tucked NE of Robber's Knob with protection from westerly winds.

(3) On the SE shore. Although the wind penetrates into the anchorage in a westerly, this is a popular spot with good holding, especially in southeasterly winds.

Port Neville extends NE. The area east beyond Robber's Knob is quite wonderful and worth exploring. Fellow boaters reported that beyond Robber's Knob the anchorage in Baresides Bay is well sheltered, although rocks are present in the shallow part of the bay. Robber's Nob has petroglyphs below the high tide line.

*Not to scale. Not to be used for navigation.*

# PORT NEVILLE PUBLIC WHARF

**APPROACH**   From the SW. The public wharf and store are conspicuous.

**ANCHOR**   Off the public wharf.

**PUBLIC WHARF**   A well-maintained dock with inside depths of a 2-m (6-ft) minimum; fishing boats have been known to raft three-deep here.

*Note: The flood and ebb current is strong in the channel; approach the wharf with the boat's bow to the current.*

*The public wharf and store sign are conspicuous on the SW shore*

**P**ort Neville was named by Captain Vancouver in 1792. Tie up at the public wharf, which dates from the Union Steamship days. The post office was closed in 2010 – it was the longest continually operating post office in the province. A caretaker now looks after the private property. There is no power and questionable water.

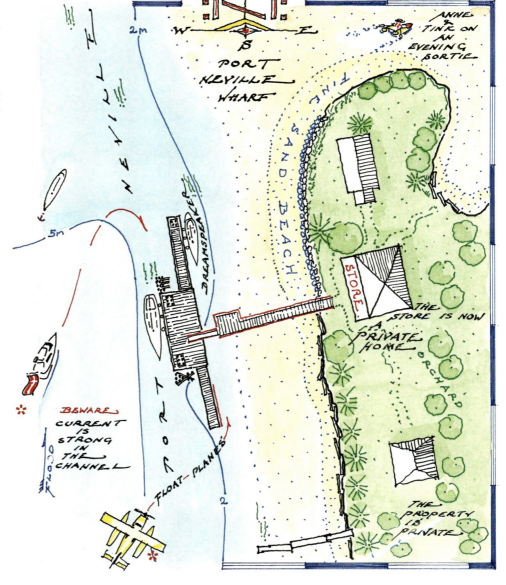

# 4.3 PORT HARVEY, EAST AND WEST CRACROFT ISLAND

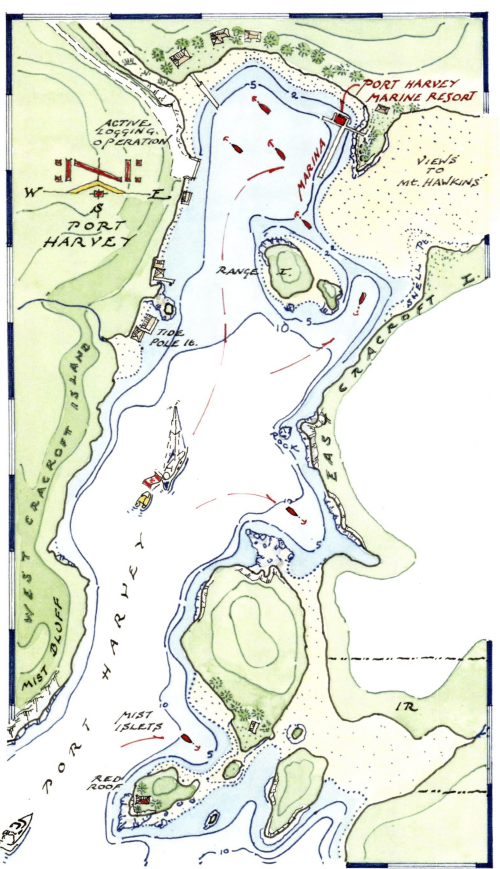

✤50°32.86'N 126°16.88'W

Not to scale. Not to be used for navigation.

## CHARTS    3545.

## APPROACH    Off Harvey Point. The run in along the W shore is clear; note the logging operations and log dumps that line the shore.

## ANCHOR    As indicated. The safest place to anchor is at the head of Port Harvey in depths of 6–8 m (19–26 ft). Excellent holding in sticky mud. *Dreamspeaker* and her crew survived a night of gale force winds in relative comfort.

## MARINA    Port Harvey Marine Resort, VHF Channel 66A or 250-902-9003, has ample moorage along 1,000 ft of well-maintained docks, potable water, power up to 30 amps, Wi-Fi, laundry, shower and washroom facilities. The marina and restaurant are popular in the summer months and booking ahead is advised.

Owned by George and Gail Cambridge since 2009, this welcoming marina has a well-stocked floating store that carries essential staples, some fresh produce, dairy products, gifts and books. They have an excellent hardware department.

Fresh cinnamon buns are baked each morning. The cozy RED SHOE PUB & RESTAURANT above the store is licensed and known for its generously-topped pizza. (Bring a red shoe for a free dessert.) Access to the shore and forest trails are just a few steps away; dig clams at LW on the beach fronting the owners' homestead.

# BURIAL COVE, 4.4
# EAST CRACROFT ISLAND

CHARTS    3545.

APPROACH    (A) From the SW, between Round Island and East Cracroft Island.

ANCHOR    In 5–10 m (16–32 ft) at the head of the cove, with holding good in mud. Well protected from westerly winds.

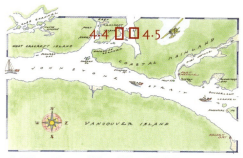

❀(A) 50°33.54'N 126°12.88'W
❀(B) 50°33.50'N 126°11.65'W

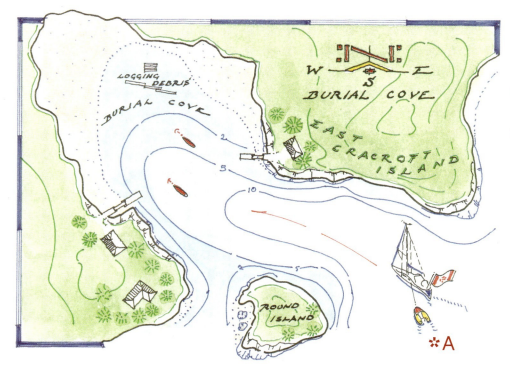

In settled weather both anchorages are fun picnic spots. For protection from westerly wind, use Burial Cove, and for easterly wind, use Matilpi Indian Islands.

# MATILPI INDIAN ISLANDS 4.5

CHARTS    3545.

APPROACH    (B) From the W. It is a clear run in 10 m (32 ft) between the northern island and the charted rocks.

ANCHOR    Off the white-shell beach in 5–10 m (16–32 ft). Holding good in mud. With a stern line ashore this anchorage is well protected from easterly winds and open to westerly winds.

The land and islands surrounding the anchorage are First Nations Reserves. The shell beach is an excellent example of a midden.

CHARTS    3545.

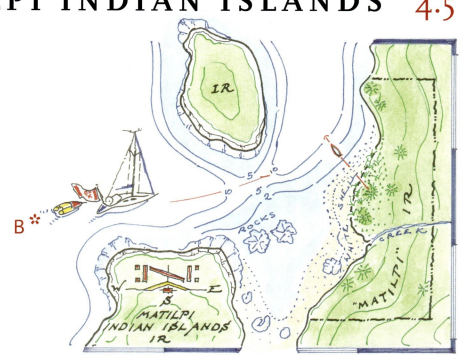

# 4.6 FORWARD BAY, WEST CRACROFT ISLAND

**APPROACH**  From the E at LW. Piles of driftwood, including whole trees, mark the HW line.

**ANCHOR**  Moderate protection from westerly winds can be had between Bush Islets and the shore in 5 m (16 ft). Holding good in sand and gravel.

❋50°31.12'N 126°24.33'W

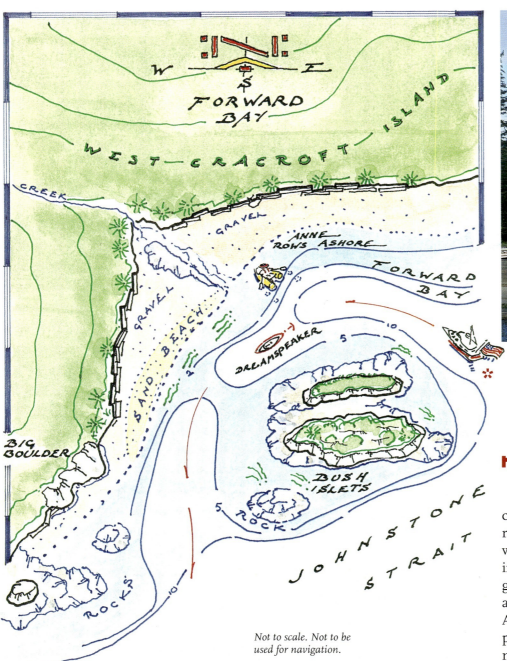

Not to scale. Not to be used for navigation.

*Beachcombing is filled with fun surprises*

Tucked behind Bush Islets is an inviting, crescent-shaped gravel beach fringed by a pine and cedar forest, with a clear-water creek running through it. Storm-tossed driftwood and entire trees with their roots intact lie beyond the HW mark – a great spot to comb for small treasures amongst the tidal flotsam and jetsam. At LW, a small white-sand beach appears beyond the gravel. Forward Bay makes for a fine picnic stop.

*Morning mist hangs in the bight off Klaoitsis Island*

**CHARTS**   3545.

**APPROACH**   From Clio Channel, the waypoint marks the initial channel prior to turning to starboard into "Laurence Passage" (named by us) or straight ahead to Potts Lagoon.

**ANCHOR**   These anchorages are best explored at LW. Locations (1) and (2) are 2 bights protected from westerly winds, while (3) gives protection from southeasterly winds.

✿ 50°34.17'N 126°28.27'W

*D*reamspeaker's crew spent an enjoyable day exploring the nooks and crannies between the islets off Klaoitsis Island, with breakfast in the northern anchorage between Wilson Pass and Laurence Passage and a picnic lunch on the semi-circular shell beach. We chose the less crowded northern basin of Potts Lagoon for an overnight anchorage, peacefully swinging to the current. From here, you can visit Potts Lagoon by dinghy or kayak, but keep an eye on the tides if you plan to explore the upper reaches with its inviting marshlands and meadows. We were cautioned to keep a lookout for visiting black bears that come to enjoy the fruits of the lagoon and its wetlands. Float homes and the ruins of an old jetty line the S shoreline.

*Not to scale.*
*Not to be used*
*for navigation.*

KLAOITSIS
ISLAND & "ISLETS"

WILSON PASS

ROCKS

ROCK

SHELL BEACH

3

2

"LAURENCE  PASSAGE"

WEST  CRACROFT  ISLAND

# POTTS LAGOON, 4.8
# WEST CRACROFT ISLAND

**CHARTS** 3545.

**APPROACH** The waypoint given is E of Klaoitsis Island. Both entrances to the N and S basins of the lagoon are quite apparent.

**ANCHOR** (4) The N basin is less crowded and more open to the W, although protected from the SE. The holding is good in sand and mud, in depths of 3–6 m (9–19 ft). (See 4.7)

(5) The popular S basin has good all-around protection with good holding in mud, in depths of 3–6 m (9–19 ft).

*Old jetty and floats in Potts Lagoon*

*A cruise liner in Broughton Strait, off Cracroft Point, prior to entering Johnstone Strait*

Chapter 5

# BROUGHTON STRAIT

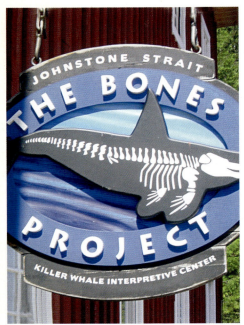

*Whale Museum, Telegraph Cove*

# Chapter 5
# BROUGHTON STRAIT

**TIDES** – *Volume 6,*
*Canadian Tide and Current Tables*
Reference Port – Alert Bay

**CURRENTS**
Reference Station – Seymour Narrows
Secondary Station – Baronet Passage

Reference Station – Johnstone Strait Central
Secondary Station – Blackney Passage, Alert Bay

Reference Station – Weynton Passage

**WEATHER**
Weather Station – WX1 162.55 MHZ
Area – Queen Charlotte Strait
Reporting Station – Alert Bay

**CAUTIONARY NOTES:** *Be aware of the large number of commercial vessels and cruise liners that ply the waters in Broughton Strait, especially in the summer months.*

*A current of up to 5 knots in Blackney Passage causes circular tide rips and turbulent water in both the passage and off Cracroft Point. Weynton Passage has a maximum 6-knot current and boaters should exercise caution when exploring the waters between Plumper and Pearse Islands, which lie on either side of the pass. Pearse Passage, between Cormorant and Pearse Islands, experiences a maximum 4–5-knot current. While docking in Alert Bay, keep in mind the 3–4-knot current in the bay.*

*This area is known for strong tidal currents and fog. Gale-force winds and accompanying seas can build at any time. Pre-planning and following marine weather predictions are essential.*

Although this area is dominated by strong currents, Broughton Strait is protected from the worst of the westerly winds and seas in Queen Charlotte Strait by Malcolm Island to the north and the string of islands that lie south of Cormorant Channel.

A good spot for whale watching is outside the boundary of Robson Bight Ecological Reserve, a favourite rubbing beach for orcas. Boat Bay and Growler Cove, on West Cracroft Island, provide convenient picnic and overnight anchorage.

Cormorant Channel Marine Park, located between Broughton Strait in the south and Cormorant Channel and Blackfish Sound in the north, encompasses Stephenson Islet in Weynton Passage and a number of islands and islets from both Pearse and Plumper Islands. This delightful park supports a rich variety of wildlife and is the primary habitat of the northern orca population. It is also well used by parties of kayakers on the Johnstone Strait sea-kayaking circuit.

The charming boardwalk village of Telegraph Cove is not always easy to visit by boat, as transient moorage is limited. The Whale Interpretive Centre's Bones Project is an educational work, fascinating for all ages.

Friendly Alert Bay offers excellent provisioning and the sweetest water on the coast. With the impressive U'mista Cultural Centre, the ceremonial "big house" and the captivating display of totem poles in the 'Namgis burial ground, this is a destination not to be missed.

Mitchell Bay, Malcolm Island, is well protected from westerly winds and seas in Cormorant Channel. *Dreamspeaker* anchored here prior to entering the Broughton Archipelago.

18    16

# FEATURED DESTINATIONS

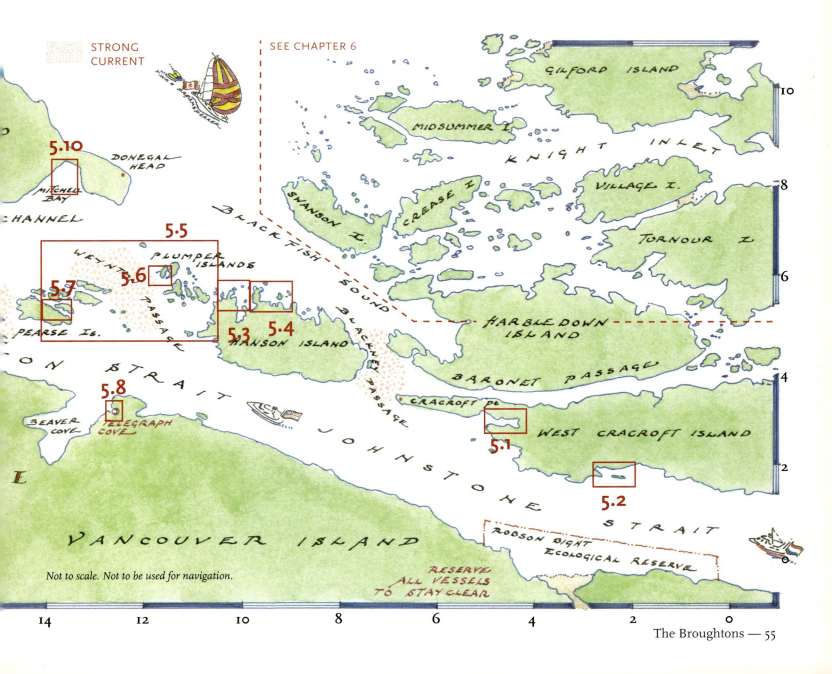

Not to scale. Not to be used for navigation.

# 5.1 GROWLER COVE, WEST CRACROFT ISLAND

✿ 50°32.36'N 126°38.16'W

**CHARTS** 3546.

**APPROACH** The waypoint lies to the N of Sophia Islands. The run lies in centre channel.

**ANCHOR** In 5–10 m (16–32 ft), below a distinctive rock cliff or farther into the head of the cove. Holding good in mud.

*Note:* Growler Cove affords moderate protection from westerly winds.

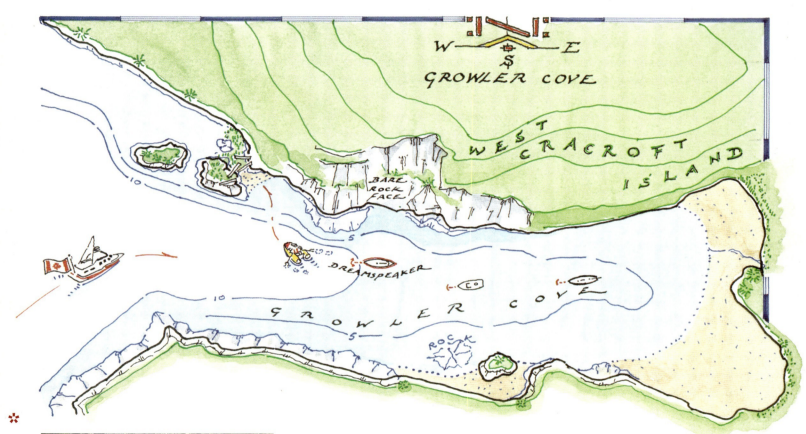

*Not to scale. Not to be used for navigation.*

*Kayakers silhouetted against the bare rock cliff*

Protected and spacious, Growler Cove is reportedly a favourite anchorage for commercial fish boats and their crews sheltering from foul weather in Johnstone Strait. The gently curved gravel beach is backed by driftwood logs, and a grassy picnic patch beside the stream is fronted by a small garden of sea asparagus. We were amused to find a concealed forest toilet, complete with an authentic seat and lid and a recycled fishnet fashioned into a hammock and slung between two trees.

# BOAT BAY, WEST CRACROFT ISLAND

**CHARTS** 3545·

**APPROACH** From the E at LW, rounding what we've named "Tink's Island" into Boat Bay. Rocks covered by kelp extend out from Camp Point, trapping driftwood logs and other debris.

**ANCHOR** There is fair protection from westerly winds, although open to the SE. Anchor in 5 m (16 ft) where holding is good in mud and sand.

*Note: The small float and camp are reserved for the wardens of the Robson Bight (Michael Bigg) Ecological Reserve (across from Boat Bay), who advise boaters of the reserve's boundaries and regulations. The two wardens who visited Dreamspeaker were knowledgeable, affable and enthusiastically committed to educating visitors on the lifestyle of killer whales.*

✳ 50°31.31'N 126°33.07'W

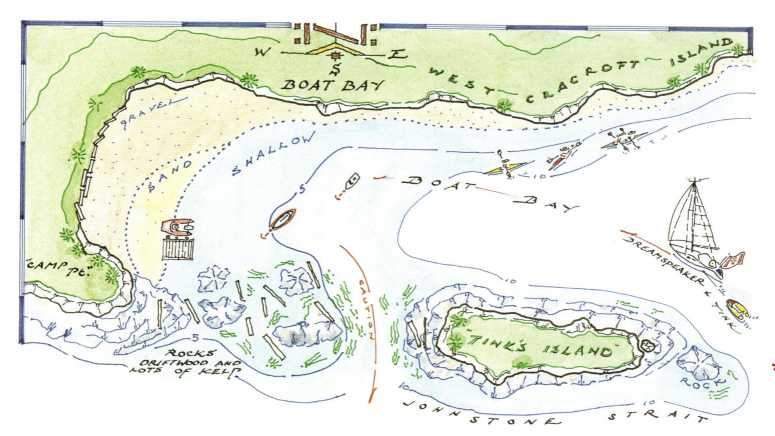

*The friendly Robson Bight wardens in Boat Bay*

The ecological reserve located on the Vancouver Island shores opposite Boat Bay was established in 1982 as a sanctuary, and to preserve an important killer-whale habitat including an upland buffer zone. Killer whales have long used Robson Bight as one of their rubbing beaches, and boats must keep at least half a nautical mile from the posted sign. Approach whales only from the side, never from the front or rear, and keep your engine in neutral or idle.

# DOUBLE BAY, HANSON ISLAND

✱ 50°35.50'N 126°45.98'W

**CHARTS**  3546.

**APPROACH**  From the N. The sign DOUBLE BAY RESORT atop a rock marks the starboard side of the entrance channel.

**ANCHOR**  In the shelter of the group of islets and rocks in 5–10 m (16–32 ft), although it's somewhat open to a swell from Blackfish Sound. Holding good in mud and shell.

*Note: The dock and moorage at PACIFIC OUTBACK RESORT is private and reserved exclusively for resort guests, though guests can purchase packages to go fishing, etc. However, the seasonal facility was not open in 2015, at time of publication.*

**A**nchorage at the head of Double Bay, below the private resort, is deep and not recommended because of the nearby noisy generator. For good depths and lovely views out to Blackfish Sound, drop the hook inside the cluster of rocks and islets to the north. The bay to the southeast is fun to investigate by dinghy at HW; at LW it dries to reveal a sizable shell-and-sand beach.

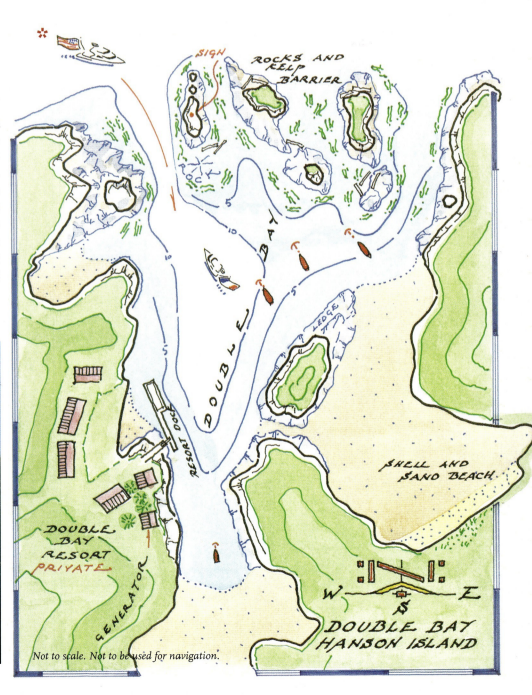

*Mother ship and tender in Double Bay*

# SPOUT ISLETS, HANSON ISLAND 5.4

**CHART** 3546.
**APPROACH** (A) From the NE at LW. The run in is clear. (B) From the NE at LW, beware of the rock ledge to the SE and isolated rock to the W.

**ANCHOR** 1) Tuck into the W shore of "Spout Bay" (named by us). (2) Anchor as indicated in "Spout Cove" (also named by us).

*Note: Both locations afford only moderate protection from swell and westerly winds.*

✤(A) 50°35.36'N 126°44.66'W
✤(B) 50°35.16'N 126°43.94'W

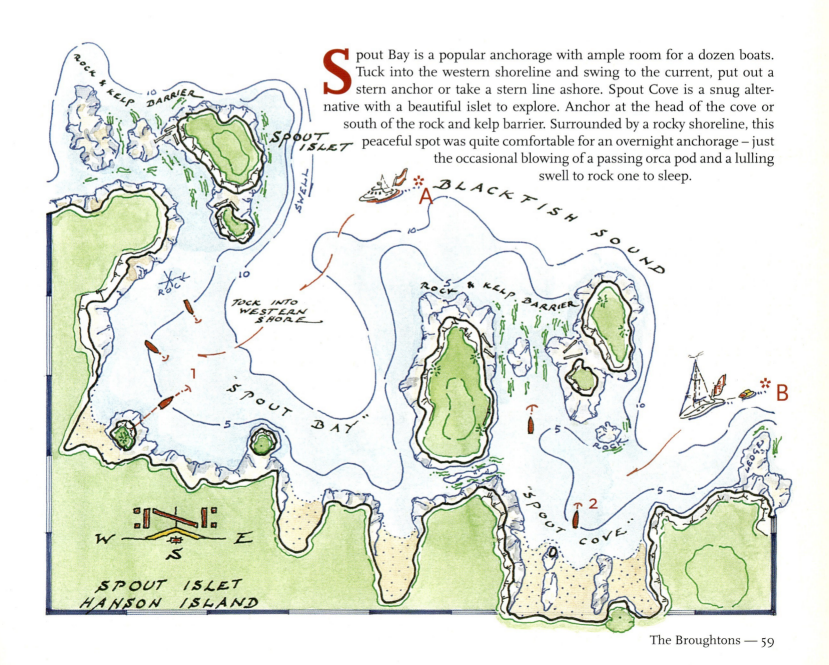

**S**pout Bay is a popular anchorage with ample room for a dozen boats. Tuck into the western shoreline and swing to the current, put out a stern anchor or take a stern line ashore. Spout Cove is a snug alternative with a beautiful islet to explore. Anchor at the head of the cove or south of the rock and kelp barrier. Surrounded by a rocky shoreline, this peaceful spot was quite comfortable for an overnight anchorage – just the occasional blowing of a passing orca pod and a lulling swell to rock one to sleep.

# 5.5 CORMORANT CHANNEL MARINE PARK

See 5.6 and 5.7 for detail opposite.

✽ (A) Plumper Islands:
   50°35.24'N 126°48.87'W
✽ (B) Pearse Islands:
   50°34.51'N 126°51.14'W

**CAUTIONARY NOTE:** *Weynton Passage is a current station. This area is known for strong tidal currents and fog. Gale-force winds and accompanying seas can build at any time. Pre-planning and following marine weather predictions are essential.*

Located between Broughton Strait in the south and Cormorant Channel and Blackfish Sound in the north, Cormorant Channel Marine Park encompasses a number of islands and islets from both Pearse and Plumper Islands. It also includes Stephenson Islet in Weynton Passage. Frequented by parties of kayakers on the Johnstone Strait sea-kayaking circuit, the park supports a rich variety of wildlife and is the primary habitat of the northern resident orca population.

*Not to scale. Not to be used for navigation.*

# PLUMPER ISLANDS, CORMORANT CHANNEL MARINE PARK 5.6

*A peaceful pool surrounded by kelp*

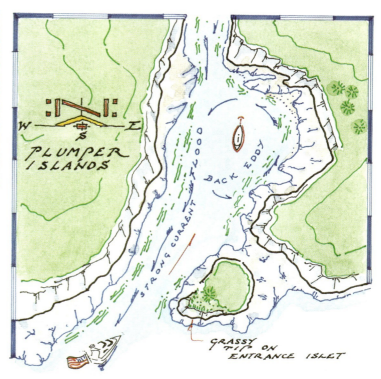

**CHARTS** 3546.

**APPROACH** From the S at LW. The two islands lie to the NW of Ksuiladas Island.

**ANCHOR** As indicated, in 5 m (16 ft); strong current is present.

**D**reamspeaker swung to the current in the small pool created by the back eddy. Some boaters might find this anchorage a little unnerving; however, there is good protection from westerly and easterly winds.

# PEARSE ISLANDS, CORMORANT CHANNEL MARINE PARK 5.7

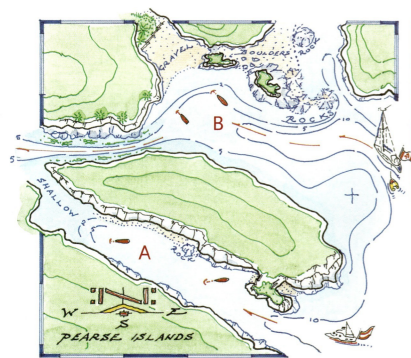
*Note: A good rendezvous spot for a number of boats.*

*A small gravel beach for stretching your legs*

**CHARTS** 3546.

**APPROACH** From the SE. Both approaches are deep and without obstruction. The channel between the two islands is navigable in the centre, although the current flows pretty swiftly.

**ANCHOR** (A) This long, narrow and deep anchorage shallows at its head. (B) Keep an eye out for rocks off the NE shore. Swing in the centre, off the gravel beach, and enjoy the open view out to Broughton Channel and the mountains beyond. Good protection from westerly winds. Depths and holding vary.

# 5.8 TELEGRAPH COVE, VANCOUVER ISLAND

✿ 50°32.89'N 126°50.08'W

*Approach to Telegraph Cove with gas dock to starboard*

*Small boat moorage backed by the whale museum*

*Little room to manoeuvre in the centre channel*

The charming boardwalk village of historic Telegraph Cove is not always easy to visit by boat; visitors often take a day-trip from Port McNeill, using public transportation, as it's well worth a visit. Taking a chance, we contacted TELEGRAPH COVE MARINA before reaching the entrance channel. It was our lucky day, and we were able to secure a slip big enough to accommodate *Dreamspeaker*'s 36-foot length for the night.

Although the architecture on this side of the cove is in total contrast to the historic village opposite, we appreciated the resort's clean shower and laundry facilities. THE SEAHORSE CAFÉ AND GALLERY at the head of Dockside 29 has a lovely view of the cove and serves great coffee and delicious breakfast and lunch dishes (a bowl of granola, fruit and yoghurt; an egg-on-a-muffin; an artichoke panini).

The cove was named in 1911 when a telegraph station was built there; it also operated as a logging camp, saltery and a sawmill, which eventually supplied lumber for the boats, docks, bridges and railways on northern Vancouver Island. At that time, the community of Telegraph Cove had over 60 residents who were served by the Union Steamship Company. Pick up the black-and-white sketchbook by Teresa Petite and relive history with an informative boardwalk tour of the original timber buildings and homes.

Provisioning is possible at the well-stocked GENERAL STORE, which also has a BC LIQUOR STORE outlet. Buy a picnic lunch and spread a blanket on the lawn, enjoy the atmosphere and some fine pub grub at the OLD SALTERY PUB or pop into the KILLER WHALE CAFÉ, which serves very tasty lunch and dinner dishes. Their patio seating is shaded by umbrellas and offers a delightful way to enjoy this historic village.

Jim and Mary Barrowman's WHALE INTERPRETIVE CENTRE is located in the old Freight Shed near the cove entrance. Dubbed the "Bones Project," this educational work-in-progress is fascinating for all ages, as skeletons are cleaned and displayed on site. Volunteers encourage visitors to ask questions and will happily take you on a tour. We left the centre far more knowledgeable about marine mammals and the fascinating internal anatomy of a diverse number of whale species.

**CHARTS** 3546.

**APPROACH** From the NW. The entrance is made obvious (in summer) by the amount of commercial and sportsboat traffic. Kayaking, whale watching and wildlife tours also operate out of Telegraph Cove.

**ANCHOR** There is no room to anchor within the cove.

**MARINA** Both TELE-GRAPH COVE MARINA (1-877-835-2683) and TELE-GRAPH COVE RESORTS (1-800-200-4665) are private, with moorage for sports fishing boats. They have no designated visitor moorage; however, slips do become available. Do not enter the cove without making prior arrange-ments, as there is little room to manoeuvre.

**FUEL** Gas is available at the northern end of the TELEGRAPH COVE RE-SORT boardwalk (although no diesel).

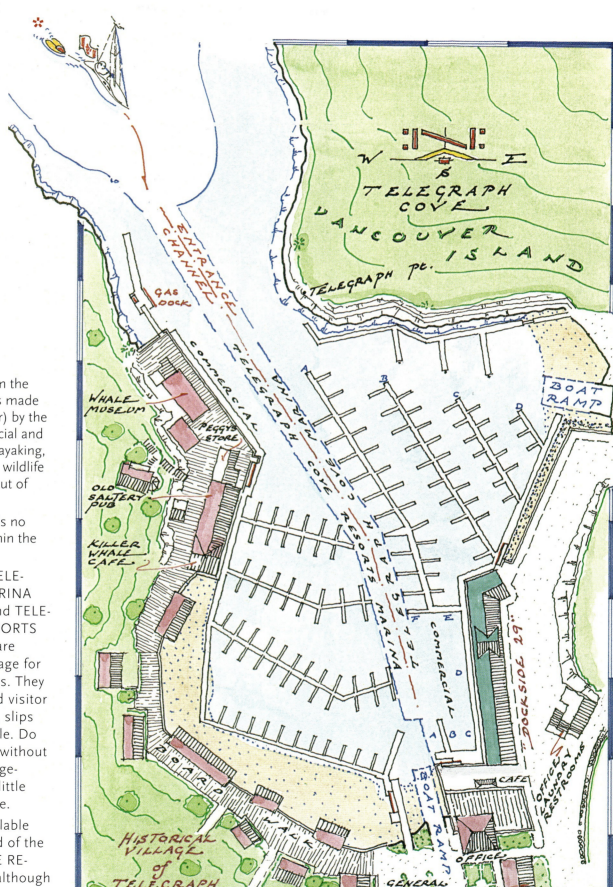

❀50°34.89'N 126°55.91'W

*Entrance to Alert Bay boat harbour*

*The colourful seawall*

*The historic waterfront with the former Nimpkish Hotel and Pub*

The historic, warm community of Alert Bay is worth a visit. With so much to see and do, stay overnight in the protected anchorage at the head of the bay or at the boat harbour inside the breakwater north of the ferry terminal. A fun alternative is to take the scheduled ferry from Port McNeill on Vancouver Island; we enjoyed both.

South of the ferry terminal, the colourful village of Alert Bay welcomes visitors to tie up at the convenient public wharf. From here, it's a short walk to Front Street and the island's ALERT BAY PUBLIC LIBRARY AND MUSEUM, which houses an excellent archival collection of historic and modern photographs. The well-appointed ALERT BAY VISITOR INFO CENTRE and art gallery offers internet access and a selection of free booklets and information leaflets. Contact them at 250-974-5024, email info@village.alertbay.bc.ca, or visit their website at www.alertbay.ca.

From the info centre, take a self-guided tour of Alert Bay's historic buildings that date back to the mid-1800s, or walk along the Ecological Park trails and boardwalk built over a natural swamp at the top of the island, which hosts birds of many species. The variety of memorial poles displayed in the nearby 'Namgis First Nation burial ground is captivating and ranges from vibrant, recently erected figures to those in the final stages of decomposition; poles are not repainted or repaired, in keeping with the belief that all things must return to nature.

Excellent provisioning is available at the supermarket and deli, where you'll find fresh produce, dry goods, hardware sections and even nautical charts. A liquor store and post office are nearby, and the sidewalk gift stores and art galleries carry local artists' works.

Front Street also offers a variety of fine, locally run cafés and restaurants, including the historic OLD CUSTOMS HOUSE RESTAURANT and the PASS'N THYME INN AND RESTAURANT, with a great view from the covered patio.

Located north of the ferry terminal, at the western end of Front Street, the U'MISTA CULTURAL CENTRE is a must-see. Built in 1980, it houses one of the finest collections of carved and decorated masks, coppers and other Kwakwaka'wakw ceremonial artifacts, which were repatriated in 1978 after being confiscated in 1921 following a traditional potlatch on Village Island. The gift shop also carries

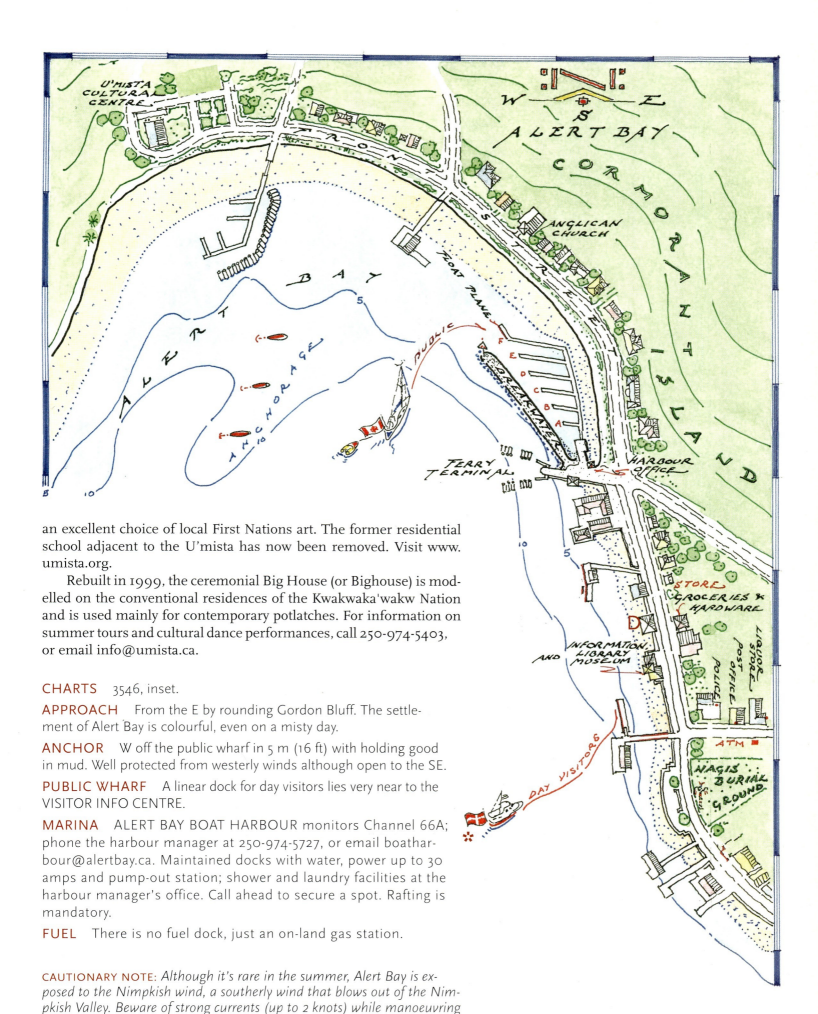

an excellent choice of local First Nations art. The former residential school adjacent to the U'mista has now been removed. Visit www.umista.org.

Rebuilt in 1999, the ceremonial Big House (or Bighouse) is modelled on the conventional residences of the Kwakwaka'wakw Nation and is used mainly for contemporary potlatches. For information on summer tours and cultural dance performances, call 250-974-5403, or email info@umista.ca.

**CHARTS**   3546, inset.

**APPROACH**   From the E by rounding Gordon Bluff. The settlement of Alert Bay is colourful, even on a misty day.

**ANCHOR**   W off the public wharf in 5 m (16 ft) with holding good in mud. Well protected from westerly winds although open to the SE.

**PUBLIC WHARF**   A linear dock for day visitors lies very near to the VISITOR INFO CENTRE.

**MARINA**   ALERT BAY BOAT HARBOUR monitors Channel 66A; phone the harbour manager at 250-974-5727, or email boatharbour@alertbay.ca. Maintained docks with water, power up to 30 amps and pump-out station; shower and laundry facilities at the harbour manager's office. Call ahead to secure a spot. Rafting is mandatory.

**FUEL**   There is no fuel dock, just an on-land gas station.

**CAUTIONARY NOTE:** *Although it's rare in the summer, Alert Bay is exposed to the Nimpkish wind, a southerly wind that blows out of the Nimpkish Valley. Beware of strong currents (up to 2 knots) while manoeuvring to dock at the public wharf and boat harbour.*

*Memorial totem poles displayed in the 'Namgis burial ground, Alert Bay*

*At anchor off the public wharf*

**CHARTS**  3546.

**APPROACH**  From the S, best at LW if intending to anchor. The public wharf and settlement are conspicuous with a logging operation, local buoys, driftwood and the coast road.

**ANCHOR**  Off the gravel beach between the boulders and seaward of the local buoys in 5–10 m (16–32 ft). Holding good in gravel and kelp.

**PUBLIC WHARF**  Local fish boats and runabouts occupy the wharf. It would be best to anchor off and take the dinghy ashore.

⚓ 50°37.78'N 126°51.26'W

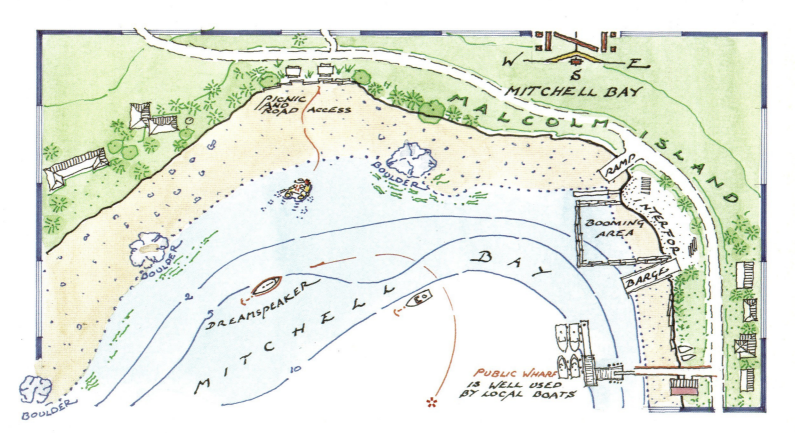

*Note: Gusty winds sweep the bay when there are strong westerly winds in Queen Charlotte Strait.*

Nestled between the trees on the southeast point of Malcolm Island lies the small, neat community of Mitchell Bay. The anchorage is backed by driftwood and a curved gravel beach, with a picnic area and public access to the island road that begins at Pulteney Point in the west and ends at Donegal Head in the east. With *Dreamspeaker* securely anchored for the night, we sat in the cockpit at sunset to witness an exhilarating and loud display of herons, bald eagles and seagulls fighting to intercept the huge schools of fish caught in the kelp and whirling cross-current. Early the next morning, we observed several locals out fishing in the traditional way – with rowboats and canoes.

# 5.11 BROUGHTON ARCHIPELAGO MARINE PARK

See chapters 6 & 7

*The Marine Park is extremely popular with kayaking enthusiasts worldwide*

*Broughton Archipelago – The perfect place to meditate on the universe*

Established in 1992 as a BC Protected Area, Broughton Archipelago Marine Park is British Columbia's largest marine park (117 square kilometres/73 square miles), and is located 30 km (18.6 mi) east of Port McNeill, on northern Vancouver Island. It is situated on the west side of Queen Charlotte Strait, near the mouth of Knight Inlet.

Broughton Archipelago Marine Park offers fabulous boating, kayaking and wildlife viewing opportunities and is extremely popular with kayaking enthusiasts worldwide. Although the many passages in the park are affected by the swift ebbing currents that force the waters of Queen Charlotte Strait through its countless islets and small islands, visitors can still find sheltered waters and a selection of protected anchorages backed by the magnificent, snow-capped coastal mountains to the east.

The area has a rich 12,000-year history, as its sheltered waters, abundant sea life and natural vegetation were the mainstay of the Kwakiutl First Nation, who established numerous village communities in the Broughton Archipelago. The many shell-midden beaches and clam gardens among the park's captivating maze of islands and islets give evidence of the bountiful lifestyle before the area was discovered by European explorers in the late 1700s, then settled by pioneers in the late 1800s and early 1900s. The remains of these sites, plus culturally modified trees (large, old red-cedar trees known as CMTs), and an ancient pictograph painted on a rock wall in Village Channel, can also be found in the park. The pictograph is on the north side of Berry Island, near a small rock pool known as the "Chief's Bathtub."

*Note that all heritage sites are protected by law – please treat these areas with respect.*

*Note: See Chapter 6 – Broughton Archipelago South (p. 71), and Chapter 7 – Broughton Archipelago North (p. 85) for details of marine park destinations.*

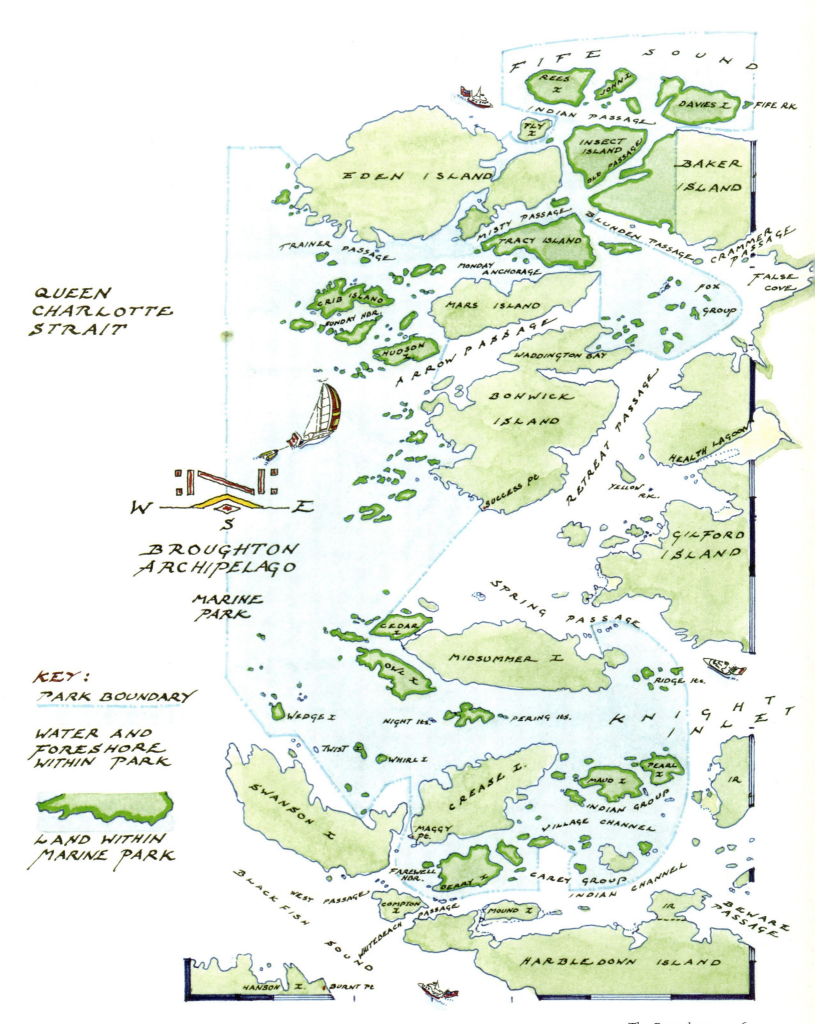

QUEEN
CHARLOTTE
STRAIT

BROUGHTON
ARCHIPELAGO

MARINE
PARK

KEY:
PARK BOUNDARY

WATER AND
FORESHORE
WITHIN PARK

LAND WITHIN
MARINE PARK

FIFE SOUND

REES I.
JOHN I.
DAVIES I. FIFE RK.
INDIAN PASSAGE
FLY I.
INSECT ISLAND
OLD PASSAGE
BAKER ISLAND
EDEN ISLAND
MISTY PASSAGE
BLUNDEN PASSAGE
CRAMMER PASSAGE
TRAINER PASSAGE
TRACY ISLAND
FALSE COVE
MONDAY ANCHORAGE
FOX GROUP
CRIB ISLAND
MARS ISLAND
SUNDAY HBR.
HUDSON I.
ARROW PASSAGE
WADDINGTON BAY
BONWICK ISLAND
RETREAT PASSAGE
HEALTH LAGOON
SUCCESS PT.
YELLOW RK.
GILFORD ISLAND
SPRING PASSAGE
CEDAR I.
MIDSUMMER I.
OWL I.
RIDGE ITS.
WEDGE I.
NIGHT ITS.
PERING ITS.
KNIGHT INLET
TWIST I.
WHIRL I.
MAUD I.
PEARL I.
IR.
SWANSON I.
CREASE I.
INDIAN GROUP
MAGGY PT.
VILLAGE CHANNEL
FAREWELL HBR.
BERRY I.
CAREY GROUP
INDIAN CHANNEL
BLACK FISH SOUND
WEST PASSAGE
COMPTON I.
WHITEBEACH PASSAGE
MOUND I.
IR.
BEWARE PASSAGE
HARBLEDOWN ISLAND
HANSON I.
BURNT PT.

*A serene evening anchorage aglow in Broughton Archipelago*

Chapter 6

# BROUGHTON ARCHIPELAGO SOUTH

## Chapter 6

# BROUGHTON ARCHIPELAGO SOUTH

**TIDES** – *Volume 6, Canadian Tide and Current Tables*

Reference Port – Alert Bay
Secondary Port – Cedar Island

**CURRENTS**

No specific reference or secondary stations cover this chapter; however, currents run swiftly through the channels and passages, creating a certain amount of current in most anchorages.

**WEATHER**

Weather Station – WX1 162.55 MHZ
Area – Queen Charlotte Strait
Reporting Station – Alert Bay

The Village of 'Mi'mkwamlis (Mamalilaculla) slowly retreating back to nature

**CAUTIONARY NOTES:** *Countless marked and unmarked rocks and reefs are scattered throughout this southern portion of the Broughton Archipelago; explore the area at low water when the dangers are visible – fog will also obscure the proliferation of rocks.*

*The presence of kelp is often a clue to the rocks and reefs below. Kelp also indicates the direction of currents; a path between kelp will often denote a deep-water passage.*

There are two routes into the southern portion of Broughton Archipelago from Blackfish Sound – the popular southern choice through Whitebeach Passage is clear and unobstructed, while the less straightforward northern route via West Passage experiences current swirls from unexpected directions and should be navigated only at LW, when the rocks are visible.

Once inside this magnificent village of islands, the uninterrupted vista of the island groups is quite breathtaking, and further exploration reveals splendid views around every headland. Cruising through the Broughton Archipelago helps to bring the area's ancient First Nations history to life, and at LW the clam gardens and middens with sun-bleached, white-shell beaches pinpoint the sites of the numerous indigenous villages and food gathering areas. Kayaking parties paddling between the islands have now replaced the hundreds of dugout canoes that plied these waters, ferrying locals and commodities between the now-deserted villages. Please treat these sites and any artifacts with respect at all times.

Located between Village and Turnour Islands, the aptly named Beware Passage – strewn with an abundance of marked and unmarked islets and rocks – has strong currents and should be navigated with caution, preferably at LW. When transiting south to Clio Channel, Beware Cove is the only suitable fine-weather anchorage in the passage.

Prior to leaving this captivating maze of islands, drop anchor off protected Crease Island and explore charming Goat Islet. Adorned with a mass of wildflowers in the springtime, this small islet provides the perfect picnic spot with a view, shaded by a single tree.

# FEATURED DESTINATIONS

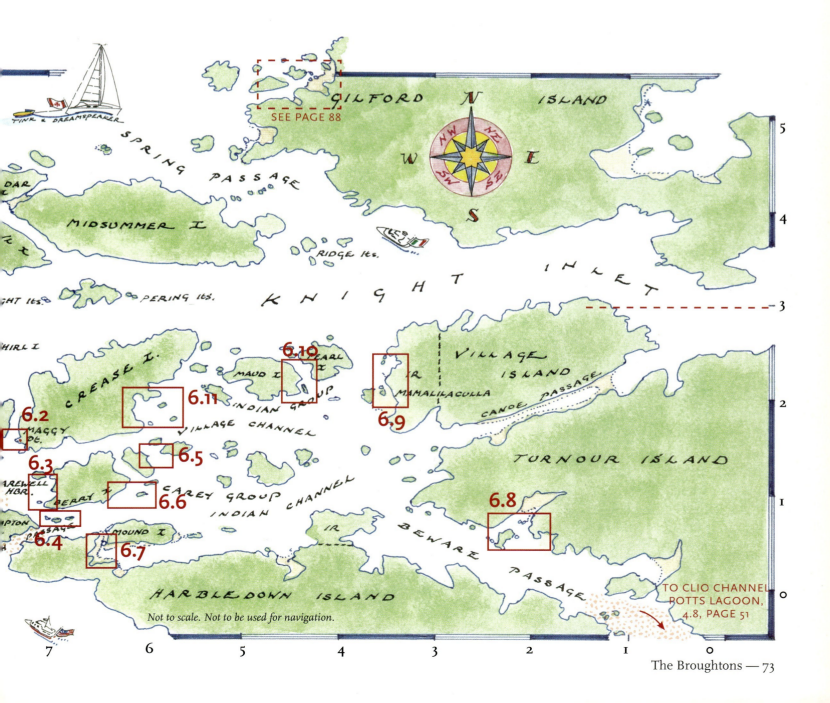

Not to scale. Not to be used for navigation.

TO CLIO CHANNEL POTTS LAGOON, 4.8, PAGE 51

SEE PAGE 88

# 6.1 WEST PASSAGE BETWEEN SWANSON AND COMPTON ISLANDS

❋ (A) 50°35.82'N 126°41.74'W
❋ (B) 50°36.46'N 126°40.90'W
❋ (C) 50°35.99'N 126°40.52'W

**CHARTS** 3546.

**APPROACH** (A) From Blackfish Sound. After rounding Slate Point with an eye out for Punt Rock to the W, leave Star Islets either to the S or to the N with caution, as this passage is navigable, but fringed with kelp.

**MARINA** KAYAKADVENTURESVILLAGE.COM RESORT is a seasonal shore-based facility for kayaks and small craft.

*Kayaks at Maggy Point*

There are two passages from Blackfish Sound into the southern part of the archipelago. Whitebeach Passage east of Compton Island is the most popular because it is clear and unobstructed. West Passage is a more direct route into Farewell Harbour; however, it requires careful navigation. Having negotiated the passage into Farewell Harbour, one immediately senses the calm of the Village of Islands. KAYAKADVENTURESVILLAGE.COM RESORT is a tent, cabin and cooking area set up in a bight on Compton Island's north shore. It is operated by a local First Nations company (Adventures Village Island) and caters to kayakers, but small visiting yachts may tie up at their dock and come ashore for a First Nations cultural and dining experience. Phone 250-488-7293.

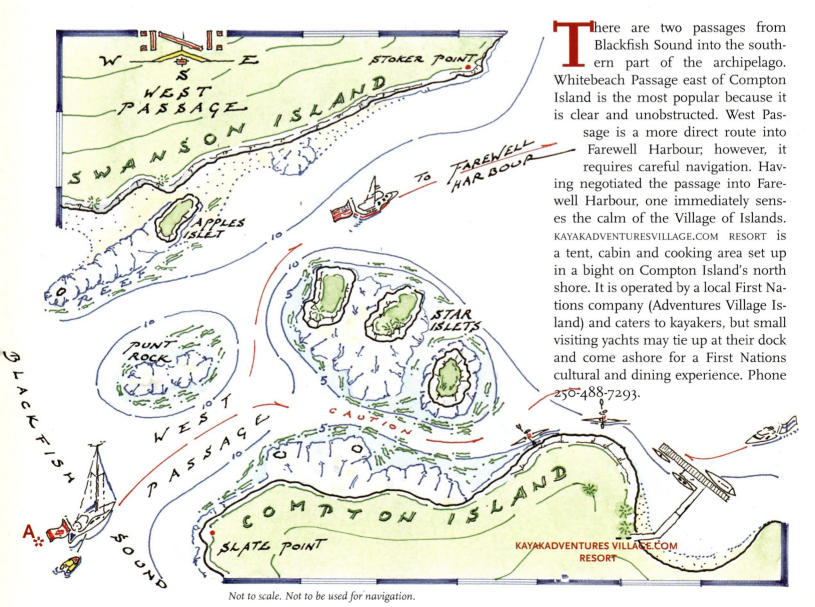

*Not to scale. Not to be used for navigation.*

# MAGGY POINT, CREASE ISLAND 6.2

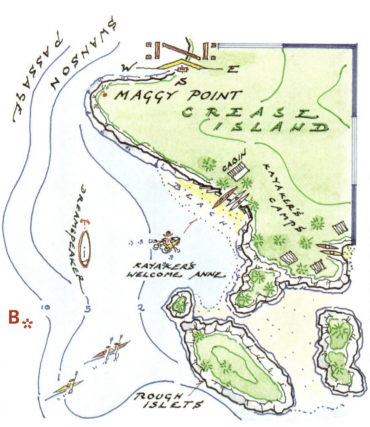

CHARTS   3546.

APPROACH   (B) From within Farewell Harbour leaving Rough Islets to the E or from Swanson Passage in the N. Both are clear and without obstruction.

ANCHOR   In depths of 3–6 m (9–19 ft) with protection from the west. Holding is good in sticky mud and kelp.

**W**ithin the Broughton Archipelago Marine Park boundaries, this delightful spot is useful as a picnic or overnight stop and is also home to an established summer kayak camp complete with a covered cookhouse just off the beach, rustic shower and toilet facilities, and tent platforms in the trees. While on a row of discovery in our dinghy, *Tink*, we were invited by a generous group of paddlers to share their happy-hour fruit cocktails and appetizers – luxury camping at its best.

For overnight anchorage in Farewell Harbour, the spots indicated S of Kumax Island give good protection.

# FAREWELL HARBOUR, 6.3
# BERRY ISLAND

CHARTS   3546.

APPROACH   (C) From the W. The private fishing lodge on a rocky point, central to the bay, is conspicuous.

ANCHOR   To the N of the lodge, S of Kumax Island in 4–10 m (13–32 ft). Excellent holding in sticky mud. Well protected from the E with moderate protection from the W.

*Note: The lodge float is private. At the time of writing, the resort was not operating and was reportedly up for sale.*

*Farewell Harbour Lodge and private dock*

# 6.4 SARAH ISLETS

6.5

6.4 — 6.6

✿ (A) 50°35.84'N 126°40.43'W
✿ (B) 50°36.55'N 126°38.77'W
✿ (C) 50°35.94'N 126°39.02'W

**CHARTS**  3546.

**APPROACH**  (A) From Farewell Harbour. The passage N of Sarah Islets is lined with kelp and the best landmark is the white-shell mound on the eastern islet.

**ANCHOR**  To the N of Sarah Islets, in a kelp-free spot. This is a comfortable anchorage in settled weather, where a boat will swing to the current in depths of 6–8 m (19–26 ft). Protected from the S with some protection from the E and W, with fair holding in sand and shell.

*Tranquility personified in Sarah Islets*

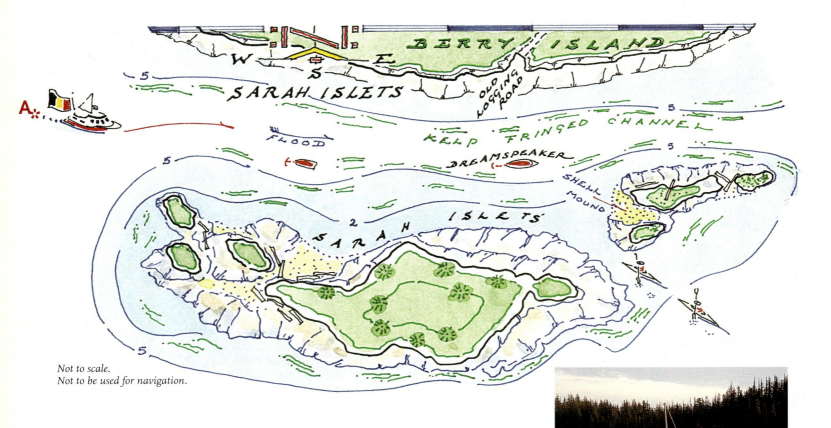

*Not to scale.*
*Not to be used for navigation.*

We found three spots in the approach to Indian Channel, Sarah Islets and the anchorages south of Madrona Island and Leone Islets. The channel between Sarah Islets and Berry Island is an ideal spot to anchor for the night in settled weather, if you're looking for a secluded alternative to Farewell Harbour. Kayakers use the narrow pass between the midden and the islets. With views east down Indian Channel, the islet and the white-shell mound are fun to explore. Take a break from the boat and beachcomb, picnic or harvest the fresh sea asparagus.

*A sunset beam illuminates Dreamspeaker*

# MADRONA ISLAND 6.5

**CHARTS**   3546.

**APPROACH**   ((B) From Village Channel or alternatively from Indian Channel.

**ANCHOR**   Between Madrona Island and the small islet to the S, in a still pool of 4 m (13 ft) with little current and fair protection all round. Holding is fair in sand, gravel and kelp. In the evening, a glowing sunset illuminates the steep rock bluff on Madrona Island.

*Note: Due to continuous generator noise from the nearby fish farm, we recommend this anchorage only when a westerly wind is blowing.*

# "LEONE ISLETS," LEONE ISLAND 6.6

**CHARTS**   3546.

**APPROACH**   (C) Named by us, these islets lie S of Leone Island and E of Berry Island. Approach from the W, out of Indian Channel.

**ANCHOR**   In depths of 3–5 m (9–16 ft) in a pool surrounded by kelp. Boats will swing to the current. A quiet 1-boat anchorage with plenty of rocks and islets to explore.

*Note: For both anchorages exploration is best made at LW. Rocks abound but are well marked by kelp.*

✿50°35.31'N 126°38.92'W

**CHARTS**   3546.

**APPROACH**   From Indian Channel. The entrance lies between two un-named islets to the E of Mound Island.

**ANCHOR**   As indicated in depths of 4–10 m (13–32 ft), this commodious bay is well protected from westerly winds with good holding in mud.

*Note:* Some shelter can be found in the bay in moderate SE winds.

*Good holding in mud with a stow-aboard sea star!*

Spacious and protected, the anchorage in what we've come to call "Mound Bay" is tucked between Mound and Harbeldown Islands and is a popular hideout for boaters during strong westerly winds. The small shell beach off Mound Island is backed by a summer kayak camp, with soft mossy rocks and islets for picnicking or setting up tents. The forest trail reportedly leads to a sanctuary of old-growth trees on the island. Please respect this area, as it is an ancient First Nations burial site.

# BEWARE COVE, TURNOUR ISLAND 6.8

**CHARTS** 3545.

**APPROACH** From the W. The entrance channel N of Cook Island is clear. The alternative entrance from the S has a narrow and kelp-lined channel.

**ANCHOR** To the NE of Cook Island in depths of 4–6 m (13–19 ft) with good holding in mud and shell. The cove is open to all winds, although it provides moderate protection from the NW.

*Note: Beware Cove is a temporary anchorage with good views out. The cove is outside the marine park boundaries.*

✳50°35.57'N 126°33.32'W

*Local knowledge helps to know where to anchor in a SE blow*

**B**eware Passage is aptly named for its strong currents and abundance of marked and unmarked islets and rocks, and therefore should be navigated with caution, preferably at low water. Beware Cove was the only suitable anchorage found in the passage on a transit south to Clio Channel on a cold and overcast day. Cook Island looked inviting to explore on a sunny day.

Dreamspeaker *anchored in the bay north of the village*

# MAMALILACULLA ('MI'MKW<u>A</u>MLIS), VILLAGE ISLAND 6.9

*A good example of a large, clam-shell midden beach*

**CHARTS**  3546.

**APPROACH**  From Elliot Passage. Pass between the makeshift breakwater and the Barrier Islets to the N.

**ANCHOR**  In approximately 5 m (16 ft) with good holding in mud and shell. Protected from all but strong NW winds.

*Note: 'Mi'mkw<u>a</u>mlis is also accessible by dinghy from many of the anchorages featured in this chapter. Village tours are available through Adventures Village Island, 250-488-7293, www.kayakadventuresvillage.com.*

❊50°37.33'N 126°35.07'W

**A**nchoring *Dreamspeaker* in the bay, we rowed *Tink* past the breakwater and the remains of a float that leads to the now-abandoned village trail. In the fine rain, a wispy mist enveloped the overgrown ruins and fallen totem poles, adding to the hushed, ghostlike mood of 'Mi'mkw<u>a</u>mlis. Fronted by a long, shell beach and somewhat protected by the island and islets to the west, this once-thriving village, built on an ancient midden, housed a large First Nations community that in the early 1900s even included a schoolhouse. The book *Totem Poles and Tea* gives Hughina Harold's honest insight into village life in the 1930s, as does an account by M. Wylie Blanchet in the classic, *The Curve of Time.*

# 6.10 "PEARL PASS" BETWEEN MAUD AND PEARL ISLANDS

❀50°37.11'N 126°35.95'W

**CHARTS**  3546.

**APPROACH**  From the S. Favour the Maud Island shore as rocks extend into the pass entrance.

**ANCHOR**  In 2–5 m (6–16 ft) between the kelp patches, as indicated. Good protection in moderate westerly winds. In strong winds, swells surge in from the north.

*Note: The kelp barrier at the head of the anchorage prevents further navigation.*

"PEARL PASS"

KELP BARRIER

MAUD ISLAND

PEARL PASS

PEARL ISLAND

BIG ROCKS

ROCK

*Not to scale. Not to be used for navigation.*

DREAMSPEAK TINK AND CREW SPEND A NIGHT HERE. ❀

*A primeval morning at low water*

Rocks and trees surround the kelp-lined but cozy two-boat anchorage that we named "Pearl Pass," tucked inside the entrance channel between Maud and Pearl Islands. With a fine view out to Village Channel, and our neighbours sharing their surprise halibut catch with us, a pleasant night was had by all.

*Not a goat in sight – but a lone tree stands proud!*

✻50°36.78'N 126°38.17'W

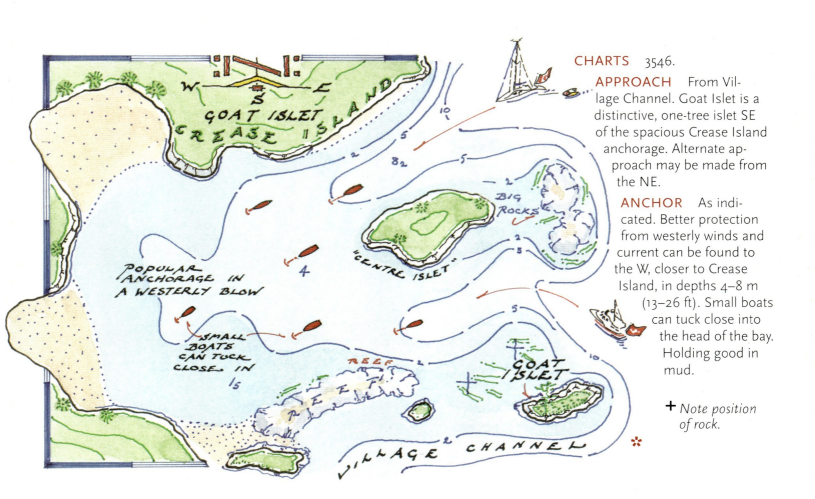

**CHARTS**   3546.

**APPROACH**   From Village Channel. Goat Islet is a distinctive, one-tree islet SE of the spacious Crease Island anchorage. Alternate approach may be made from the NE.

**ANCHOR**   As indicated. Better protection from westerly winds and current can be found to the W, closer to Crease Island, in depths 4–8 m (13–26 ft). Small boats can tuck close into the head of the bay. Holding good in mud.

+ *Note position of rock.*

Adorned with a mass of wildflowers in the springtime, charming Goat Islet provides boaters with the perfect spot to picnic in the summer months. Explore the small island and enjoy the view out to Village Channel before spreading a blanket on the soft grass, shaded by a single tree. An experienced and friendly fisherman named Jim Davis, who anchors his boat there in the summer months, recommended this sheltered anchorage.

Ocean Dawn, *Anne and Goldy, Billy and* Dreamspeaker *in "Proctor Bay" backed by Bill Proctor's homestead and museum*

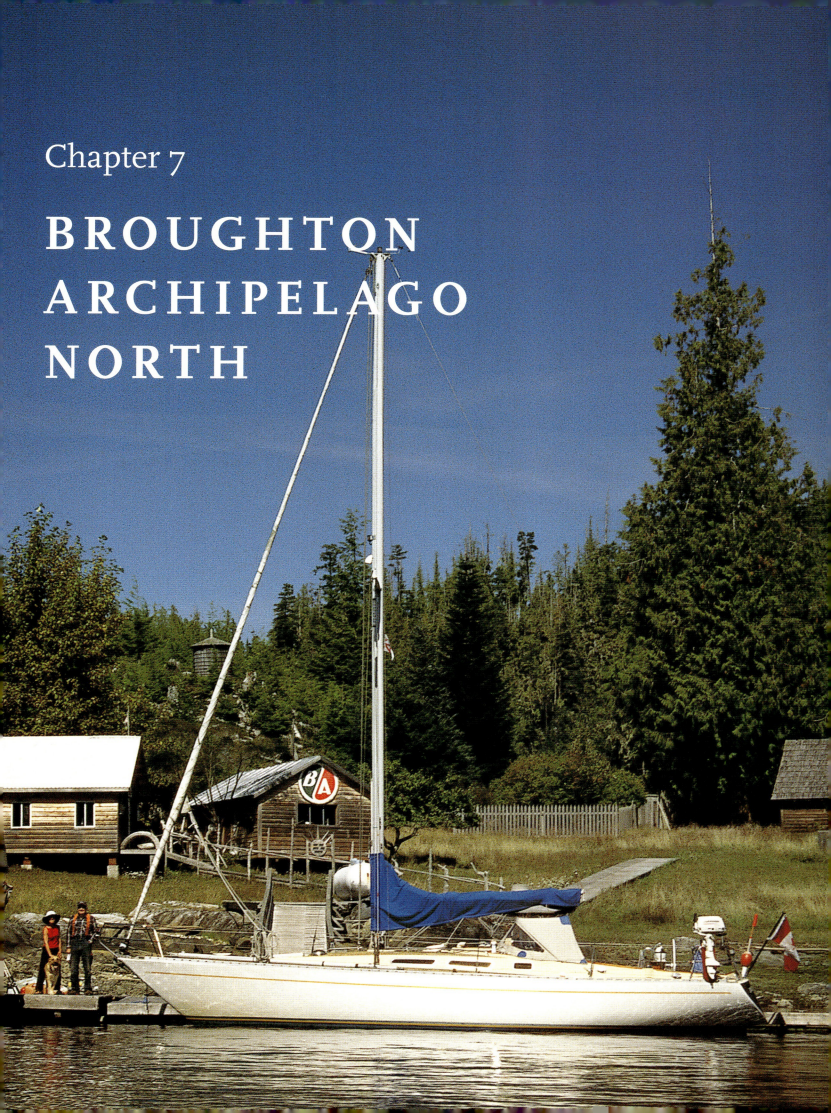

Chapter 7

# BROUGHTON ARCHIPELAGO NORTH

# Chapter 7

# BROUGHTON ARCHIPELAGO NORTH

**TIDES** – *Volume 6,*
*Canadian Tide and Current Tables*
Reference Port – Alert Bay
Secondary Port – Sunday Harbour

**CURRENTS**

No specific reference or secondary
stations cover this chapter; however,
currents run swiftly through the channels and passages, creating a certain
amount of current in most anchorages.

**WEATHER**

Weather Stations – WX1 162.55 MHZ
Weather Radio Canada 103.70 MHZ
Area – Queen Charlotte Strait
Reporting Stations – Alert Bay,
Port Harvey

*Venturing into fog*

**CAUTIONARY NOTES:** *The outer islands
of the Broughton Archipelago that
fringe Queen Charlotte Strait offer little
protection from summer westerly winds;
shelter should be found before wind and
seas build. Although this northern section of the Broughton Archipelago is well
charted, there are many unmarked rocks
and it is best navigated at LW when the
majority of dangers are visible. Morning
fog is a prevailing condition in this area.*

Squeezed between Queen Charlotte Strait and Gilford
Island, the northern isles of the Broughton Archipelago offer picturesque anchorages with snug coves
east of Seabreeze Island, Health Bay and Lagoon, and the
inviting islets hugging Bonwick Island's western shore.
Dusky Cove is a delight to explore in settled weather.

Waddington Bay, wedged into the northern tip of
Bonwick Island, is well protected but a little crowded
in the summer. Nearby is a small anchorage we named
"Kelp Bight," where we overnighted with great views.

Gilford Island – home to the now legendary fisherman, storyteller, author and environmental advocate Bill
Proctor – is the largest in the enchanting Broughton region. Echo Bay provides a sheltered harbour, small marine park, and a marina with transient moorage, along
with showers, laundry, provisioning and fuel. There is a
breathtaking, 200-foot sheer cliff on the eastern shoreline of the bay, and the view out to Cramer Passage is
sensational.

West via Indian Passage takes you to Eden Island
and "Lady Boot Cove," Monday Harbour and Joe Cove –
a quiet, sheltered anchorage.

9     8

# FEATURED DESTINATIONS

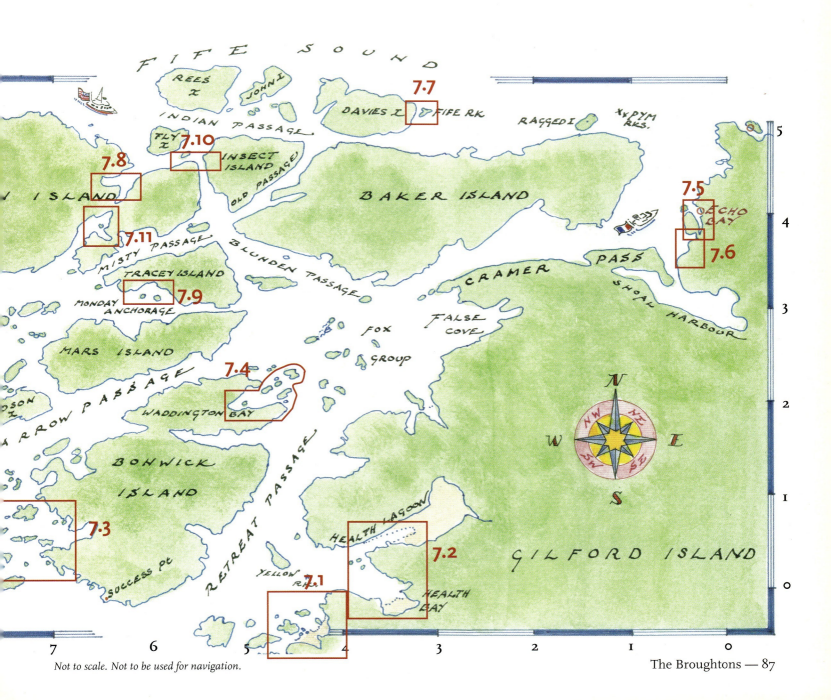

*Not to scale. Not to be used for navigation.*

# 7.1 COVES EAST OF SEABREEZE ISLAND

✤50°40.79'N 126°36.79'W

**CHARTS** 3546.

**APPROACH** Best approached at LW. The waypoint lies just S of Gilford Rock. When heading S, thread your way slowly between Islet 1 and 2. For the northern anchorages, head E between Islet 2 and 3.

**ANCHOR** In any of the four small coves indicated. Holding is excellent in mud with depths of 4–8 m (13–26 ft). Suitable for one or two boats; all anchorages offer good protection from the SE and moderate protection from the W.

*A sea breeze ripples the water*

It was a pleasant sail from Success Point to the snug coves east of Seabreeze Island. Black bears, previously sighted by our boat neighbours, were being elusive, although watchful bald eagles and osprey looked on while Bonaparte gulls indulged in a one-legged nap, and sleepy seals lazed on the warm rocks. Illuminated by the sun's radiant afterglow, this cluster of islets provided the perfect setting for an overnight stay.

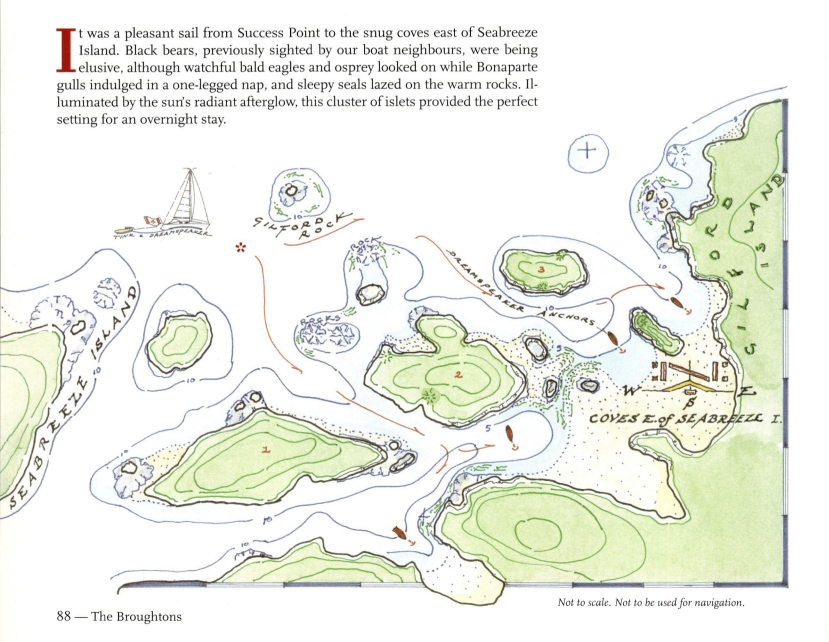

*Not to scale. Not to be used for navigation.*

# HEALTH BAY
# AND HEALTH LAGOON

7.2

**CHARTS** 3546.

**APPROACH** Health Bay and Lagoon from the W. Health Bay lies to the SE of "Centre Islets" (named by us). The run in is clear. Health Lagoon lies to the NE of "Centre Islets." Enter N of the rock in the entrance for a picnic stop, or anchor overnight in settled weather. The head of the lagoon shallows rapidly, revealing a muddy foreshore at LW.

**ANCHOR** As indicated, in depths of 3–6 m (9–19 ft) where holding is excellent in sticky mud. Health Bay offers good protection from the SE and with moderate protection from the W.

✳50°41.14'N 126°35.35'W

**D**rop anchor in the good, sticky mud of Health Bay and explore the lagoon by dinghy or kayak. Alternatively, laze in the cockpit surrounded by the bay's tree-lined and rocky shore, well patronized by the local community of basking seals and their doe-eyed pups.

# DUSKY COVE, BONWICK ISLAND

✳ 50°40.88'N 126°40.19'W

**CHARTS**   3546.

**APPROACH**   At LW, between the Leading Islets. Be aware that the islets' ledges, like icebergs, extend farther out below water.

**ANCHOR**   (1, 2, & 3) Alternate temporary anchorages. (4) In Dusky Cove, depths of 3–6 m (9–19 ft) where holding is good in sand. The anchorage is surprisingly commodious and well protected from the SE. The ring of islets breaks the swell and light winds from the W. This is not a good spot in a moderate-to-strong westerly blow.

*A lot of rocks and Christmas trees!*

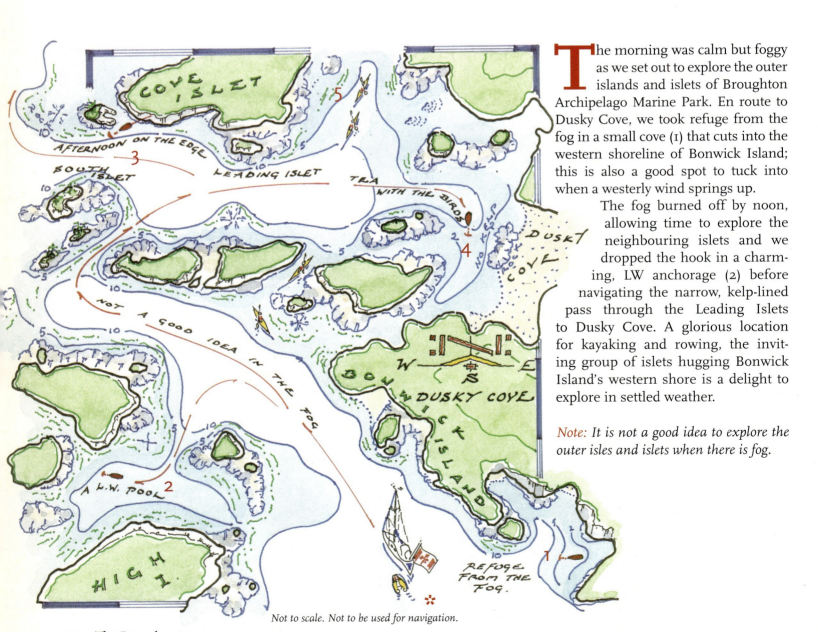

*Not to scale. Not to be used for navigation.*

The morning was calm but foggy as we set out to explore the outer islands and islets of Broughton Archipelago Marine Park. En route to Dusky Cove, we took refuge from the fog in a small cove (1) that cuts into the western shoreline of Bonwick Island; this is also a good spot to tuck into when a westerly wind springs up.

The fog burned off by noon, allowing time to explore the neighbouring islets and we dropped the hook in a charming, LW anchorage (2) before navigating the narrow, kelp-lined pass through the Leading Islets to Dusky Cove. A glorious location for kayaking and rowing, the inviting group of islets hugging Bonwick Island's western shore is a delight to explore in settled weather.

*Note: It is not a good idea to explore the outer isles and islets when there is fog.*

# WADDINGTON BAY, BONWICK ISLAND

**CHARTS**   3546.

**APPROACH**   (A) From Arrow Passage. Leave "Fox Island" to starboard. (B) From Retreat Passage, leave the rocks and reef that extend well off "Fox Islet" (named by us) to port. The entrance channel is clear.

**ANCHOR**   Good holding in mud in depths of 4–8 m (13–26 ft). The alternative anchorages outside Waddington Bay should be approached cautiously and at LW.

*A tree can be a useful perch when catching up on notes*

❀ (A) 50°43.37'N 126°36.00'W
❀ (B) 50°42.92'N 126°36.07'W

**A**n orderly semi-circle of neatly positioned power- and sailboats, and a sleek motor yacht, anchored stern-to on the islet, glistened in the sunlight as we entered popular Waddington Bay. A small alternative anchorage south of "Fox Island" provided a quiet overnight stop with fine views out. We spent a blissful morning exploring the islets in *Tink*, lounging on grassy picnic rocks with the fragrance of wild onion and mint, shaded by a lone tree. At LW, a small shell beach is revealed between the two rocks.

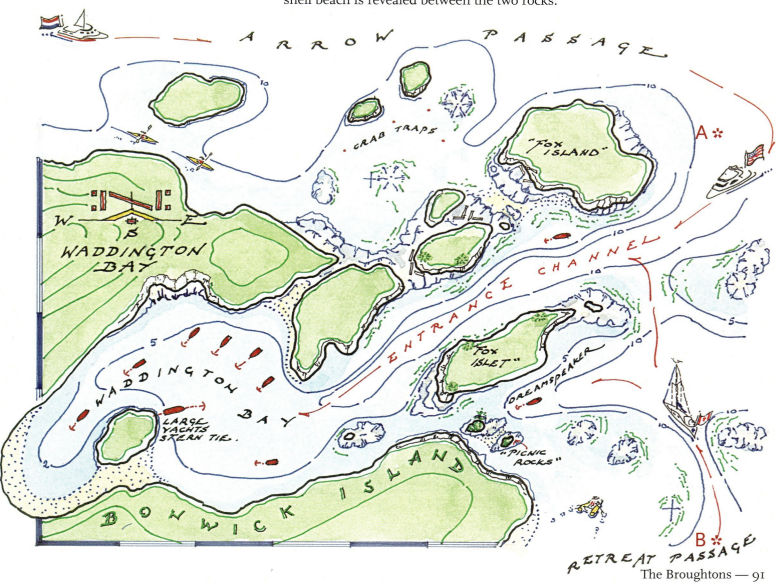

# 7.5 ECHO BAY, PIERRE'S LODGE & MARINA, GILFORD ISLAND

❁50°45.34'N 126°29.95'W

*The entrance to Echo Bay is highly conspicuous (Peter Robson photo)*

*Visitor moorage at Pierre's Echo Bay Lodge and Marina*

*Saturday night pig roast – Three would-be Mexicans, one named Pierre!*

Accessible by boat or float plane, Gilford Island is the largest of the islands that make up the enchanting Broughton Archipelago. Echo Bay, originally called Echo Cove, provides a sheltered harbour and memorable vistas.

The bay was occupied by First Nations communities for over 10,000 years until the devastating smallpox epidemic. Those who survived moved away 150 years ago, leaving rust-coloured pictographs on the steep cliff face and an extensive midden that forms a lovely white-shell beach at the head of the bay – part of Echo Bay Marine Park.

Since 1910, the bay has been home to pioneers and their families who ran the store and fuel dock. It also housed a fish-buying camp, a shingle mill and a beer parlour. The school, located in the park, has been removed.

A cruise in the Broughton Islands would not be complete without a night or two at PIERRE'S ECHO BAY LODGE & MARINA. Owners Pierre and Tove Landry delight in special events and theme evenings. Happy hour social gatherings are frequent – relax in the wood-fired hot tub or end the evening chatting around the community fire pit.

Their renowned Pig Roast Saturdays are highly popular and reserving your moorage and meal is essential during the busy summer months. Pierre cooks the roast to perfection while Tove keeps everything and everyone shipshape. Guests provide potluck side dishes to share along with personal beverages, crockery and cutlery. Check their weekly dinner schedule at www.pierresbay.com.

The well-stocked store has a post office and carries all the staples including fresh produce and dairy products, frozen meat and chicken, bread, baked goods, snacks and ice cream. Ice, books, handmade gifts and cards are also available. Tove and Pierre are also proud of their skookum book exchange.

For a must-have experience, visit legendary Bill Proctor. His intriguing local history museum is filled with items collected over the years he has lived and worked on this coast (see pages 94–95). A trail from Pierre's makes for easy access (about 15 minutes) to Bill's property.

*Note: Please be sure to slow down well before reaching the entrance to Echo Bay. The surge from a boat's wake can roll into the bay, making the marina floats rock and roll – uncomfortable for all.*

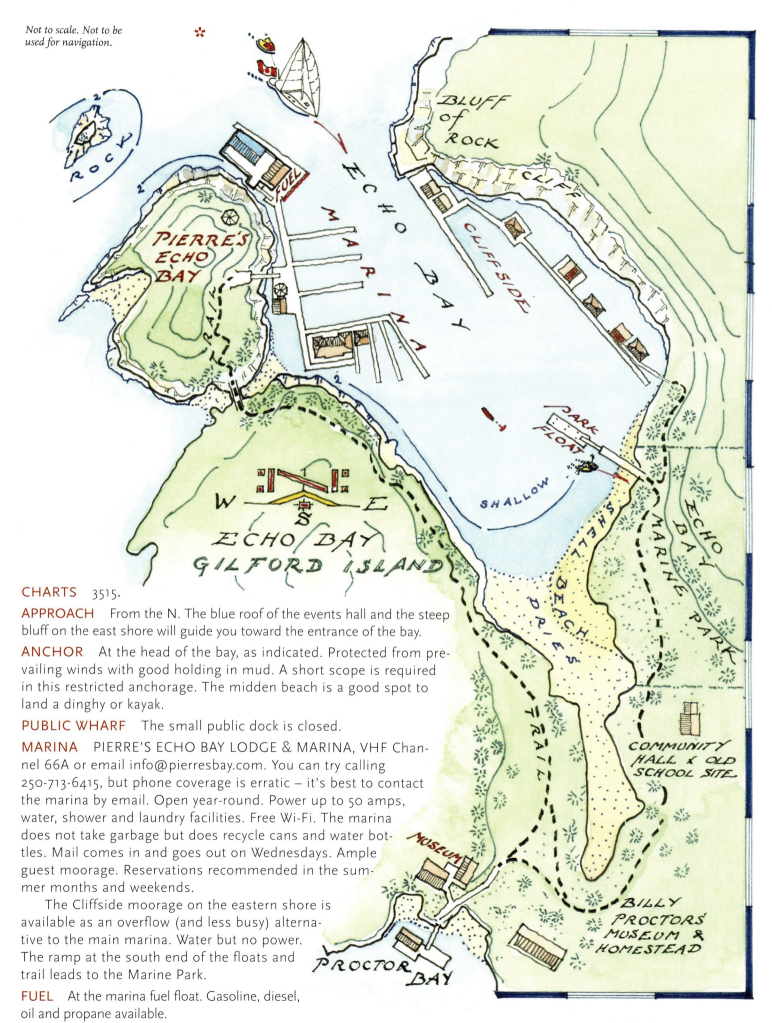

*Not to scale. Not to be used for navigation.*

ROCK

PIERRE'S ECHO BAY

FUEL

BLUFF of ROCK

ECHO BAY MARINA

CLIFFSIDE

PARK FLOAT

SHALLOW

TRAIL

ECHO BAY GILFORD ISLAND

SHELL BEACH MIDDEN

ECHO BAY MARINE PARK

COMMUNITY HALL & OLD SCHOOL SITE

TRAIL

MUSEUM

BILLY PROCTORS MUSEUM & HOMESTEAD

PROCTOR BAY

**CHARTS**   3515.

**APPROACH**   From the N. The blue roof of the events hall and the steep bluff on the east shore will guide you toward the entrance of the bay.

**ANCHOR**   At the head of the bay, as indicated. Protected from prevailing winds with good holding in mud. A short scope is required in this restricted anchorage. The midden beach is a good spot to land a dinghy or kayak.

**PUBLIC WHARF**   The small public dock is closed.

**MARINA**   PIERRE'S ECHO BAY LODGE & MARINA, VHF Channel 66A or email info@pierresbay.com. You can try calling 250-713-6415, but phone coverage is erratic – it's best to contact the marina by email. Open year-round. Power up to 50 amps, water, shower and laundry facilities. Free Wi-Fi. The marina does not take garbage but does recycle cans and water bottles. Mail comes in and goes out on Wednesdays. Ample guest moorage. Reservations recommended in the summer months and weekends.

The Cliffside moorage on the eastern shore is available as an overflow (and less busy) alternative to the main marina. Water but no power. The ramp at the south end of the floats and trail leads to the Marine Park.

**FUEL**   At the marina fuel float. Gasoline, diesel, oil and propane available.

✿ 50°46.26'N 126°29.09'W

*Billy Proctor's place with his popular collection of artifacts in the centre (Yvonne Maximchuk photo)*

*Billy relaxing in front of his museum (Yvonne Maximchuk photo)*

*Naturalist Nikki van Schyndel, "The Forest Dweller" (Yvonne Maximchuk photo)*

Fisherman, storyteller, author and environmental activist BILL PROCTOR has homesteaded in the bay for over 40 years, so it was natural for the local community to name it "Proctor Bay" in his honour. Billy's personal museum is filled with hundreds of eclectic artifacts that he has collected, and every treasure has a story. Bill celebrated his eightieth birthday in 2014.

His small gift shop sells books that he has authored and co-authored (see p. 188) and a fine selection of work by local authors and by artist Yvonne Maximchuk. His latest project is a miniature schoolhouse to commemorate the Echo Bay School. Four years ago he produced a replica of a hand logger's cabin, circa 1900, constructed from a single cedar log. The museum is open from 10.00 a.m. to 5.00 p.m. daily.

Naturalist NIKKI VAN SCHYNDEL (known as "the forest dweller") built her home in Proctor Bay, close to Billy's homestead, in 2007. She offers one-woman Eco Ventures, custom tours that can be booked at the marina. Let Nikki take you deep into the forest to learn about the wildlife (including the greens and berries that you can pick and eat), how to make a fire without matches and how to cook lunch in a skillet while sipping on warm spruce tea. Her popular book, *Becoming Wild*, is available at Bill's gift store. wwwbecomingwild.com.

In October 1984, whale researcher ALEXANDRA MORTON and her late husband, Robin, fell in love with all that the Broughton Archipelago had to offer them. They built their home a short distance from Bill Proctor. Environmentalist and philanthropist Sarah Haney purchased the house, enabling Alexandra's vision to develop it into a scientific research station. Andrea moved to Sointula eight years ago and devotes her energies to addressing the problems created by the salmon farms, which have affected the region's ecosystem (for both salmon and whales). THE SALMON COAST FIELD STATION has grown to become a leading biological research station. It is independent and non-profit and relies on donations. To book a date and time to visit, call 250-974-7171 or VHF Channel 16, Salmon Coast. www.salmoncoast.org.

Author and artist YVONNE MAXIMCHUK is prolific when it comes to ceramic art and painting – from seascapes, landscapes and portraits to wildlife in acrylic and watercolour. She works with her husband, Al Munro, creating a great va-

# GILFORD ISLAND

riety of porcelain tableware and one-of-a-kind art objects. She also offers lessons, workshops and art retreats. SEAROSE STUDIO and the enchanting gardens serve as her home, studio and gallery – it's open to all appreciative art lovers. She also sells her colourful artwork at Billy's gift store. Call Yvonne on VHF Channel 16, SeaRose or 250-974-8134.     www.yvonne maximchuk.com.

**CHARTS**   3515.

**APPROACH**   "Proctor Bay" lies due S of Echo Bay. It is a local name and not marked on the chart.

**DEPTH**   The depth contours are as indicated on the chart.

*Note: Two trails from Echo Bay lead to Billy's Museum. You can also dinghy over – call ahead to "Ocean Dawn" on VHF Channel 16. The Salmon Coast Field Station and SeaRose Studio can only be reached by boat or seaplane. Call ahead if planning to visit by dinghy from Echo Bay.*

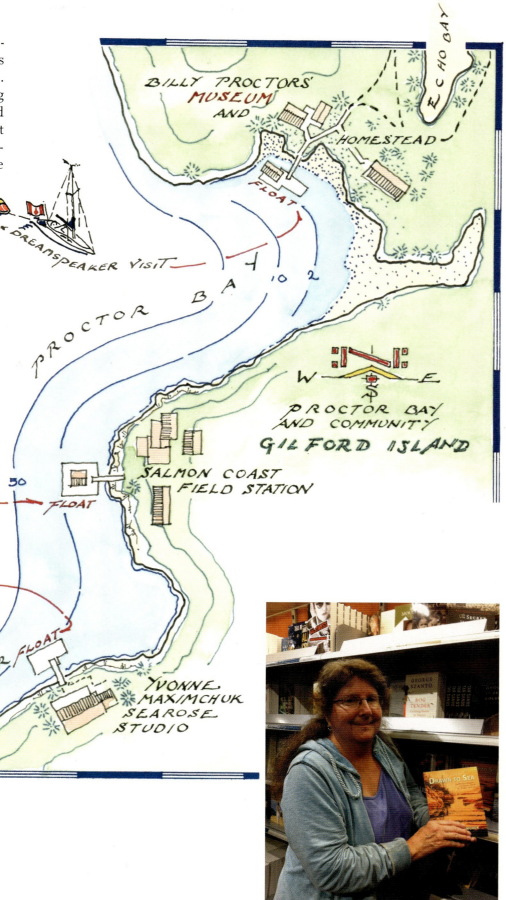

*Artist Yvonne Maximchuk*

# 7.7 FIFE ROCK, DAVIES ISLAND

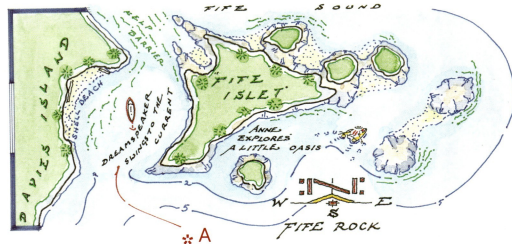

✿(A) 50°46.04'N 126°34.29'W
✿(B) 50°45.45'N 126°39.03'W

**APPROACH**   (A) From the S. The gap between Davies Island and Fife Rock has no obstructions. The presence of kelp suggests that a passage N, beyond the shell beach, may not be possible.

**ANCHOR**   A one-boat day stop best explored at LW. Great for a picnic or shelter from westerly winds; if the winds are strong, however, swells

from Fife Sound would curl around Davies Island into the anchorage. Holding good in shell, mud and kelp in depths of 3–7 m (9–23 ft).

*Note: Fife Rock is the size of an islet with trees and grass, rocky outcrops and isolated rocks.*

A little oasis adjacent to Davies Island, Fife Rock offers calm waters for rowing or kayaking, a shell beach to stretch your legs and many delightful pocket-beaches to explore at low water.

# 7.8 "LADY BOOT COVE," EDEN ISLAND

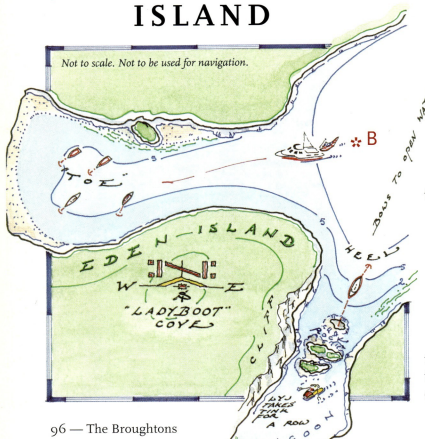

**CHARTS**   3547.

**APPROACH**   (B) From the NE. After rounding Fly Island, 2 coves form the chart profile of a lady's stiletto-heeled boot. Both approaches are free of obstruction.

**ANCHOR**   *Heel* – A great day stop; drop the hook at LW and stern-tie to the rock.

*Toe* – A sizeable overnight basin. Both are well protected from westerly winds, although open to the NE. Holding is good in mud, shell and kelp, in depths of 4–8 m (13–26 ft).

"Lady Boot Cove," aptly named by the Douglasses in *Exploring the South Coast of British Columbia* (see p. 188), provides sheltered, overnight anchorage at the head of the *toe*. Although there is little room to swing at the entrance to the *heel*, this cozy picnic stop offers lovely views out and is fun to explore by dinghy.

# MONDAY ANCHORAGE, TRACEY ISLAND 7.9

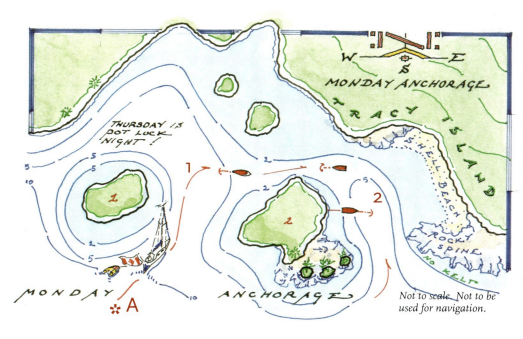

Not to scale. Not to be used for navigation.

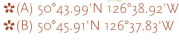

❀(A) 50°43.99'N 126°38.92'W
❀(B) 50°45.91'N 126°37.83'W

**CHARTS**   3546.

**APPROACH**   (A) From the W at LW. The islets have a clear passage between them.

**ANCHOR**   (1) With protection from Islet 1.
(2) With protection from Islet 2. Shelter from a westerly blow would be marginal unless anchored with a stern line as shown; this indicates the best spot to drop the hook. Holding in mud 4–6 m (13–19 ft).

In her book *The Curve of Time*, Muriel Wylie Blanchet describes how their small boat was blown into Monday Anchorage after dragging anchor in Sunday Harbour. There, she took shelter in a small anchorage she called "Tuesday Cove." On a sunny day, the white-shell beach on the eastern shoreline of Monday Anchorage is perfect for picnicking and beachcombing. We like to think that it is the same cove that Muriel and her family enjoyed.

# "EDEN'S POOL," EDEN ISLAND 7.10

**CHARTS**   3546.

**APPROACH**   From Indian Pass. Head for the passage between Insect and Eden Islands. Rocks lie to the NE of "Fly Islet" (named by us).

**ANCHOR**   In a pool of calm water between "Fly Islet" and Eden Island. Swing to the current in depths of 6–8 m (19–26 ft). Good protection from westerly winds.

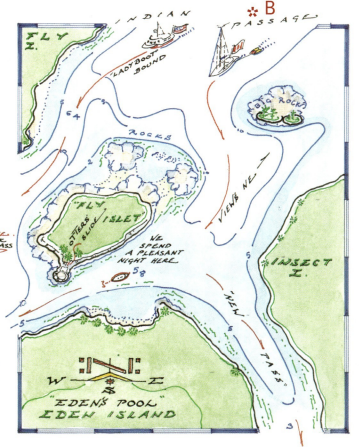

With views out to the northeast and southwest, we dropped anchor in a small anchorage that we named "Eden's Pool" and spent a peaceful night swinging to the current. Boats en route to "Lady Boot Cove" from Indian Passage take the pass between Fly Island and "Fly Islet" while boats heading to Monday Anchorage make use of "New Pass" (also named by us) between Insect and Eden Islands.

*The wood float in the east finger of the cove provides a convenient tie-up.*

**CHARTS**   3547.

**APPROACH**   From the SE; the entrance and run into the anchorage at the head of the cove is clear without obstructions until you reach the two rocks at the entrance to the anchorage (sometimes marked with a can or buoy).

**ANCHOR**   In the N finger in depths of 3–5 m (9–16 ft). Holding in mud. The old wooden float in the east finger provides a spot for boats up to 10.5 m (35 ft) to tie up on either side.

✱ 50°44.92'N 126°39.70'W

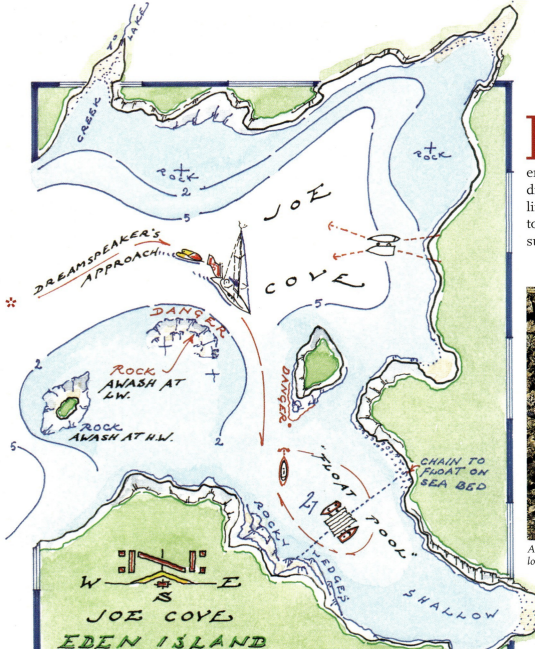

Not to scale. Not to be used for navigation.

Long and slim, Joe Cove has a protected anchorage at its head that is popular with recreational boaters seeking a quiet, sheltered spot to drop the hook or even tie up. A stern line to the shore will allow more boats to enjoy this peaceful spot in the busy summer months.

*A sunflower star (twenty-rayed sea star) exposed at low water*

A stormy evening in Broughton Strait, looking out from the anchorage in Port McNeill.

Chapter 8

# QUEEN CHARLOTTE STRAIT SOUTH

# Chapter 8
# QUEEN CHARLOTTE STRAIT SOUTH

**TIDES** – *Volume 6,*
*Canadian Tide and Current Tables*
Reference Port – Alert Bay
Secondary Ports – Port Hardy, Port McNeill

**CURRENTS**

Reference Station – Johnstone Strait Central
Secondary Station – Pulteney Point, Masterman islands.

**WEATHER**

Weather Station – WX1 162.55 MHZ
Area – Queen Charlotte Strait
Reporting Station – Alert Bay

*Cottage craft, Malcolm Island*

CAUTIONARY NOTES: *Swift currents appear to be ever present in Broughton Strait; these currents can run up to 3 knots in the channel off Pulteney Point.*

*Take the ebb tide north, to Beaver Harbour and Port Hardy, remembering that wind against current always makes for an uncomfortable trip. Travelling on an ebb tide with an easterly wind in Queen Charlotte Strait would be ideal.*

This chapter primarily covers the northern Vancouver Island shore and includes the urban amenities of Port McNeill and Port Hardy, and a visit to Sointula on Malcolm Island.

Port McNeill proclaims to be the "gateway to the Broughtons" and is conveniently situated with protected moorage and all amenities and services within two blocks of downtown. Port McNeill Harbour and the North Island Marina are well patronized by transient boaters. Downtown includes a hospital, pharmacy, post office, banks, ATMs, art galleries, gift stores, restaurants and cafés, marine stores and two supermarkets. This is a major provisioning stop, and the scheduled ferry service connects with nearby Alert Bay and Sointula on Malcolm Island. Boaters will find deluxe laundry facilities with complimentary Wi-Fi service.

The thriving community of Sointula was established in 1901 by Finnish settlers planning to build a socialist utopia – the meaning of "sointula" in Finnish is "harmony." Visitors are welcome at the nearby public wharf. Take advantage of the fine Malcolm Island trails, and rent a bike or hike to Bere Point and the whale-rubbing rocks.

Once a Hudson's Bay Company trading post, fort and coal mining site, and now a thriving First Nations reserve, the Village of Fort Rupert welcomes visitors to its art galleries where you can experience traditional crafters at work. Lovely Beaver Harbour fronting the village has a choice of small, cozy anchorages; our favourite was tucked between the beautiful white-shell beaches of Cattle and Shell Islands and is a terrific spot for beach-hopping and wildlife.

A comprehensive service centre for boaters and fishermen, Port Hardy has an airport nearby, and Bear Cove is the southern terminal for the Vancouver Island–Prince Rupert ferry. The town is a popular rendezvous stop for visitors and crew.

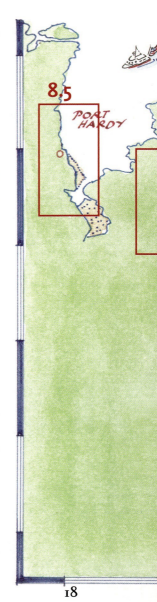

# FEATURED DESTINATIONS

The town centre around Market, Rupert and Granville Streets has every type of shop or service including supermarkets, hardware and marine stores, a post office, hospital and pharmacy. Gift stores and art galleries are in abundance and the museum is excellent. Restaurants in the area are highly recommended for their choice of fresh fish and seafood. The more protected Inner Basin offers boaters moorage at the public wharf and THE QUARTERDECK INN AND MARINA RESORT comes complete with clean shower and laundry facilities and restaurant. Fuel is also available.

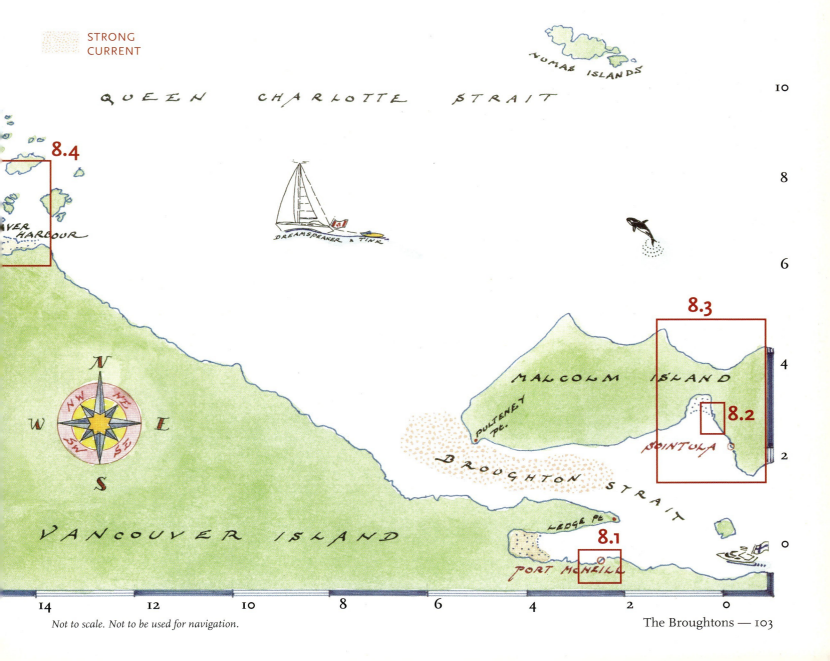

STRONG CURRENT

*Not to scale. Not to be used for navigation.*

# 8.1 PORT MCNEILL, VANCOUVER ISLAND

❀50°35.64'N 127°05.09'W

*Looking south from the anchorage to Port McNeill Boat Harbour*

*Gateway to the Broughtons*

*Dreamspeaker rafted at the commercial public wharf*

At the western entrance to Broughton Strait, on the eastern Vancouver Island shoreline, lies the bustling community of Port McNeill. The town is perched on a gently sloping escarpment overlooking the harbour. With the amenities of a small city, a regional airport close by and floatplane connections to and from Vancouver and Seattle, Port McNeill is the cruising boater's "Gateway to the Broughtons."

Shower, laundry and provisioning facilities as well as shops, restaurants and art galleries are conveniently situated within walking distance of the harbour. PORT MCNEILL HARBOUR OFFICE is in the VISITOR CENTRE building on Beach Drive. Spacious laundry facilities with free internet service are located on the corner of Beach and Broughton and operated by CAB INDUSTRIAL AUTOMOTIVE SUPPLY, which also carries marine supplies.

While your washing dries, visit the excellent HERITAGE MUSEUM, housed nearby, in a handsome log structure; here you will be introduced to a plethora of forestry and logging implements and a collection of historic photographs and objects from Port McNeill's pioneering days. A short walk from the museum will take you to a great Vancouver Island photo op – the world's largest burl.

Port McNeill has a hospital, pharmacy, post office, banks and ATM facilities. The scheduled ferry service connects with nearby Alert Bay and Sointula; both are well worth the trip (see p. 64 & 106). Provisioning is a breeze in the downtown core and you can transport your goods to the boat, and then neatly park your trolley at the top of the dock for pickup. The IGA MARKETPLACE in Pioneer Mall also offers free delivery to either marina.

The BC LIQUOR STORE carries a fine selection of wines and THE BEAD LADY'S GALLERY, owned by Carol Ellison, is a treasure trove of her own delicate beadwork and jewellery, in addition to pieces by other various artists. SHOPRITE OUTDOOR SPORTS MARINE & LOGGING is the can't-miss spot for one-stop-shopping and is filled with a diverse selection of products, clothing and shoes.

A few favourite eateries include TIA'S CAFÉ for a hearty breakfast; SPORTSMAN'S STEAKHOUSE serves pizza, pasta and Greek dishes; and NORTHERN LIGHTS RESTAURANT at the HAIDA WAY INN offers excellent fresh fish and seafood dishes. (Reservations are recommended; call 250-956-3263.)

**CHARTS**   3546, inset.

**APPROACH**   From the E, north of the ferry terminal. Seaplanes operate frequently in this area and take off and land parallel to the breakwater.

**ANCHOR**   Good anchorage can be found in the bay N of the shoreside facilities. Favour the ledge point shoreline. Good holding in mud, in depths of 5–8 m (16–26 ft). (See Cautionary Note.)

**MARINA**   PORT MCNEILL HARBOUR lies behind the rock breakwater. The marina is efficient and open year-round. They monitor VHF Channel 66A for slip assignment prior to arrival. Limited reservations are accepted May through September – call 250-956-3881. There is visitor moorage at the municipal floats, while commercial vessels moor at the federal docks. Water, power up to 100 amps, wireless internet service, pay phones, a pump-out station and shower facilities are available. Pay a deposit and receive your key and unlimited showers for a very reasonable price.

NORTH ISLAND MARINA is well run and welcoming. Open year-round. The marina is protected by a breakwater to the W. They monitor VHF Channel 66A. Reservations recommended, call 1-855-0008-622. Marina office 250-956-4044. Water, 30, 50 (120/208 volt)) and 100 (single and three-phase) amp power and free Wi-Fi. Convenient in-berth fuelling available. Garbage and recycling at the top of the dock. You will need a pass code from the marina office for the security gate. Shared showers at Port McNeill Harbour. A courtesy car, and airport pickup and drop-off, are available.

**FUEL**   Fuel dock at North Island Marina. Gasoline, diesel, propane and stove oil available. The small dock store carries ice, lubricants and a small selection of marine parts.

CAUTIONARY NOTE: *The anchorage is well sheltered from the W. Ensure that your anchor is well set, as dead kelp is layered over the mud. Although open to the SE, seas appear to disperse in the bay.* Dreamspeaker, *along with many other boats, survived a night of gale-force winds.*

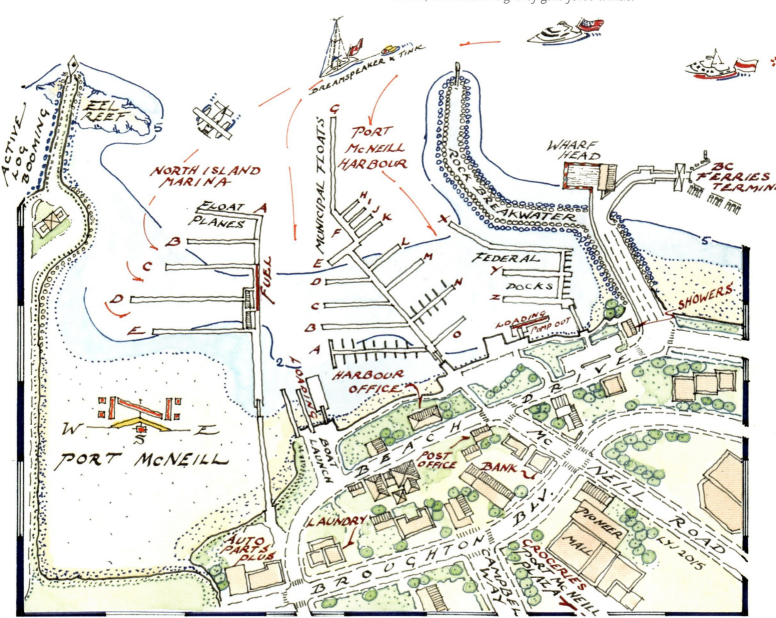

*Not to scale. Not to be used for navigation.*

# 8.2 SOINTULA HARBOUR, MALCOLM ISLAND

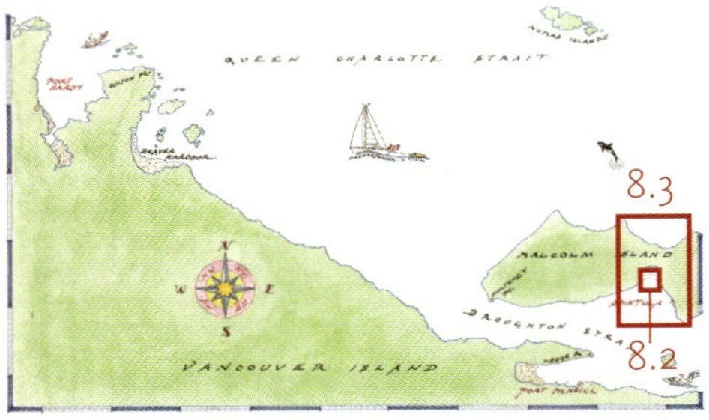


✲50°38.34'N 127°01.99'W

CHARTS 3546.
APPROACH To the W of Dickenson Point. Stay clear of the ferry route. The public wharf in Rough Bay lies NW of Sointula and the ferry terminal.
PUBLIC WHARF N of the village of Sointula. Managed by the Malcolm Island Lions Harbour Authority. This is an efficient but laid-back facility. VHF 66A or call 250-973-6544. Water and power up to 30 amps. Laundry, showers, ice, garbage drop-off and Wi-Fi. First-come, first-served basis. Side tie; rafting possible.

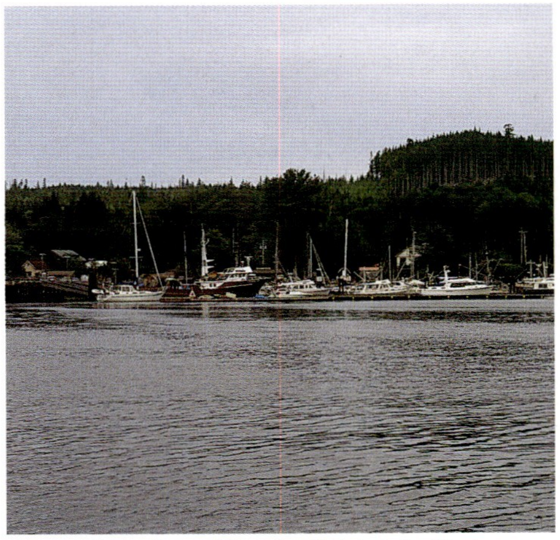

*Approaching the public wharf, Sointula Harbour*

*Note: You can also visit Sointula by ferry from Port McNeill.*

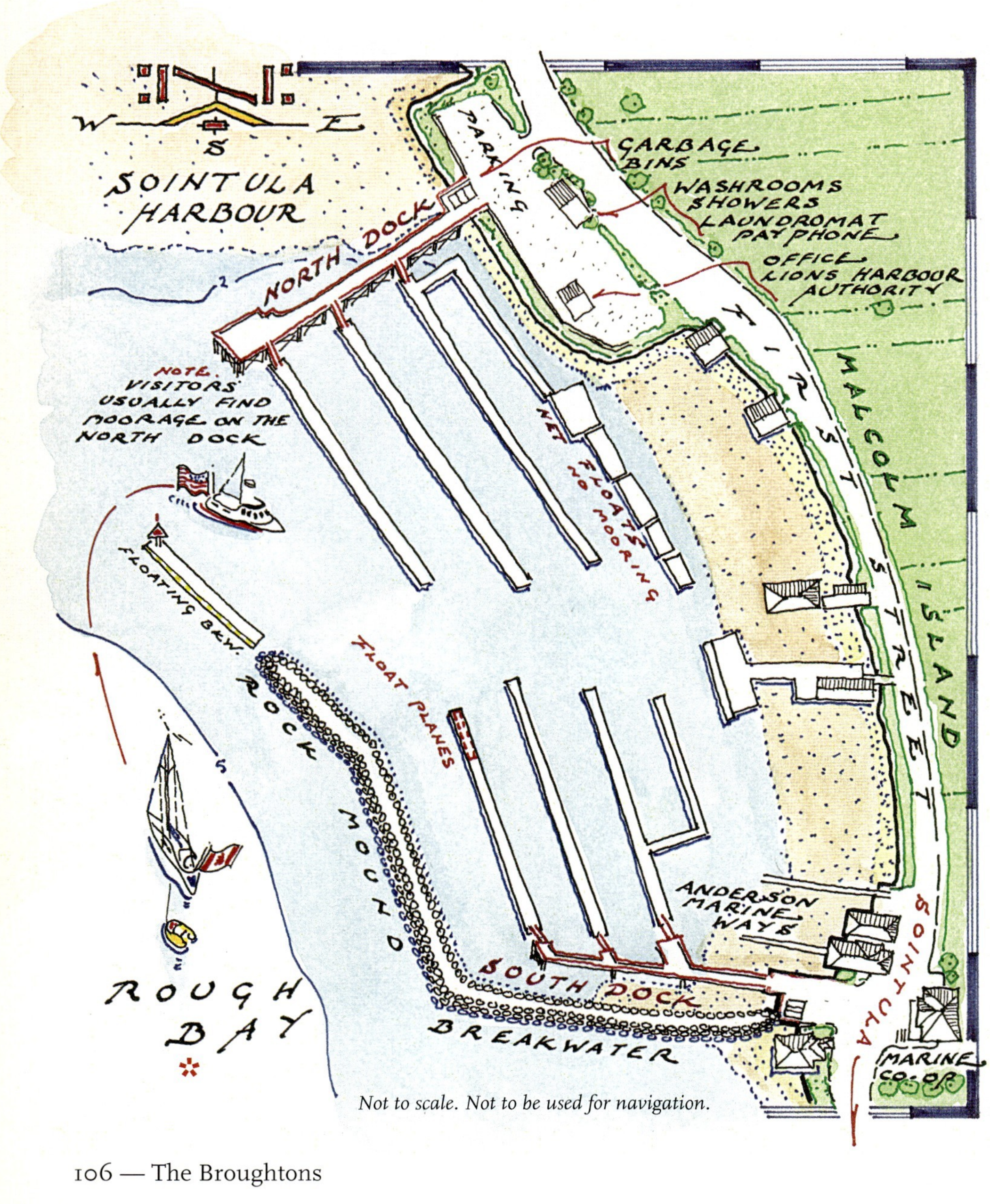


*Not to scale. Not to be used for navigation.*

Sointula was established by a group of Finnish utopians led by journalist and idealist Matti Kurikka. It's a thriving community where the cooperative movement is still strong.

Clean shower and laundry facilities welcome boaters at the public wharf; they are well used by locals so it's first-come, first-served.

Take a pleasant 2-km (1.2-mi) walk into the Village of Sointula; browse in the SOINTULA CO-OPERATIVE STORE, stock up at SOINTULA WILD SEAFOODS & SMOKEHOUSE and pop into the enticing arts and crafts studios along the way. The locals have a fascinating pastime of creating personalized fence designs to front their properties.

At the UPPER CRUST BAKERY AND CAFÉ, relax over lunch before visiting the fascinating SOINTULA MUSEUM. To provision go no further than the historic, well-stocked CO-OPERATIVE STORE (with ATM). The liquor store is downstairs; upstairs there's a selection of homewares, toys and clothing. There is another ATM in the MALCOLM ISLAND INN, as well as an after-hours liquor store at the pub. It's great fun to tour the island using the free "green bikes" from the RESOURCE CENTRE across from the ferry terminal.

# MALCOLM ISLAND TRAILS 8.3

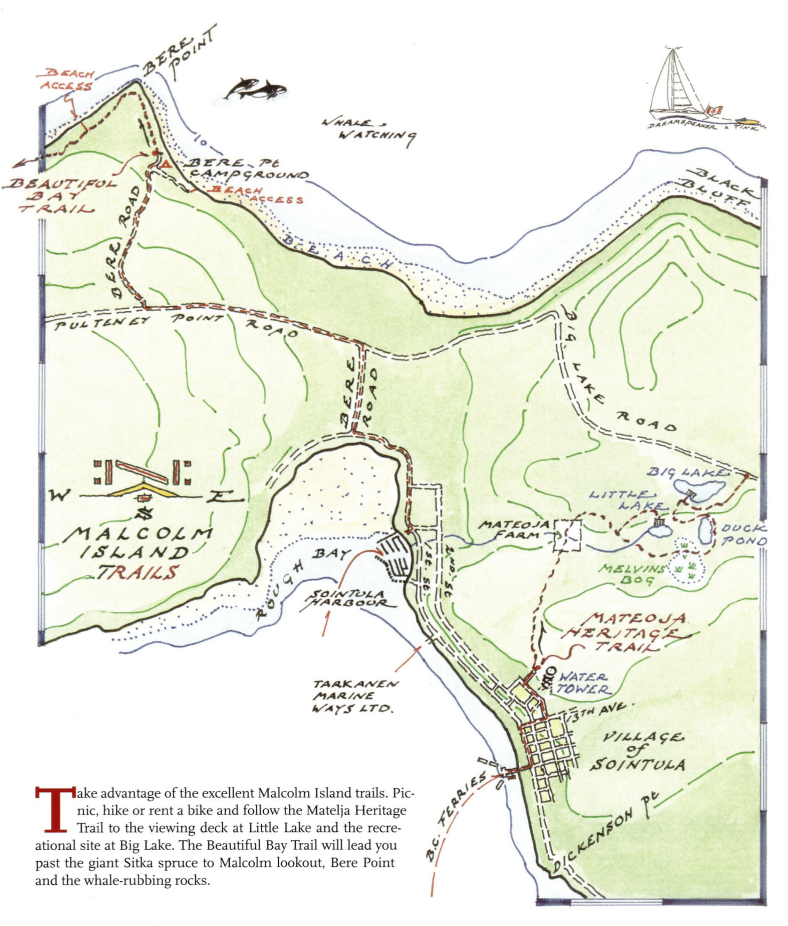

BERE POINT

BEACH ACCESS

WHALE WATCHING

DREAMSPEAKER & TINK

BLACK BLUFF

BEAUTIFUL BAY TRAIL

BERE PT CAMPGROUND

BEACH ACCESS

BEACH

BERE ROAD

PULTENEY POINT ROAD

BERE ROAD

BIG LAKE ROAD

BIG LAKE

LITTLE LAKE

DUCK POND

W E N S

MALCOLM ISLAND TRAILS

MATEOJA FARM

MELVINS BOG

ROUGH BAY

SOINTULA HARBOUR

1st ST

2nd ST

MATEOJA HERITAGE TRAIL

TARKANEN MARINE WAYS LTD.

WATER TOWER

13TH AVE.

VILLAGE OF SOINTULA

B.C. FERRIES

DICKENSON PT

**T**ake advantage of the excellent Malcolm Island trails. Picnic, hike or rent a bike and follow the Matelja Heritage Trail to the viewing deck at Little Lake and the recreational site at Big Lake. The Beautiful Bay Trail will lead you past the giant Sitka spruce to Malcolm lookout, Bere Point and the whale-rubbing rocks.

# 8.4 BEAVER HARBOUR, VANCOUVER ISLAND

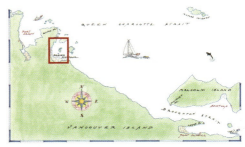

❋ 50°42.40'N 127°23.07'W

**CHARTS**  3548.
**APPROACH**  From the E, between Thomas Point and Deer Island. An alternative approach may be made via Daedalus Passage.

**ANCHOR**  There are a number of anchor spots off the shell beaches and the Vancouver Island shoreline. Well-protected from the W and moderately sheltered from the E, anchor in depths of 4–10 m (13–32 ft) with holding good in mud.

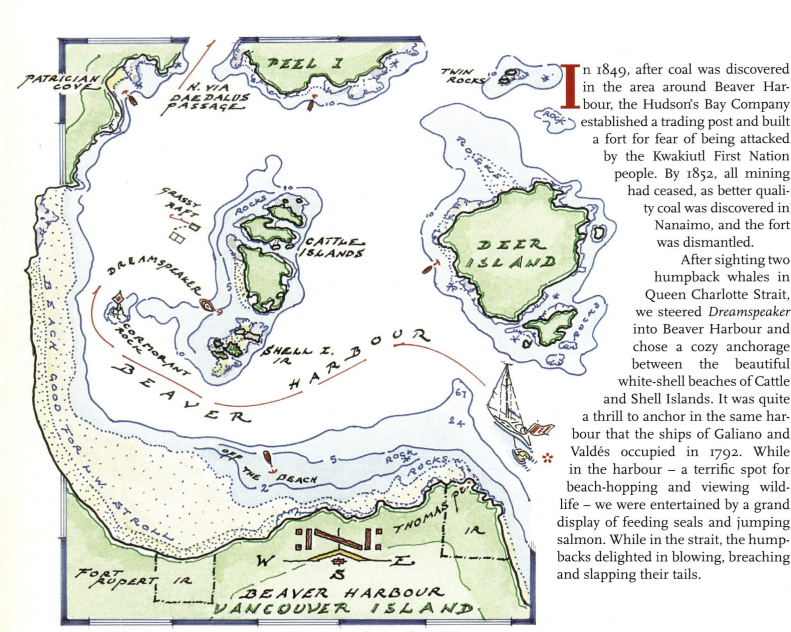

*Not to scale. Not to be used for navigation.*

In 1849, after coal was discovered in the area around Beaver Harbour, the Hudson's Bay Company established a trading post and built a fort for fear of being attacked by the Kwakiutl First Nation people. By 1852, all mining had ceased, as better quality coal was discovered in Nanaimo, and the fort was dismantled.

After sighting two humpback whales in Queen Charlotte Strait, we steered *Dreamspeaker* into Beaver Harbour and chose a cozy anchorage between the beautiful white-shell beaches of Cattle and Shell Islands. It was quite a thrill to anchor in the same harbour that the ships of Galiano and Valdés occupied in 1792. While in the harbour – a terrific spot for beach-hopping and viewing wildlife – we were entertained by a grand display of feeding seals and jumping salmon. While in the strait, the humpbacks delighted in blowing, breaching and slapping their tails.

*A tranquil evening in Beaver Harbour*

# 8.5 PORT HARDY, VANCOUVER ISLAND

✽ 50°43.80'N 127°28.68'W

*Seagate Wharf from Carrot Park*

*Downtown Port Hardy*

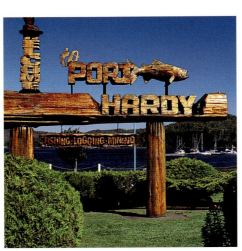

*Chainsaw-carved signs are a local specialty*

Once a comprehensive commercial service centre for boaters and fishermen, Port Hardy is the northernmost community on Vancouver Island and was our last big stop before crossing Queen Charlotte Strait to Blunden Harbour. Nearby Bear Cove is the southern terminal for the Vancouver Island-Prince Rupert ferry. Here you will find COASTAL MOUNTAIN FUELS, who monitor VHF Channel 09 (or call 250-949-9988). They have gasoline, diesel and propane available. The local airport makes Port Hardy a good rendezvous stop for visitors and crew.

The small public wharf (A) at the end of Granville Street is the most convenient spot to tie up and walk into town. The area around Market, Rupert and Granville Streets has a variety of shops and services; pop into the VISITOR INFO CENTRE on Market and pick up a downtown map, which will direct you to the post office, hospital, pharmacy, gift store, liquor store and art galleries – some of the best First Nations art is produced on northern Vancouver Island. The small museum on Main Street is a delight and worth a visit. The OVERWAITEA supermarket is in the Thunderbird Mall. If you are a non-member ask for a tourist card to receive their discounts. They will deliver large orders by taxi.

There are several good restaurants to choose from, including CAPTAIN HARDY'S (for a hearty breakfast) and CAFÉ GUIDO (for a delicious selection of espressos, teas, baked goods and paninis). Local artisan work can be found at the WEST COAST COMMUNITY CRAFT SHOP. Downstairs in the BOOK NOOK you will find an excellent selection of books, unique gifts and clothing. Don't forget to visit HARDY BUOYS SMOKED FISH for the best Atlantic Maple Candy and fresh crab.

Enjoy a leisurely stroll along the waterfront sea walk, which is amber-lit at night and connects to the green lawns of CARROT PARK, and the notorious chainsaw-carved "Welcome to Port Hardy" sign.

The more protected "Inner Basin" (a local name) offers moorage at the public wharf or at THE QUARTERDECK INN AND MARINA RESORT, which provides all the necessities – fuel, clean shower and laundry facilities, a small fishing tackle store and the QUARTERDECK PUB AND RESTAURANT. To visit the downtown shops and restaurants from here, take an invigorating walk along Hardy Bay Road, and then treat yourself to a taxi home.

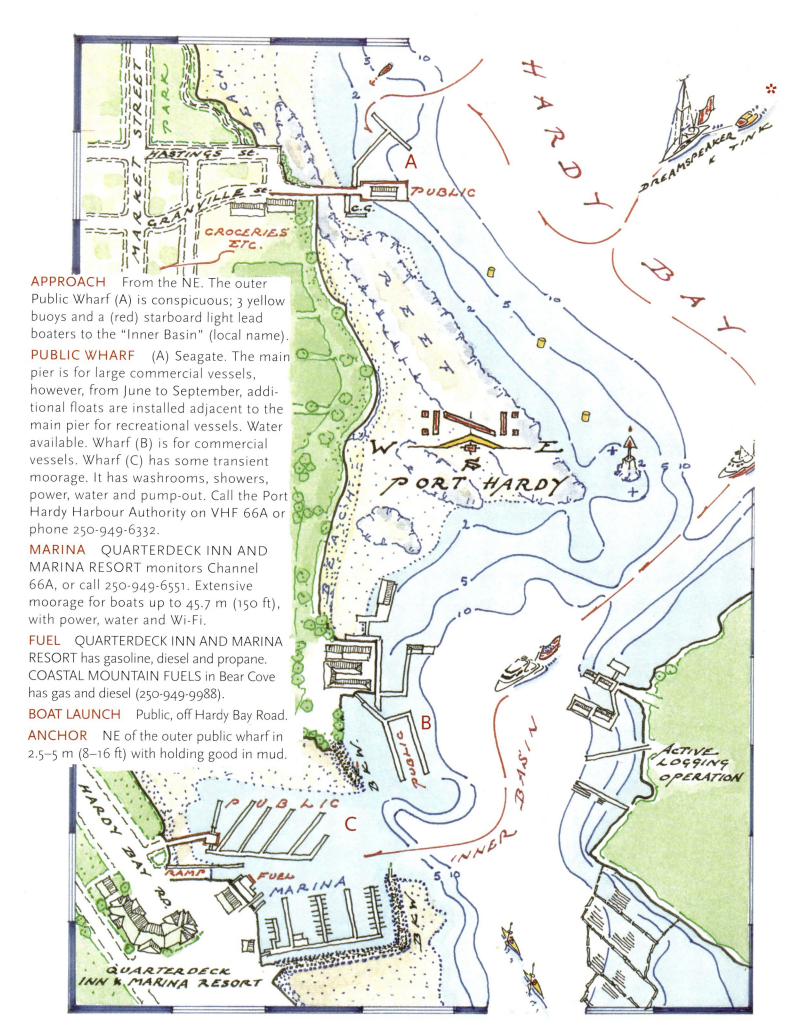

**APPROACH**   From the NE. The outer Public Wharf (A) is conspicuous; 3 yellow buoys and a (red) starboard light lead boaters to the "Inner Basin" (local name).

**PUBLIC WHARF**   (A) Seagate. The main pier is for large commercial vessels, however, from June to September, additional floats are installed adjacent to the main pier for recreational vessels. Water available. Wharf (B) is for commercial vessels. Wharf (C) has some transient moorage. It has washrooms, showers, power, water and pump-out. Call the Port Hardy Harbour Authority on VHF 66A or phone 250-949-6332.

**MARINA**   QUARTERDECK INN AND MARINA RESORT monitors Channel 66A, or call 250-949-6551. Extensive moorage for boats up to 45.7 m (150 ft), with power, water and Wi-Fi.

**FUEL**   QUARTERDECK INN AND MARINA RESORT has gasoline, diesel and propane. COASTAL MOUNTAIN FUELS in Bear Cove has gas and diesel (250-949-9988).

**BOAT LAUNCH**   Public, off Hardy Bay Road.

**ANCHOR**   NE of the outer public wharf in 2.5–5 m (8–16 ft) with holding good in mud.

# Chapter 9
# QUEEN CHARLOTTE STRAIT NORTH

*Sailing southwest to the Polkinghorne Islands. Mount Mitchell overlooks Wells Passage*

# Chapter 9
# QUEEN CHARLOTTE STRAIT NORTH

**TIDES** – *Volume 6, Canadian Tide and Current Tables*
Reference Port – Alert Bay
Secondary Port – Raynor Group

**CURRENTS**
Secondary Station – Browning Island, NW of Blunden Harbour. This station will give a good indication of the strength of current flooding or ebbing along the Northern Queen Charlotte Strait shore.

**WEATHER**
Weather Station – WX1 162.55 MHZ
Area – Queen Charlotte Strait
Reporting Stations – Alert Bay, Herbert Island

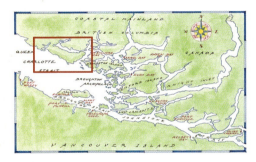

**CAUTIONARY NOTES:** *Explore the destinations in this chapter with great caution, as there are shallows and rocks just waiting for a fresh keel. Best to run aground at dead slow on a rising tide, when patience will be the requirement for a safe recovery.*

New adventures around every corner

**P**ort Hardy to Blunden Harbour on the coastal mainland is 15 nautical miles northeast across Queen Charlotte Strait. A boater's haven, this sheltered anchorage is protected by a barrier of islands and islets. Here, you will find an inviting, white-shell beach backed by a deep midden and a colourful fisherman's cabin. The small anchorage near the entrance to Bradley Lagoon allowed us a day of exploration and sweet tranquility.

When unpleasant wind and sea conditions prevail in Queen Charlotte Strait, nip into the sheltered passage between the Raynor Group of islands and the coastal mainland to explore the choice of one-boat anchorages and mini shell beaches. Alternatively, visit the unexpected and beautifully rugged anchorage that lies further south, in sheltered Lewis Cove. With a wonderful view out to Queen Charlotte Strait, laze in the cockpit and watch the distant cruise liners heading north and south. If time and weather permit, don't miss a stopover in the charming Polkinghorne Islands near the entrance to Wells Passage in Queen Charlotte Strait; they offer an inviting cluster of rocks, islets and white-shell beaches to explore and a well-protected anchorage for an overnight.

Southeast of Wells Passage on Dickson Island, "Deep Cove" offers a fair-sized anchorage with good protection from westerly winds. It's often popular with club flotillas and boat rendezvous. Less crowded and more scenic options are the sheltered anchorages in Carter Passage, where you can sit back, relax and immerse yourself in the area's beauty and tranquility. Commodious and peaceful anchorage is also possible in Tracey Harbour, Broughton Island, where we found protection from all winds and experienced one of the most brilliant scarlet sunsets.

# FEATURED DESTINATIONS

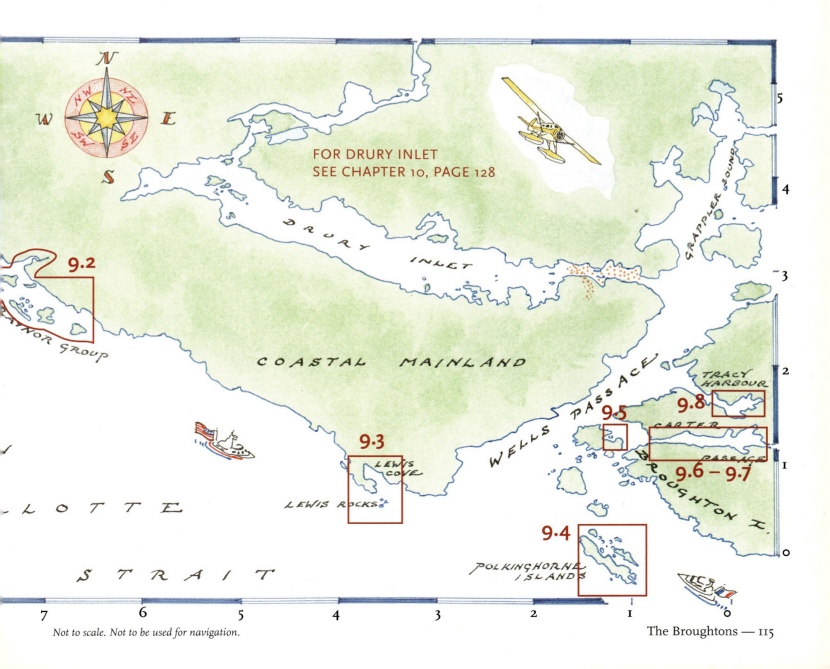

FOR DRURY INLET
SEE CHAPTER 10, PAGE 128

*Not to scale. Not to be used for navigation.*

# 9.1 BLUNDEN HARBOUR

✻ 50°53.89'N 127°16.18'W

**APPROACH** From the SE. Enter between Barren Rock and Shelf Head. A course mid-channel is clear and free of obstructions.

**ANCHOR** The outer harbour, W of the Augustine Islands, is roomy and protected from all quarters. Take your pick in depths of 5–7.5 m (16–24 ft), where the holding is good in mud. The spot we call "Kingfishers Pool," in the upper reaches of Blunden Harbour, is totally protected, with anchorage for one to two boats. Swing to the current in depths of 2–3 m (6–9 ft) with good holding in mud.

*Note: Entrance into Bradley Lagoon is possible only at HW and best explored by dinghy and outboard with reserve fuel.*

A barrier of islands and islets, with plenty of room to swing, protects the sheltered anchorage of Blunden Harbour, a boater's haven. We took *Tink* to investigate and found beautifully marbled granite and sandstone shorelines, and boulders resembling petrified chocolate-chip cookie dough.

The wide, inviting shell beach is backed by a midden and massive nurse logs from the now abandoned village. Follow the salmonberry and salal bordering the beach to a colourful fisherman's cabin with a rope swing and picnic table.

The silence and tranquility in the small anchorage near the entrance to Bradley Lagoon is often interrupted by the piercing screech of the resident kingfishers – hence our name for it.

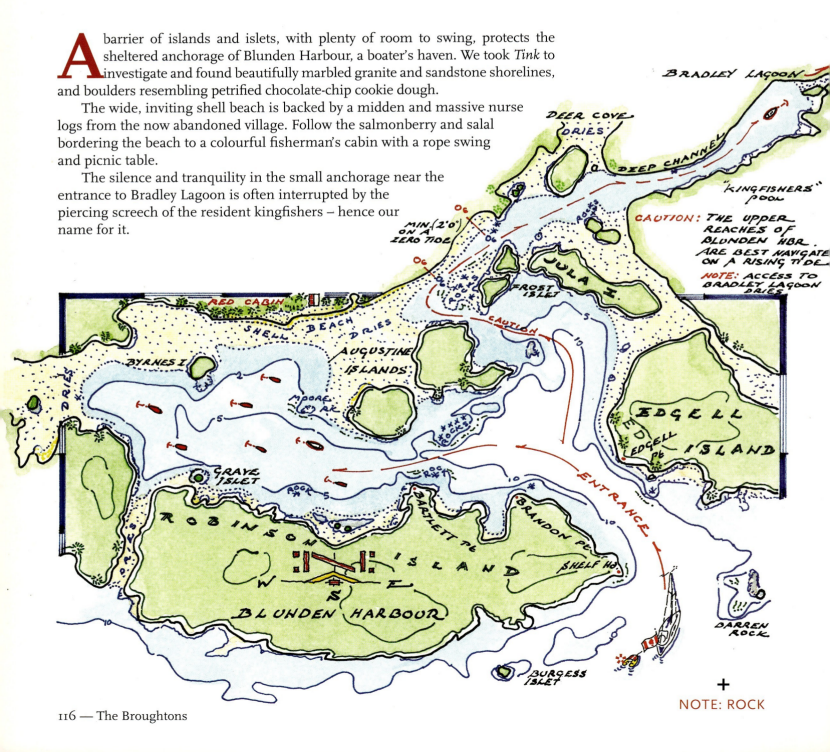

*Stairs from the shell beach lead to a colourful cabin*

**CHARTS**   3548.

**APPROACH**   From the N. Follow the route as indicated, and navigate with care as there are many unmarked rocks (kelp is a good indicator of their position). Alternate approach from the S; there is deep water between the rocks and the SW island that forms the entrance to the inside passage, which is also deep and clear of obstructions.

**ANCHOR**   Temporary, as indicated, in 5–10 m (16–32 ft). Holding varies.

✷ 50°53.82'N 127°15.30'W

**W**hen unpleasant wind and sea conditions prevail in Queen Charlotte Strait, nip into the sheltered passage between the Raynor Group of islands and the coastal mainland; explore the choice of one-boat anchorages and small, shell beaches from Cohoe Bay to Akam Point. Drop a hook and beachcomb, or enjoy an expansive view out to the strait while tucked into one of the delightful picnic stops.

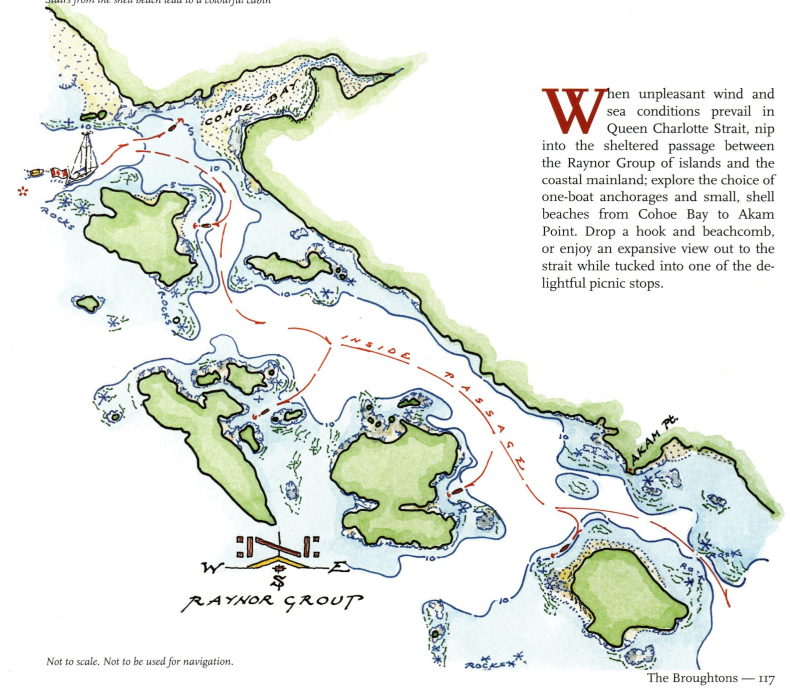

*Not to scale. Not to be used for navigation.*

# 9.3 LEWIS COVE

✽ 50°49.03'N 127°03.32'W

**CHARTS** 3547.

**APPROACH** From the SW between a large marked rock and the peninsula, or from the SE with a straight run in. Best approached at LW.

**ANCHOR** Along the western shore or as indicated. Good protection from westerly wind although open to the SE. Holding good in shell and mud in depths of 5–10 m (16–32 ft).

*One of the tide-trimmed, rocky islets*

A beautifully rugged and unexpected anchorage lies north of Lewis Rocks in sheltered Lewis Cove. With a wonderful view out to Queen Charlotte Strait, laze in the cockpit and watch the distant cruise liners heading north and south, or dinghy over to the three lovely islets topped with tide trimmed salal bushes. Feast with the birds on ripe salal berries in season, or explore the shallows and sandy beach beyond the rocks. For the ultimate birdwatching experience, stand on the highest point of the first islet (all three dry at LW) and watch as the tide falls and the sky fills with gulls gliding on the wind currents before diving and fishing just beyond the shallows.

**CAUTIONARY NOTE:** *Kelp indicates the outward reach of Lewis Rocks, S of the peninsula; these are a birder's paradise.*

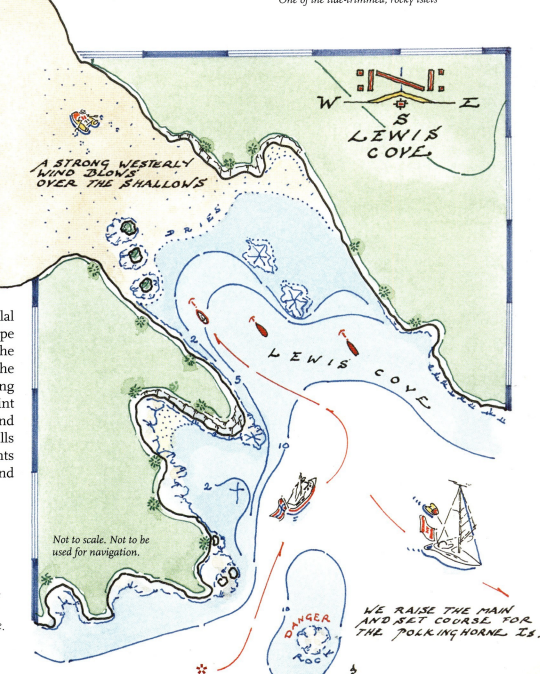

*Not to scale. Not to be used for navigation.*

# THE POLKINGHORNE ISLANDS

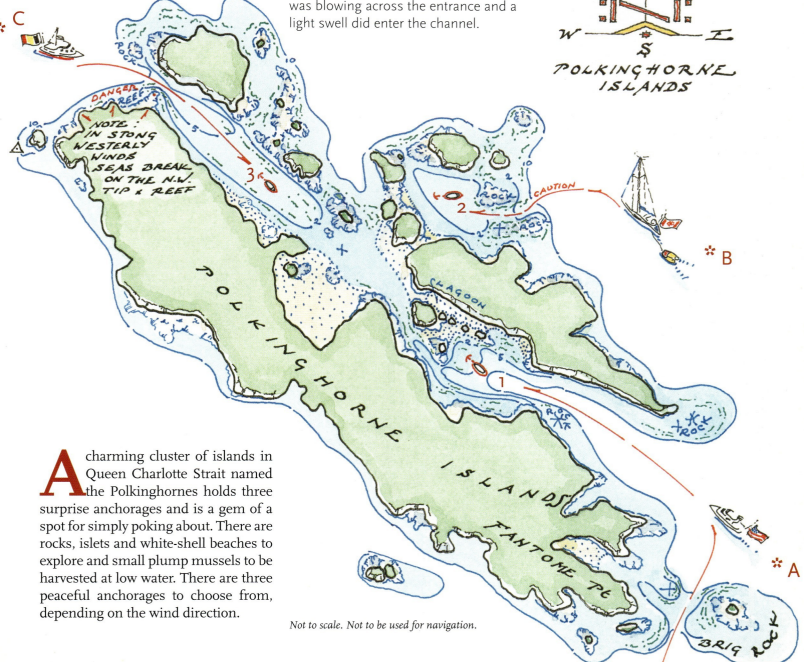

**CHARTS** 3547.

**APPROACH**   (A) From the SE; the run in is clear. (B) On a rising tide and with extreme caution, from the E. A shallow bar runs a short distance south of the rock. (C) From the N, at the entrance, run in close to the E side. Look out for patches of kelp in the channel because a reef extends out from the western shore.

**ANCHOR**   (1) SE of the islet and rock crescent, with the best protection from strong westerly winds. Holding good in sand/shell/kelp in depths of 7–10 m (22–32 ft). Open to the SE.
(2) On a rising tide, in the small pool surrounded by rocks; navigate with caution. Good protection from strong westerly winds in depths of 3–5 m (9–16 ft). Open to the SE.
(3) In the channel as indicated. Better protection in a southeasterly. Holding good in depths of 2–5 m (6–16 ft). When *Dreamspeaker* was at anchor, a strong 20-knot westerly wind (or more) was blowing across the entrance and a light swell did enter the channel.

✽(A) 50°47.40'N 126°54.62'W
✽(B) 50°47.91'N 126°54.94'W
✽(C) 50°48.33'N 126°56.72'W

A charming cluster of islands in Queen Charlotte Strait named the Polkinghornes holds three surprise anchorages and is a gem of a spot for simply poking about. There are rocks, islets and white-shell beaches to explore and small plump mussels to be harvested at low water. There are three peaceful anchorages to choose from, depending on the wind direction.

*Not to scale. Not to be used for navigation.*

# 9.5 "DEEP COVE," DICKSON ISLAND

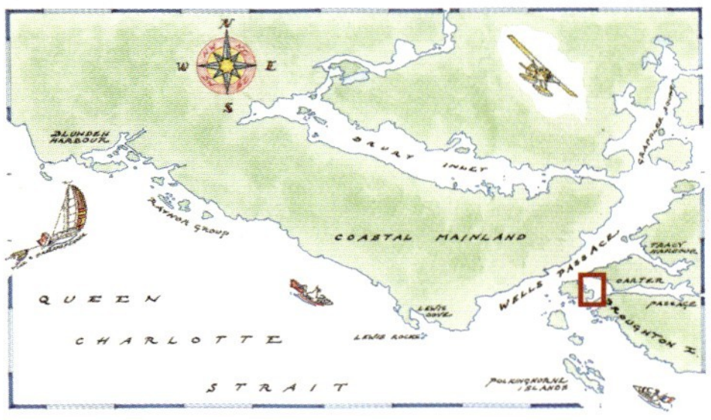


✲50°50.35'N 126°55.38'W

APPROACH From the NE. A rocky shallow area with a depth of 2.1 m (6.8 ft) extends out from the N shore.

ANCHOR The spot we call "Deep Cove" is a fair-sized anchorage with good protection from westerly winds. The cove is 10 or more metres deep (32 ft), and convenient rope loops secured on shore make stern-tying a possible option if crowded. Holding and bottom condition not recorded.

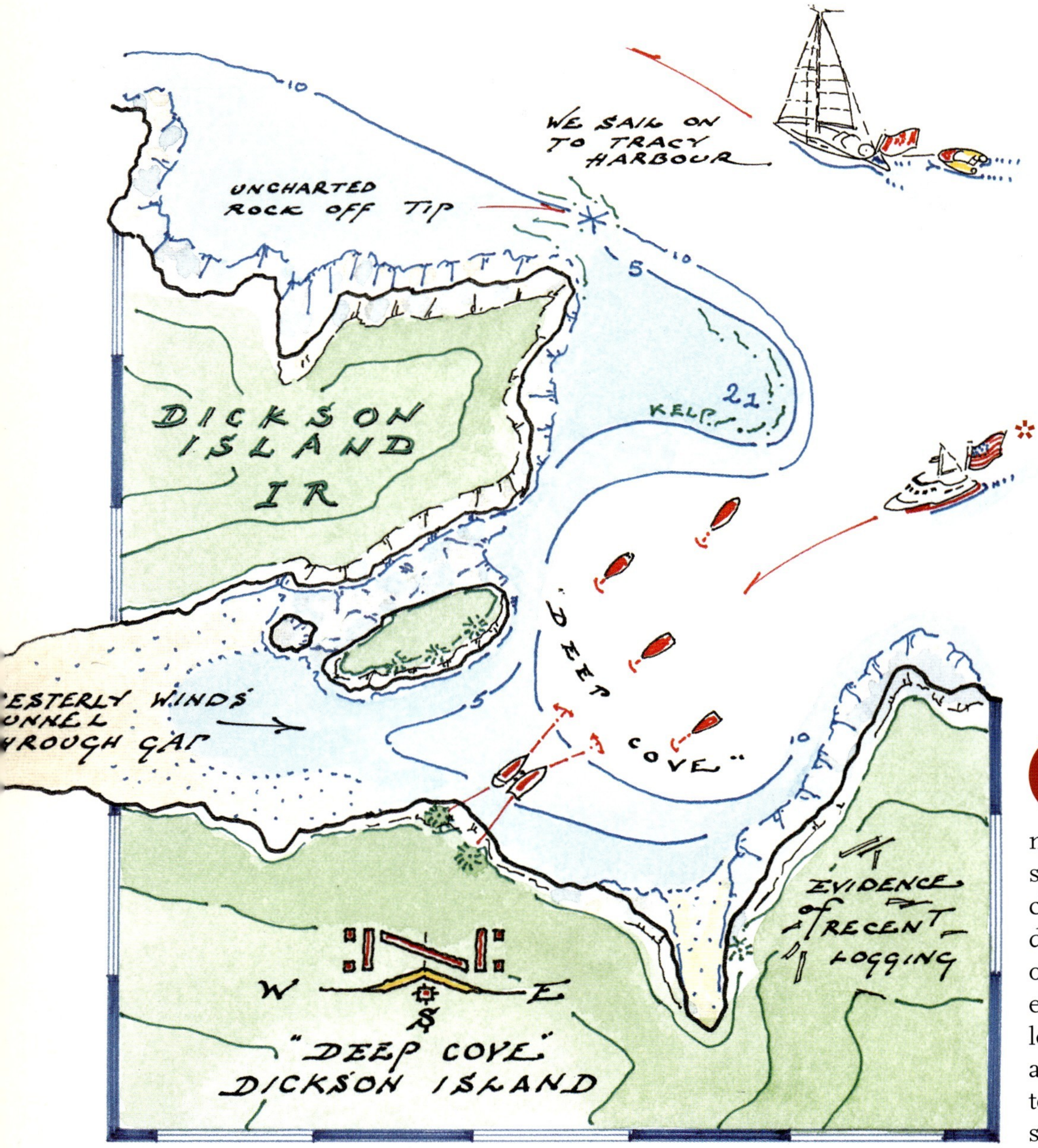


*Not to scale. Not to be used for navigation.*

Often popular with club flotillas and boat rendezvous, "Deep Cove" was busy with boaters manoeuvring, anchoring or taking stern lines ashore as we dropped anchor close to the cove entrance. With depth sounder in hand, we took *Tink* on an exploratory row, stopping off to enjoy a picnic lunch on the rocks overlooking the anchorage. Encouraged by an afternoon westerly wind, we left our temporary anchorage to enjoy a fine sail to Tracey Harbour.

*Seawind illuminated in Napier Bay, Tracey Harbour*

# 9.6 ENTRANCE TO CARTER PASSAGE, BROUGHTON ISLAND

✿50°50.19'N 126°54.83'W

**CHARTS** 3547.

**APPROACH** With caution, as large rocks are centrally located prior to the entrance. Best approached at LW or HW slack. The pass and centre channel are clear. Although rocks on the S shore are marked by kelp, favour the N shore.

**CAUTIONARY NOTE:** *The pass at the eastern end, beyond the anchorage, dries at 3.7 m (12 ft). Do not attempt transit to Greenway Sound.*

**F**rom a distance, the narrows into Carter Passage look a little daunting. However, once inside, they are much wider than they appear, with equally navigable depths.

*Bow-watch at the entrance to Carter Passage*

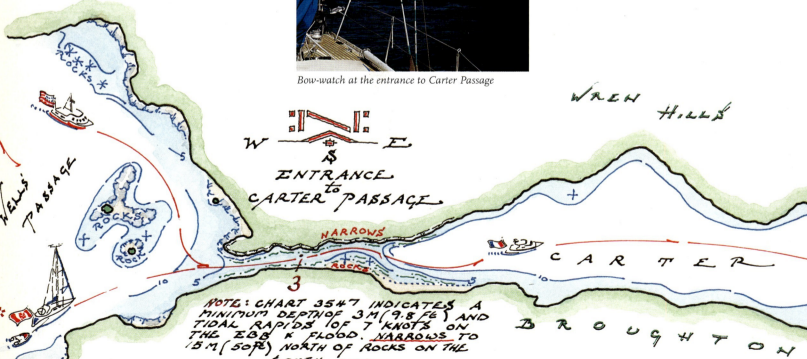

*Seals laze on rocks awash in Wells Passage*

# ANCHORAGES IN CARTER PASSAGE, BROUGHTON ISLAND 9.7

**ANCHOR** At the E end of the pass where depths are more suitable in 8–10 m (26–32 ft) and holding is good in mud. The anchorages in Carter Passage are well protected from all directions, although westerly winds do funnel through, keeping boats steady.

This is a commodious, peaceful and highly scenic anchorage. There are two small coves and one large bay to give boaters their choices of where to drop the hook – then sit back, relax and immerse yourself in the area's beauty and tranquility.

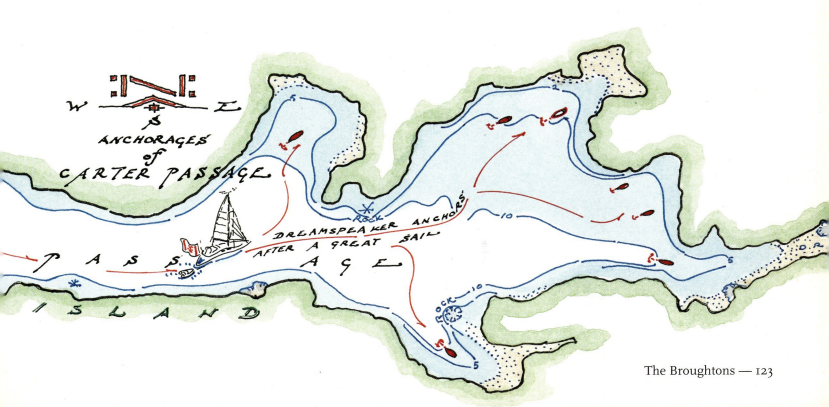

*Looking west – Tracey Harbour aglow*

# NAPIER BAY, TRACEY HARBOUR, BROUGHTON ISLAND

**CHARTS**   3547.

**APPROACH**   The centre channel in Tracey Harbour is clear of obstructions. When approaching the anchored-log breakwater off Carter Point, take the northern route into Napier Bay, or take the southern route to what we call "Little Napier Bay."

**ANCHOR**   In Napier Bay, where you will find protection from all winds in depths of 5–12 m (16–39 ft) with holding good in mud. Be aware of the submerged pipeline near the head of the bay. "Little Napier Bay" is big enough for only two or three boats with depths of 5–10 m (16–32 ft). Holding is good in mud.

✿50°50.90'N 126°51.83'W

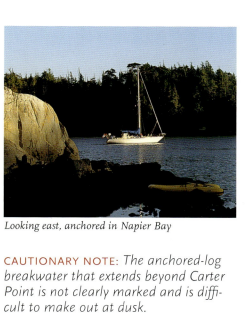

*Looking east, anchored in Napier Bay*

**CAUTIONARY NOTE:** *The anchored-log breakwater that extends beyond Carter Point is not clearly marked and is difficult to make out at dusk.*

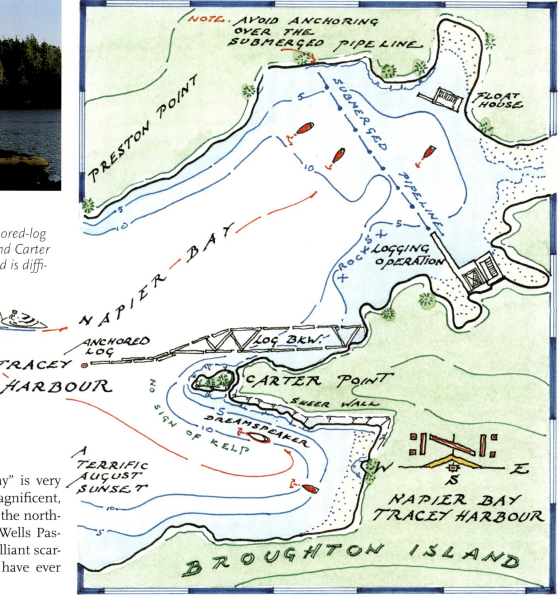

Cozy "Little Napier Bay" is very scenic with a magnificent, sheer wall of rock on the northern shoreline, views out to Wells Passage and one of the most brilliant scarlet and copper sunsets we have ever experienced.

*Drury Inlet – a quiet sense of mystery*

# Chapter 10
# DRURY INLET

*Anne investigates Sutherland Bay*

# Chapter 10
# DRURY INLET

**TIDES** – *Volume 6,*
*Canadian Tide and Current Tables*
Reference Port – Alert Bay
Secondary Ports – Stuart Narrows,
Jennis Bay

**CURRENTS**
Reference Station – Stuart Narrows on
Alert Bay
Reference Port (tide) – Alert Bay

**WEATHER**
Weather Station – WX1 162.55 MHZ
Area – Queen Charlotte Strait
Reporting Stations – Alert Bay

**CAUTIONARY NOTES:** *Currents are strong in Stuart Narrows at the entrance to Drury Inlet – up to 6 knots on the flood tide and 7 knots on the ebb. Note the position of "Centre Reef" in the narrows, as it can come as a surprise with all the deep water around. Be aware of strong and turbulent currents, especially around Dove Island and off Charters Point at the entrance to Actress Passage – best transited at slack water or with the tide in your favour.*

Drury Inlet, with its quiet sense of mystery, is certainly the place to explore when planning a few days away from the more crowded anchorages. Although the current runs swiftly in Stuart Narrows, with a small amount of turbulence at the entrance, it is still best to run into the inlet with the flood, and out with the ebb tide. Although there are anchorages in Davis and Richmond Bay on the southern shoreline, they both become uncomfortable at its head when a strong westerly picks up in the inlet.

Jennis Bay is a well-protected anchorage. Jennis Bay Marina has 350 ft (107 m) of dock space and several guest cabins. There is no power or water, but there is Wi-Fi and showers. A logging-road walking trail leads to beautiful Huaskin Lake, 5 km away. The marina owners are planning a number of improvements. For updated information, visit their website, www.jennisbay.com.

To find placid waters, head up to the peaceful Muirhead Islands where you will find a snug and protected anchorage with a collection of islets, rocks and pocket shell beaches worth exploring by dinghy and kayak.

Sutherland Bay, at the head of the inlet, offers peace and quiet, a lovely view to Mount Ellis and an abundance of wildlife. The bay has excellent anchorage for large and small boats, with plenty of room to swing. *Dreamspeaker*'s crew did not venture past Skeene Point into Actaeon Sound because of the iffy weather forecast. "Bond Basin" provides a calm, sheltered anchorage between Actress Passage and Actaeon Sound and a staging point for those travelling farther north to explore Bond Lagoon and Actaeon Sound.

# FEATURED DESTINATIONS

**CHARTS**   3547, inset Stuart Narrows.

**APPROACH**   Best at LW slack; the flooding current will assist one into the inlet.

**ENTRANCE TO DRURY INLET**

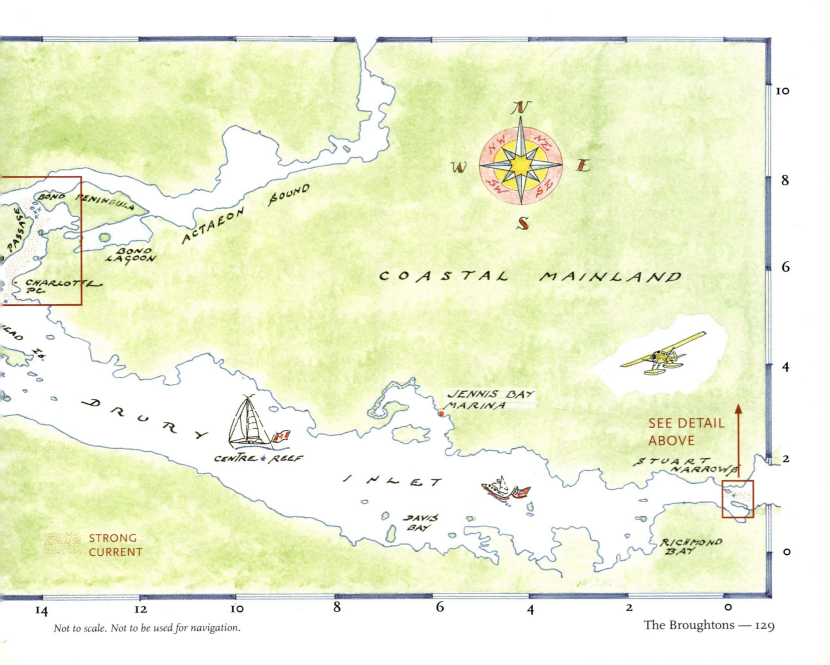

*Harmony in the Muirhead Islands*

# MUIRHEAD ISLANDS 10.1

**CHARTS**   3547.

**APPROACH**   From the E at LW. Clear the rocks to the S, prior to heading N into the small cove formed by the Muirhead Islands to the E and N and the rocks and islets to the W.

**ANCHOR**   Ample room for 2-–3 boats with a stern line ashore. Well sheltered from prevailing E and W winds, with holding good in gravel/mud/shell.

✳50°55.15'N 127°08.59'W

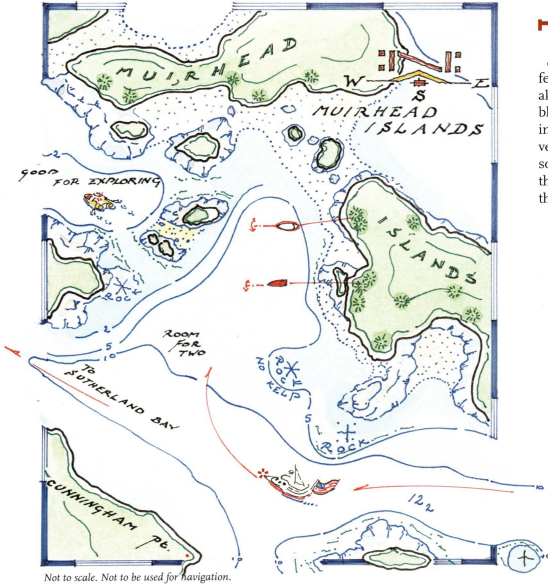

*Not to scale. Not to be used for navigation.*

This delightful cluster of islands, islets and rocks forms a snug and protected anchorage, perfect for exploring by dinghy and kayak. Low water exposes pockets of sun-bleached shell fragments, and a closer inspection of the islands and islets reveals ripe, plump salal berries in season. After a day's adventuring, relax in the cockpit with a cool drink, enjoying the sunset and serenity.

## IO.2 SUTHERLAND BAY

❀ 50°55.58'N 127°10.70'W

**CHARTS** 3547.

**APPROACH** Sutherland Bay lies at the head of Drury Inlet. The bay is free of obstructions.

**ANCHOR** In depths of 2–5 m (6–16 ft) with good holding in mud. The anchorage is quite spacious with protection from westerly winds.

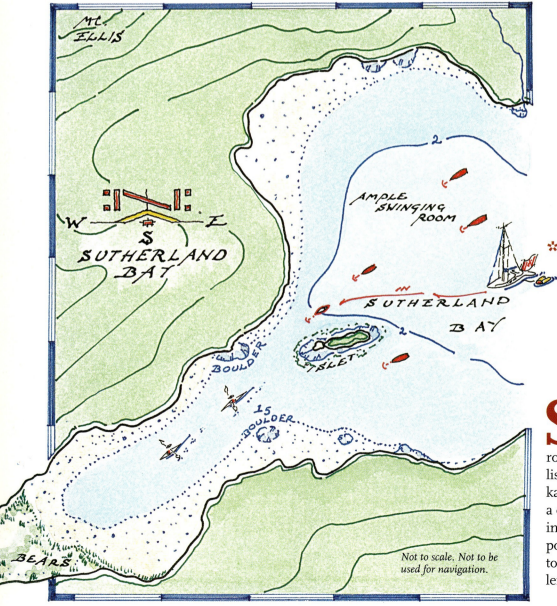

Not to scale. Not to be used for navigation.

Sutherland Bay offers peace and quiet and excellent anchorage for larger boats, with plenty of room to swing and a view to Mount Ellis. Explore the shoreline by dinghy or kayak and observe the wildlife – from a charming family of mergansers feeding in the shallows, to curious seals popping up beside your craft. The trails to Bradley Lagoon should definitely be left to the bears that use them!

# "BOND BASIN," ACTRESS PASSAGE 10.3

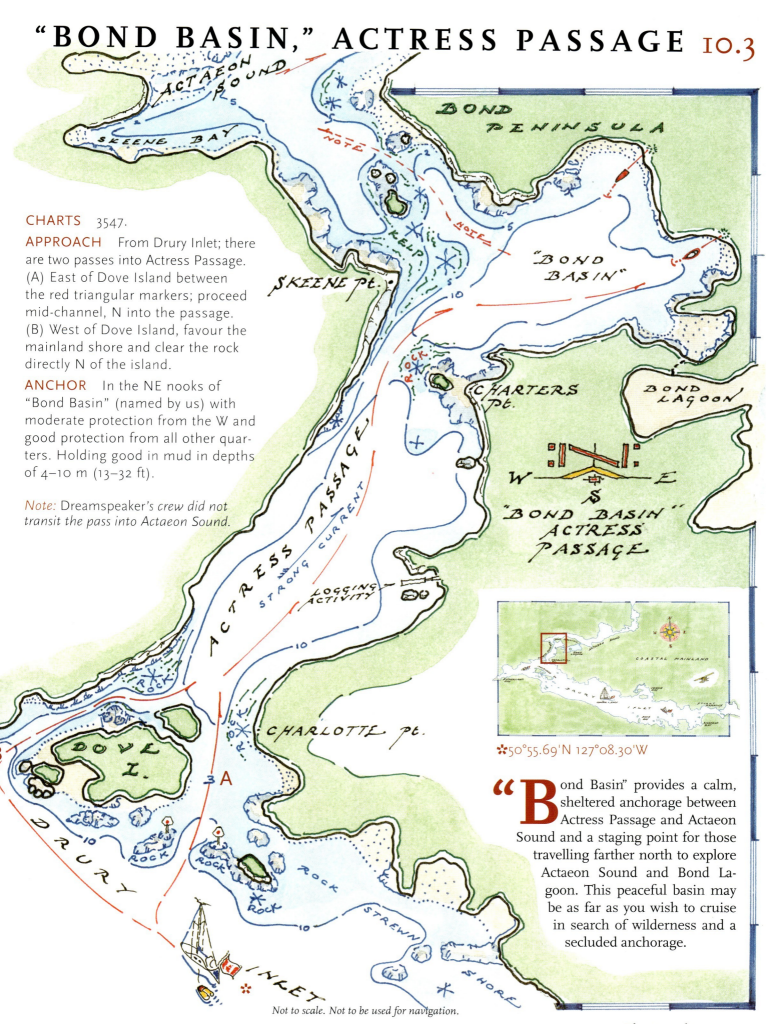

**CHARTS**   3547.

**APPROACH**   From Drury Inlet; there are two passes into Actress Passage. (A) East of Dove Island between the red triangular markers; proceed mid-channel, N into the passage. (B) West of Dove Island, favour the mainland shore and clear the rock directly N of the island.

**ANCHOR**   In the NE nooks of "Bond Basin" (named by us) with moderate protection from the W and good protection from all other quarters. Holding good in mud in depths of 4–10 m (13–32 ft).

*Note: Dreamspeaker's crew did not transit the pass into Actaeon Sound.*

✽ 50°55.69'N 127°08.30'W

"Bond Basin" provides a calm, sheltered anchorage between Actress Passage and Actaeon Sound and a staging point for those travelling farther north to explore Actaeon Sound and Bond Lagoon. This peaceful basin may be as far as you wish to cruise in search of wilderness and a secluded anchorage.

*Not to scale. Not to be used for navigation.*

*The arrival of a Canadian Naval vessel in Sullivan Bay*

Chapter 11

# GRAPPLER AND MACKENZIE SOUND

# Chapter 11

# GRAPPLER AND MACKENZIE SOUND

*Stairs to a heavenly freshwater dip in Turnbull Cove*

**TIDES** – *Volume 6,*
*Canadian Tide and Current Tables*
Reference Port – Alert Bay
Secondary Ports – Sullivan Bay, Jessie
Point (entrance to Kenneth Passage)

**CURRENTS**

No specific reference or secondary
stations cover this chapter. Slack water
in the passages off both Watson Point
and Jessie Point are similar to slack at
Roaringhole Rapids (see note chart
3547).

**WEATHER**

Weather Station – WX1 162.55 MHZ
Area – Queen Charlotte Strait
Reporting Station – Alert Bay

**CAUTIONARY NOTES:** *Currents run
swiftly through all the channels and
passages, creating a certain amount of
current in all the destinations covered in
this chapter. Do not be tempted to take
the shortcut through Hopetown Passage into Mackenzie Sound at HW, and
note the position of the rock off Watson
Point in Grappler Sound – this one was
a near miss for Dreamspeaker's keel!
An excursion into Nepah Lagoon is not
recommended due to the Roaring Hole
Rapids and the lack of suitable anchorage depths.*

The community of Sullivan Bay is conveniently situated on northern Broughton Island and historic
Sullivan Bay Marine Resort is a relaxed place full of
character. The floating village is an eclectic mix of colourful
float homes from the early 1940s and offers the cruising
boater facilities to fuel, provision, shower, throw in a load or
two of laundry and rendezvous with friends. It's the perfect
spot to begin your cruise into the scenic waters of Grappler
and Mackenzie Sound – the start of the coastal mainland's
labyrinth of passages and channels.

Hopetown Passage north of Sullivan Bay offers a small,
peaceful anchorage. Swing to the current and savour the
magnificent views, with mighty Mount Stephens stand-
ing guard. Note that the narrow, boulder-strewn pass into
Mackenzie Sound has a very strong current and can only
be navigated by shoal draft boats at HW. The comfortably large anchorage in Claydon Bay is backed by Mount
Emily. Explore Embley Lagoon and navigate the tidal falls
into Overflow Basin by dinghy.

Surrounded by a rocky shoreline and steep forested
sides, harbour-sized Turnbull Cove offers good anchorage
and an invigorating hike to lovely Huaskin Lake, where
you can take a freshwater swim.

En route from Steamboat to Nimmo Bay, look out for
the spectacular cliff face at Anne Point; an inconspicuous
nook east of Turner Island also reveals a cozy one-boat
anchorage. The prettiest spot to anchor in Burly Bay is
tucked in behind Blair Islet.

In settled weather westerly winds tend to die off at
the end of the day, making the anchorage at the head of
Mackenzie Sound a peaceful spot to drop the hook for
the night.

The mirror-calm of mornings in Nimmo Bay is an experience not to be missed.

# FEATURED DESTINATIONS

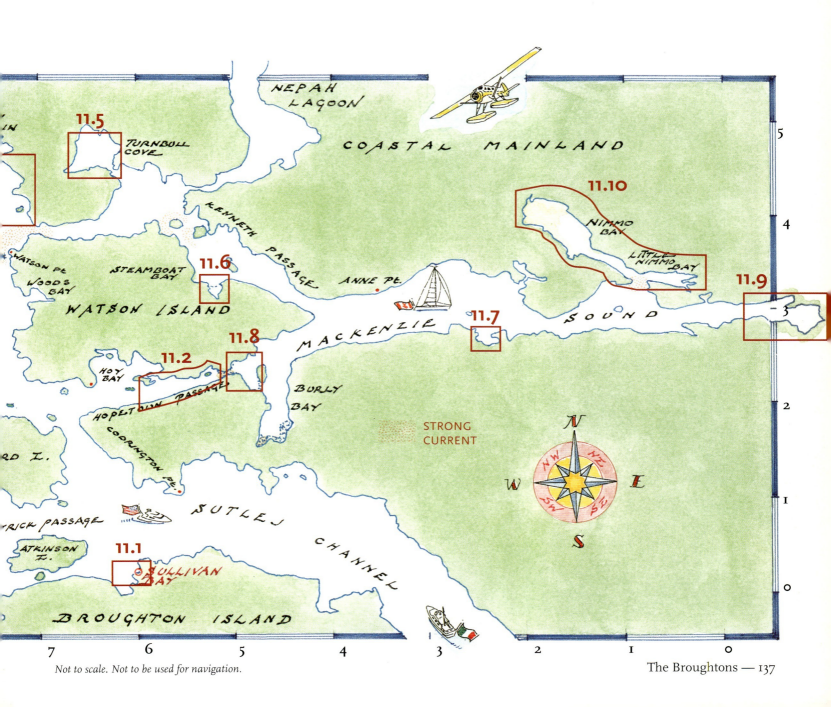

*Not to scale. Not to be used for navigation.*

# SULLIVAN BAY, BROUGHTON ISLAND

❋ 50°53.29'N 126°49.81'W

*"The International Airport," fuel tanks and fuel dock*

*The store is a focal point*

*The Town Hall Restaurant serves tasty, hearty meals*

Historic SULLIVAN BAY MARINE RESORT is relaxed, friendly and full of character. The unique floating village is an eclectic mix of wooden structures and float homes brought into the bay during the early 1940s, and its fun, quirky personality endures today. Almost everything is painted with vibrant murals, and the charming gardens and planters along the boardwalk overflow with flowers. A community of vacation float homes is situated southwest of the resort.

The resort has a postal drop and an excellent store with fresh produce brought in every two or three days in high season. The BC LIQUOR STORE outlet is well stocked. Cozy but clean showers offer hot water, although the laundry facilities supply only cold. (Prepay for both at the store.) There is also an exercise room. Garbage disposal is for recycling only (beer cans, pop cans, water bottles); a large tin drum is provided for dry burnable garbage only. The village's smokehouse is available by reservation.

The TOWN HALL floating restaurant is licensed and features a popular limited menu of specials every other night. This cozy spot makes a welcome addition to the village amenities, with a Saturday evening menu that might include prime rib and Yorkshire pudding or a fresh halibut special. Boaters often gather for happy hour at the "Sullivan Square" float. On display are historic photographs of Sullivan Bay between the mid-'40s and late-'50s, when it was one of the main fuelling stops on the coast for floatplanes and biplanes. Passengers and employees of Queen Charlotte Airlines – once the third-largest airline in Canada, owned by entrepreneur Jim Spilsbury – were frequent visitors. His fascinating and entertaining book, *Spilsbury's Coast*, is a must-read for any boater cruising this coast (see Selected Readings, p. 188).

Floatplane services to and from the resort can be found on Sullivan Bay's website (www.sullivanbaymarina.com), as well as information on summer events, including the famous July 4th Fireworks Parade and potluck dinner.

**CHARTS** 3547.

**APPROACH** The floating village, and its colourful roofs, is easily spotted as you enter Sullivan Bay. The run in is free of obstructions.

**MARINA** Sullivan Bay Marine Resort offers extensive visitor moorage with power, Wi-Fi and unlimited water. Fifteen-, 30-, 50-, 100-amp and 240-volt service is available. They monitor Channel 66A (or phone 604-484-9193); a dock attendant is nearly always on call. Debbie Holt and Chris Scheveers are the managers.

**FUEL** At the resort's fuel float – gasoline, diesel and propane are available.

**CAUTIONARY NOTE:** *Do not underestimate the force of the cross-current at the docks. Come to a full stop prior to making the run in and assess the current's direction and strength.*

*The float home that sports both flags!*

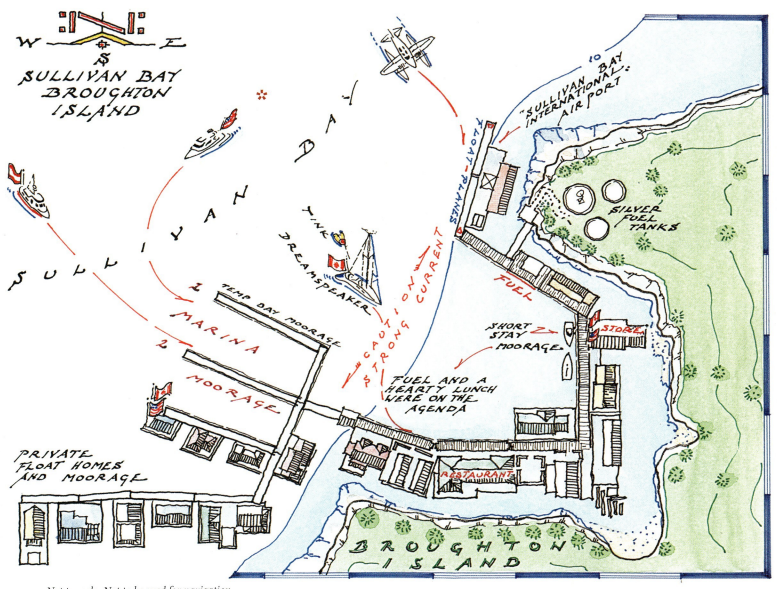

*Not to scale. Not to be used for navigation.*

# HOPETOWN PASSAGE, HOY BAY

✿ 50°55.06'N 126°49.28'W

**CHARTS** 3547.

**APPROACH** From the W, along the steep southern shoreline of Hopetown Passage which lies S of the First Nations community.

**ANCHOR** As indicated in (1), which has less current; or in (2) in settled weather, between the kelp. Swing to the current in depths of 2.5–4 m (8–13 ft), with fair holding in gravel and rock.

*Note: Anchorage (2) is only for boaters who feel comfortable anchoring in the current, between kelp.*

Tuck into the kelp-free nook on the northern shoreline of Hopetown Passage, or drop anchor in a snug pool beyond the big rock in the narrow section of the pass. Swing to the current and savour the solitude and the magnificent views of mighty Mount Stephens. Large trees overhang the water's edge, where darting kingfishers dive for their supper, and the quiet is occasionally disturbed by the soft splash of leaping salmon.

*Mighty Mount Stephens*

# CLAYDON BAY 11.3

**CHARTS** 3547.

**APPROACH** From the SE out of Grappler Sound. Favour the W shore, as rocks lie to the NE. If anchoring NE of the islet, favour the W shore.

**ANCHOR** Good protection from westerly winds can be found in the N basin and from SE winds in the S basin. Holding good in mud in depths of 3–6 m (9–19 ft).

✳50°55.56'N 126°93'W

I n both of the finger-like coves, ruins of trestle structures that once formed logging jetties add a little history to Claydon Bay. The comfortably large anchorage, backed by Mount Emily, is a very pleasant spot to spend the day or to overnight. Explore the grassy islet or visit the ruins and beachcomb at leisure while graceful sandpipers feed on the rising tide.

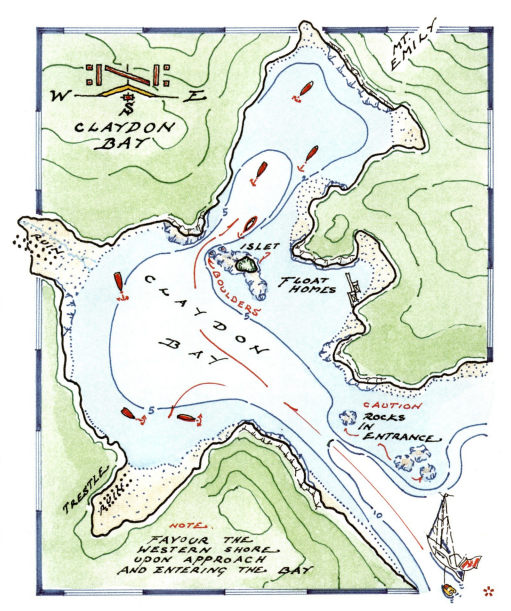

*Ruins of the trestle structures*

# THE HEAD OF GRAPPLER SOUND

✿ 50°56.41'N 126°51.85'W

**CHARTS** 3547.

**APPROACH** From the S. Clear the rock off Watson Point and keep the strong currents in mind.

**ANCHOR** (1) N of the islet on the E shore, with a stern line ashore. (2) E of the gap to Overflow Basin, with a taut stern line ashore. (3) Drop anchor along the 10 m (32 ft) sounding on the W shore. A lovely anchorage in settled weather with holding good in mud, in depths of 6–10 m (19–32 ft).

*Note: It is necessary to have a reliable outboard and dinghy if you plan to navigate the tidal falls into Overflow Basin before or after HW slack. The gap dries at LW.*

*A large section of Embley Lagoon dries at LW, although the entrance is shallow but navigable by dinghy.*

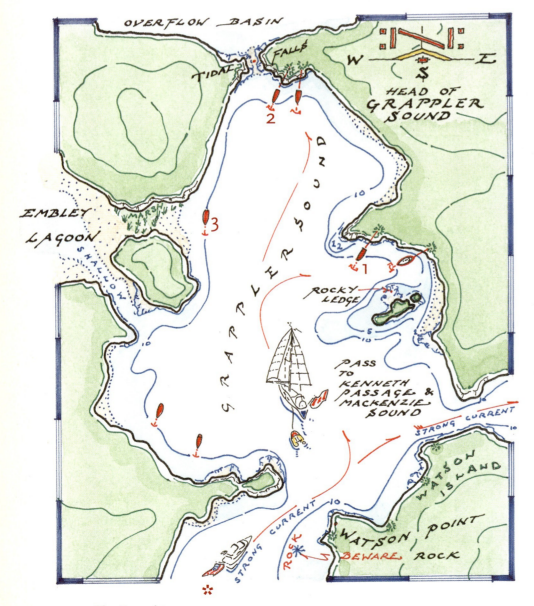

*A lucky boat anchored adjacent to the tidal falls*

Each of the three anchorages at the head of Grappler Sound has its own personality; the cozy nook north of the small islet keeps the light longest, while anchoring close to the tidal falls at the entrance to Overflow Basin is a dramatic and much coveted overnight spot. Anchoring off the western shoreline will include a fine view into peaceful Embley Lagoon, where the marsh is home to a large family of flighty mergansers.

*Tink* took us on a thrilling and fun trip through the tidal falls. Once inside, the basin was sunny and tranquil; it was an exhilarating experience being flushed out with the ebb, before it became too strong.

**CHARTS** 3547.

**APPROACH** From the head of Grappler Sound. The entrance is lined with kelp, although the centre channel gives a clear run in.

**ANCHOR** No need to crowd your neighbours in this commodious and protected anchorage. Take a stern line or swing in depths of 5–10 m (16–32 ft), as easterly winds tend to swirl around. Holding good in mud.

*Note: Westerly winds will funnel through the gap in the SW corner.*

✷50°57.26'N 126°93'W

*Shoreline access to base of the steep trail*

**H**arbour-sized Turnbull Cove – surrounded by a rocky shoreline and steep, forested sides – offers good anchorage and a hike to Huaskin Lake, which was once home to a large logging camp. The trail is maintained by the Ministry of Forests, allowing your crew to hike, go for a freshwater swim off the wooden raft and enjoy a picnic lunch.

Pull your dinghy up to the rock-strewn beach and walk to the base of the steep trail; help yourself to one of the many recycled walking sticks, which are a great help during the often slippery uphill climb. The descent to the lake is via dozens of stairs cut into a secured, sturdy log covered with a non-slip surface (a thoughtful modification, indeed).

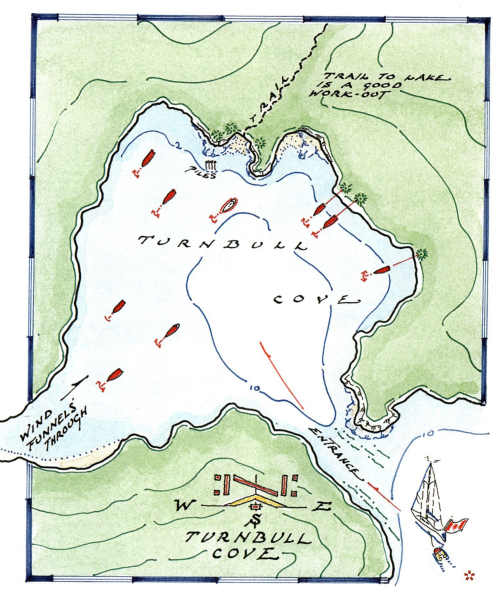

Dreamspeaker *glides past Anne Point*

# STEAMBOAT BAY, KENNETH PASSAGE 11.6

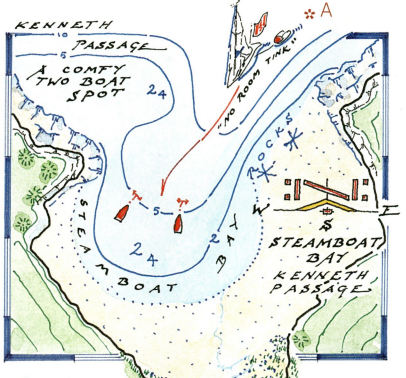

❋(A) 50°56.26'N 126°48.21'W
❋(B) 50°55.84'N 126°43.89'W

*Two lucky boats in Steamboat Bay*

**S**teamboat Bay is a little gem of an anchorage. On our visit, however, two boats were anchored there and there wasn't room for a third, so we moved on.

**CHARTS** 3547, inset Kenneth Passage.
**APPROACH** From the N. At LW, kelp marks the rocks to the E.
**ANCHOR** Two boats comfortably in depths of 4–8 m (13–26 ft).

# "ANNE COVE" 11.7

**M**idway between Steamboat Bay and the head of Mackenzie Sound, an inconspicuous nook east of Turner Island revealed a pocket paradise, which we named "Anne Cove." The small beach is backed by a stream and a patch of crisp sea asparagus. The lone tree on what we've dubbed "Crabapple Islet" provided a hatful of the tart fruit for crabapple jelly and a spot of shade for our picnic.

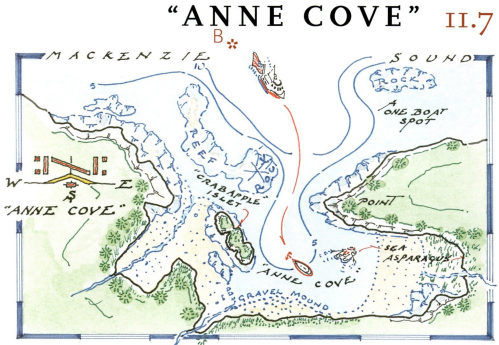

**CHARTS** 3547.
**APPROACH** As indicated, mid-channel between Turner Island and the S shore of Mackenzie Sound. Best approached at LW when rocks are visible.

**ANCHOR** A one-boat anchorage in depths of 4–6 m (13–19 ft), sheltered from westerly and easterly winds. Holding good in mud and shell.

# II.8 "BLAIR COVE," BURLY BAY

❉ 50°55.45'N 126°47.45'W

**CHARTS** 3547.

**APPROACH** From the NE. The run in is free of obstructions.

**ANCHOR** As indicated, in depths of 4–8 m (13–26 ft). Holding good in mud and gravel.

*Note:* Do not attempt to pass through to Hopetown Passage or between Blair Islet and the mainland, as both are boulder-strewn.

*Company in lovely "Blair Cove"*

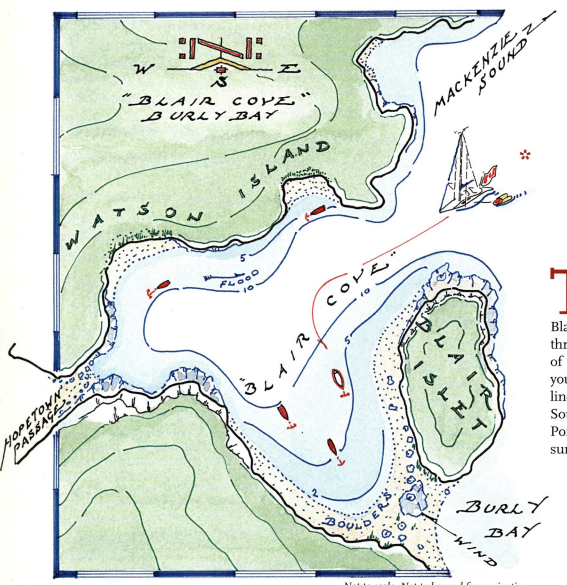

The prettiest place to anchor in Burly Bay is a spot we've named "Blair Cove," tucked in behind Blair Islet, with a dramatic outlook through the gap to the Coastal Range of mountains. Alternatively, drop your hook along the northwest shoreline with a clear view into Mackenzie Sound, and take in the beauty of Anne Point and the sheer rock face aglow at sunset.

*Not to scale. Not to be used for navigation.*

MV Sir James Douglas

**CHARTS** 3547.

**APPROACH** From the W. Logging operations were evident to us on both the N and S shore. The entrance lies mid-channel between remnants of a log breakwater.

**ANCHOR** Although the anchorage is open to the W, reasonable protection in a strong westerly can be found into the N or S corners. Holding is good in mud and gravel, in depths of 4–6 m (13–19 ft).

✿ 50°55.98'N 126°39.07'W

In settled weather, westerly winds tend to die off at the end of the day, making the anchorage at the head of Mackenzie Sound a peaceful spot to drop the hook for the night. The stream that flows from Mackenzie Lake into the basin has created a small beach for exploring at LW.

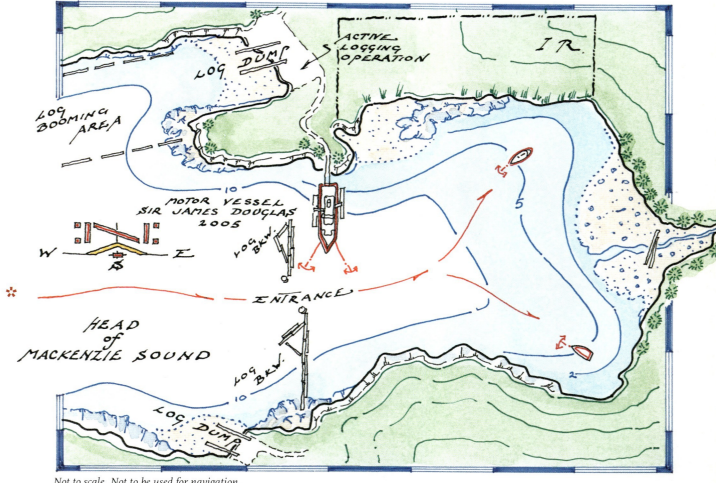

Not to scale. Not to be used for navigation.

# LITTLE NIMMO BAY AND NIMMO BAY

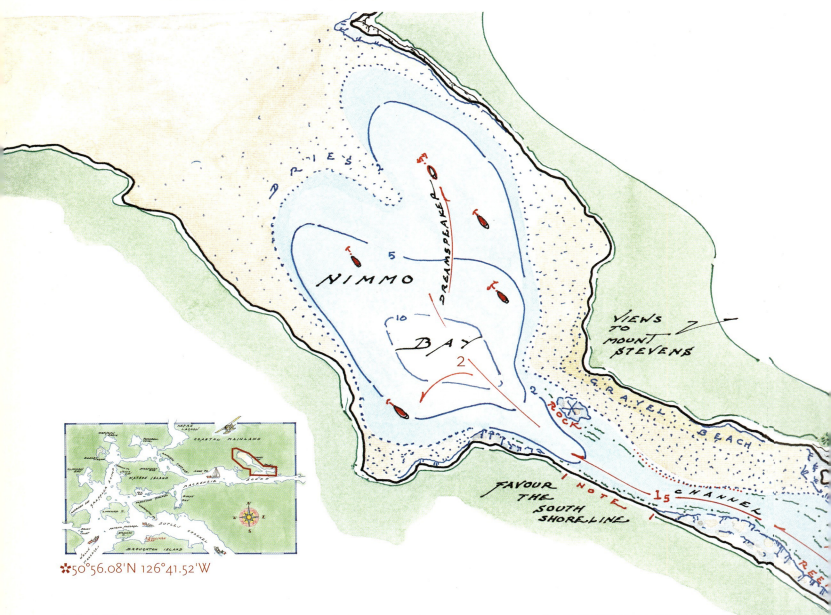

NIMMO BAY

DREAMSPEAKER

VIEWS TO MOUNT STEVENS

GRAVEL BEACH

ROCK

FAVOUR THE SOUTH SHORELINE

NOTE

CHANNEL

15

REEF

COASTAL MAINLAND

MACKENZIE SOUND

BROUGHTON ISLAND

❀50°56.08'N 126°41.52'W

**H**aving negotiated the entrance into Little Nimmo Bay, we anchored south of the lodge, then moved to a quieter anchorage west of the entrance for the night. The following morning on a rising tide, dead slow, we crept west along the channel into Nimmo Bay, which is a glorious spot to anchor – tranquility at its best. We discourage an excursion ashore, as the shoreline is home to bears.

If space is available, the NIMMO BAY RESORT is happy to offer boaters day adventure tours or fishing by helicopter; limited transient moorage (no power); or a gourmet breakfast or dinner by reservation. For general inquiries call 800-837-4354 or use VHF Channel 10. Visit their website, www.nimmobay. com, for tour information.

*The resort's red-roofed cabins indicate the entrance*

MA

*Glassy calm in Nimmo Bay*

**CHARTS**   3547.

**APPROACH**   (A) From the S. The resort's colourful cabins are noticeable on approach. The entrance to Little Nimmo Bay is best navigated on a rising tide. The clear channel is W of centre and best transited when the rocks on the western shore are still visible. Beware the nugget of rock E of centre, and the reef that extends N off Nimmo Point. Note that the local consensus is that the charted least depth of 30 cm (1 ft) lies E of the entrance channel. (B) Nimmo Bay, on a rising tide. Leave the rock in the centre channel to the N and take a curve around the edge of the reef extending out from the S shore; favour the S shore upon entering the bay. Note that it is easy to run aground on the gravel that extends off the N shore.

**ANCHOR**   (1) E or W of the entrance in depths of 4–8 m (13–26 ft), with holding good in mud. (2) Drop your hook in Nimmo Bay, as indicated. Holding good in mud. Watch your depth sounder as the head dries extensively.

*Note: The water was glassy calm when Dreamspeaker was anchored in Nimmo Bay, although a moderate westerly was blowing in Mackenzie Sound. Local knowledge reports that Little Nimmo Bay has good protection from westerly winds, while Nimmo Bay has reasonable protection.*

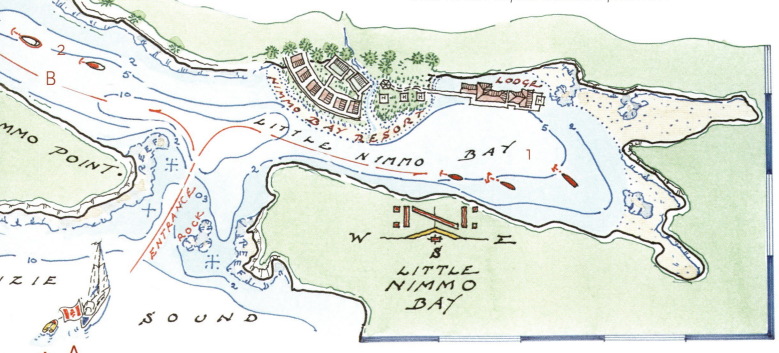

# Chapter 12

# BROUGHTON ISLAND, GREENWAY SOUND TO CULLEN HARBOUR

*Looking up Penphrase Passage (Peter A. Robson photo)*

*Elusive winds in Fife Sound*

# Chapter 12

# BROUGHTON ISLAND, GREENWAY SOUND TO CULLEN HARBOUR

### TIDES – *Volume 6, Canadian Tide and Current Tables*

Reference Port – Alert Bay
Secondary Port – Sunday Harbour

### CURRENTS

No specific reference or secondary stations cover this chapter; however, currents run swiftly through the channels and passages, creating a certain amount of current in most anchorages.

### WEATHER

Weather Station – WX1 162.55 MHZ
Area – Queen Charlotte Strait
Reporting Station – Alert Bay

**CAUTIONARY NOTES:** *Beware – a rock in "Laura Cove" is situated between the islet and Trivett Island. At the entrance to Booker Lagoon, Booker Passage has a reef that extends out from Long Island. Look for the stone man Inukshuk on the reef tip.*

Greenway Sound off Sutlej Channel runs east, then south, and almost cuts Broughton Island in two. Although it is deep, it has few anchorages from which to choose. At the entrance to the sound, tucked behind Cecil Island, are two nooks that provide comfortable day and overnight anchorage. When the sun sets, the westerly winds in Greenway Sound die off and the northeast outflow winds take over, making this a protected, cozy corner.

Nearby Broughton Lakes Marine Park offers a maintained trail and traditional log road that allows boaters to stretch their sea legs with a scenic walk.

Behind Broughton Point, at the east end of Carter Passage, you will find a small anchorage that affords good protection for the night. Tucked into the head of Berry Cove, enjoy a picnic lunch in the cockpit. For an alternative overnight anchorage, pop into sheltered Stopford Bay and sleep soundly in its all-around protection.

One of the more popular anchorages on the eastern shore of Broughton Island is in Laura Bay, off Penphrase Passage. Locally called "Laura Cove," it's an unexpectedly wonderful anchorage tucked behind a grassy islet off Trivett Island. Enjoy a stunning view of Wishart Peninsula and Kingcome Inlet.

In Fife Sound, west of Pearse Peninsula, a fringe of islands and islets protect roomy Cullen Harbour from westerly winds. The anchorage provides a convenient staging point for boaters cruising east or west through the Broughtons, and access to Booker Lagoon via Booker Passage.

# FEATURED DESTINATIONS

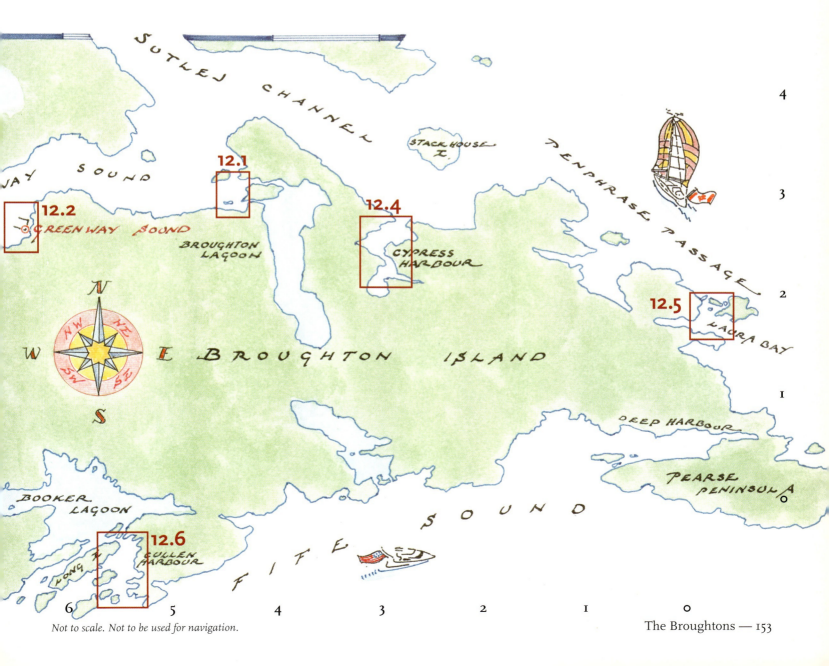

*Not to scale. Not to be used for navigation.*

# 12.1 ENTRANCE TO BROUGHTON LAGOON, GREENWAY SOUND

✿ 50°50.71'N 126°43.00'W

**CHARTS**  3547.

**APPROACH**  From the W out of Greenway Sound. A large fish farm on the NW side of Cecil Island is highly conspicuous.

**ANCHOR**  (1) In the current, just outside the tidal rapids; room for one or two boats and protected from westerly winds.

(2) Behind "Lion Islet" (named by us), pass to port or starboard. There is room for two to four boats, and although it's a little bumpy during a westerly, things calm down when the evening outflow winds begin.

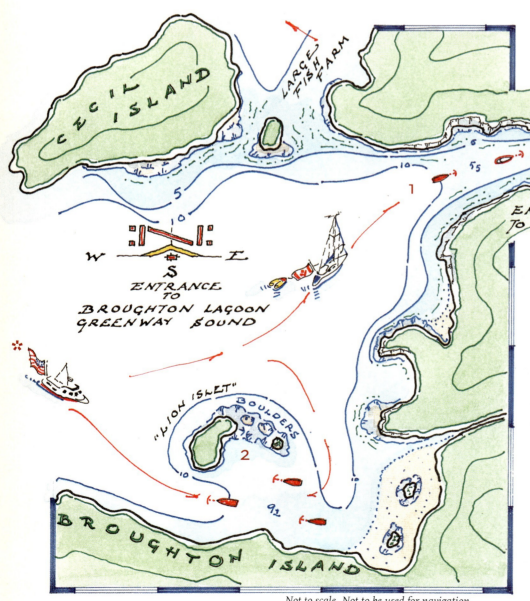

Not to scale. Not to be used for navigation.

Greenway Sound is deep with few anchorages from which to choose. At the entrance to the sound, tucked behind Cecil Island, two convenient nooks provide comfortable day and overnight stops. When the sun sets, the westerly winds in Greenway Sound die off and the NE outflow winds take over, making this a protected and cozy corner.

Exploring the lake-like Broughton Lagoon is best done at HW slack with a reliable outboard and reserve fuel.

*A friendly red trawler tucked in behind the islet*

# GREENWAY SOUND MARINE RESORT 12.2

CHARTS 3547.

✽50°50.48'N 126°46.57'W

*Boats gather in Greenway Sound prior to the closing of the Marine Resort*

Unfortunately, this once popular destination has been closed for a number of years – the owners, Tom and Ann Taylor, decided to retire and have been unable to find a buyer. As of 2015, the marina was still for sale, but the docks and floating buildings were in bad repair and vandals had been at work. Perhaps in the coming years someone will able to revive the marina. For updates, visit the Friends of Greenway Sound facebook page, www.facebook.com/greenwaysound.

While the marina has closed down, nearby Broughton Lakes Marine Park has a dinghy dock, maintained trails and a traditional log road that allows boaters to stretch their sea legs with a scenic walk. Give yourself a few hours to hike through the forests of Mount Ick to Beaver Dam Lake and Broughton Lake Viewpoint, take a refreshing dip in the tannic waters of Broughton Lake, and picnic on the grassy shore while enjoying the stillness of nature at its best.

# 12.3 BROUGHTON POINT, GREENWAY SOUND

✽ 50°50.31'N 126°48.70'W

**CHARTS** 3547.

**APPROACH** From the E. The cut to Carter Passage lies S of Broughton Point; a clear view W opens up. Keep S of the islet on approach. The E entrance to Carter Passage dries and is strewn with boulders.

**ANCHOR** In a pool NW of the islet or in the channel, as indicated. There is room for two or three boats to swing to the current in depths of 4–10 m (13–32 ft). Holding is good in mud and gravel. Protected from northeast outflow winds by the point and islet.

*Typical rainforest shoreline*

After a glorious day's sail exploring every nook and cranny in Greenway Sound, we tucked *Dreamspeaker* behind Broughton Point at the east end of Carter Passage and dropped our hook for the night. This anchorage affords good protection, as westerly winds do not funnel this far into the channel. The odd sports fishing boat zooming by might be the only disturbance. We experienced a tranquil evening and glassy- smooth waters in the morning.

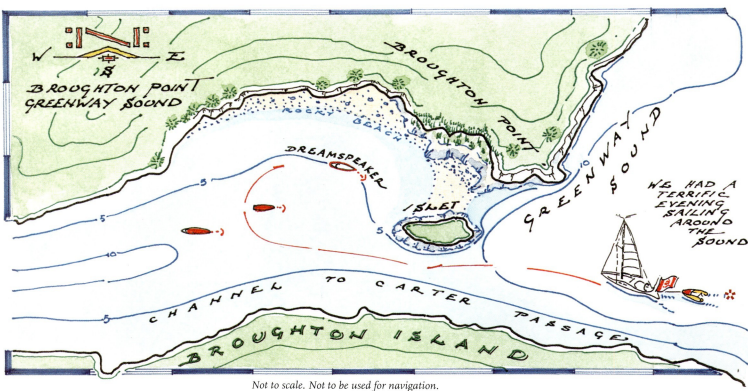

*Not to scale. Not to be used for navigation.*

# CYPRESS HARBOUR 12.4

**CHARTS**   3547.

**APPROACH**   From Sharp Passage; enter between Fox Rock and Donald Head. The fish farm in Miller Bay is mighty conspicuous. The run in to Berry Cove and the channel to Stopford Bay are clear.

**ANCHOR**   In Berry Cove, which is open to the NE and outflow winds in 4–8 m (13–26 ft) with good holding in gravel and mud. For all-around protection, anchor in Stopford Bay, the harbour's inner basin, in depths of 2–5 m (6–16 ft) with holding good in mud.

*Note: Miller Bay is in the lee of the fish farm, which operates 24 hours a day.*

✳50°50.53'N 126°39.62'W

Tucked into the head of Berry Cove, we enjoyed lunch in the cockpit. For an alternative overnight anchorage, drop anchor in sheltered Stopford Bay, explore the shoreline by dinghy or kayak and sleep soundly in its all-around protection. Be aware of the possibility of logging debris on the bottom of the bay.

*Rock bluffs backing Berry Cove*

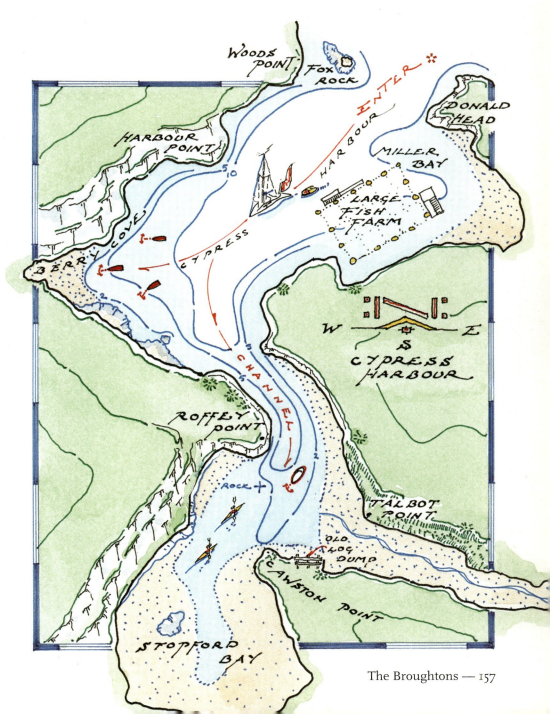

*A beach fire completes the day in Laura Cove*

**CHARTS** 3515.

**APPROACH** From the E, along the S shore of Trivett Island. Enter the cove leaving the islet to the E.

**ANCHOR** In popular "Laura Cove" as indicated, in 2–4 m (6–13 ft) with a stern line ashore.

*Note:* A rock lies between the islet and Trivett Island.

✷50°49.20'N 126°33.79'W

**O**ne of the more popular anchorages on the eastern shore of Broughton Island is in Laura Bay. It's referred to by locals as "Laura Cove" and is an unexpected little gem tucked behind a grassy islet off Trivett Island. To accommodate as many boats as possible during the busy summer season, it's best to take a stern line ashore. Beach your dinghy on the isthmus that connects Broughton and Trivett Island to enjoy a stunning view over Penphrase Passage, across to Wishart Peninsula and north to Kingcome Inlet.

*Not to scale. Not to be used for navigation.*

# 12.6 CULLEN HARBOUR, BOOKER PASSAGE

✿50°45.88'N 126°44.49'W

**APPROACH** From the S, favour the Nelly Islet shore. The centre channel of Cullen Harbour is clear. Booker Passage is deep but best transited at LW slack. Kelp fringes the channel with a minimum charted depth of 6.4 m (21 ft).

**ANCHOR** In commodious Cullen Harbour with good protection from all prevailing winds. Dreamspeaker held well on a rocky/gravel bottom in 4–8 m (13–26 ft).

*Note: If transiting Booker Passage to Booker Lagoon, look out for the stoneman Inukshuk on the tip of the reef that extends out from Long Island.*

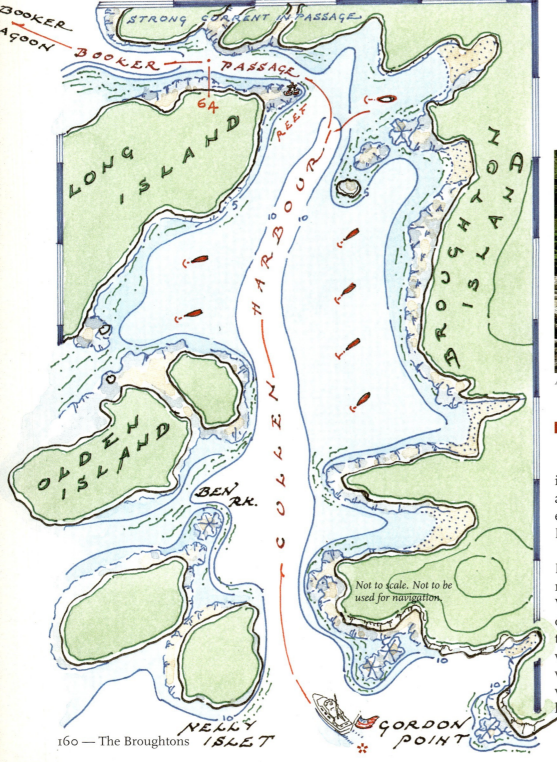

*An Inukshuk marks the tip of the reef*

The fringe of islands and islets protects roomy Cullen Harbour from the westerly winds in Queen Charlotte Strait and provides a convenient staging point for boaters cruising east or west through the Broughtons.

Access to extensive Booker Lagoon, which for some is great exploration territory, is via Booker Passage. We entered at LW slack and popped out before the flood got too strong, then dropped anchor in the harbour's very northern nook, with a lovely view into the passage, marked to the west by a navigational stone structure known as an Inukshuk.

# SHAWL BAY, TRIBUNE CHANNEL TO KWATSI BAY AND BOND SOUND

*Quite the photo opportunity at "Lacy Falls," Tribune Channel*

# Chapter 13

# SHAWL BAY, TRIBUNE CHANNEL TO KWATSI BAY AND BOND SOUND

*Anne discovers the waterfall at Kwatsi Bay*

**TIDES** – *Volume 6,*
*Canadian Tide and Current Tables*
Reference Port – Alert Bay

**CURRENTS**

No specific reference or secondary stations cover this chapter. However, currents run swiftly through the channels and passages, creating a certain amount of current in most anchorages.

**WEATHER**

Weather Station – WX1 162.55 MHZ
Area – Queen Charlotte Strait
Reporting Station – Alert Bay

**CAUTIONARY NOTES:** *The pass between Shawl and Moore Bay should only be navigated on a rising tide when it is half-tide or above. The Burdwood Group of Islands are better protected from westerly winds with little protection from the east.*

Because there really are no suitable anchorages in Wakeman Sound and Kingcome Inlet, Moore Bay offers a good base for day trips up the inlets and channels, or to use as a staging point.

Shawl Bay has always been a meeting place for loggers and fishermen; today cruising boaters meet at Shawl Bay Marina to rendezvous with friends, share potlucks and indulge in the complimentary pancake breakfasts. Fed by the glacial waters of Kingcome River, the converging waters at the junction of Wakeman Sound and Kingcome Inlet take on a milky-green hue. A short detour south will take you into Belleisle Sound. Backed by lofty Mount Mathison and the conical-shaped mounds of Craig Hills, this is one of the most spectacular settings to drop your anchor.

Stunning Simoom Sound is dominated by the mask-like, black-granite face of Bald Mountain. Although the sound appears calm, strong winds can find their way in.

The Burdwoods are a group of low-lying islands, islets and rocks in the west end of Tribune Channel and were home to the Kwakiutl people around 8,000 years ago. They offer a myriad of pocket shell beaches and are pure heaven for kayaking parties and the boat-bound crew.

Kwatsi Bay Marina, tucked into the northwest portion of this bay off Tribune Channel, welcomes visitors to share in the peaceful wilderness setting. Wide docks and shaded lounging areas invite fun, relaxing interaction with visiting boaters.

The Ahta River, at the head of magnificent Bond Sound, has its headwaters in British Columbia's Coast Mountains and is the only major watershed south of Cape Caution that still remains un-logged.

# FEATURED DESTINATIONS

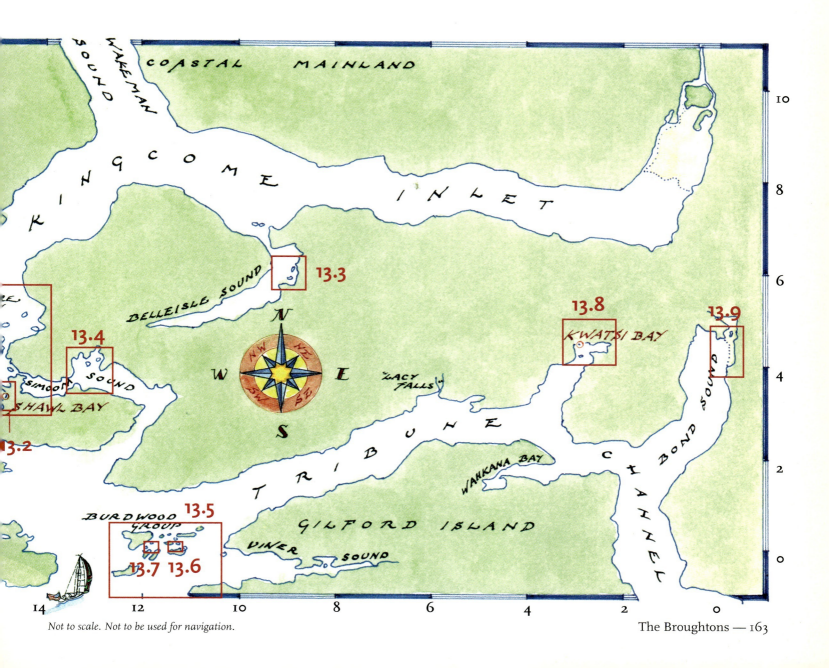

*Not to scale. Not to be used for navigation.*

# SHAWL BAY AND MOORE BAY

✿(A) 50°50.96'N 126°35.45'W
✿(B) 50°52.84'N 126°33.36'W

**CHARTS**  3515 Knight Inlet

**APPROACH**  (A) Shawl Bay from Penphrase Passage. The approach to the marina is deep and without obstructions. The pass between Gregory Island and the mainland is used frequently by small craft. The chart indicates a minimum depth of 0.6 m (2 ft) – favour the mainland shore after half-tide plus. (B) Moore Bay from Kingcome Inlet. Beware of the three major rocks that straddle the entrance.

**ANCHOR**  There is no suitable anchorage in Shawl Bay; however, in Moore Bay there are three Forestry Service buoys and numerous spots indicated in which to anchor in depths of 6–12 m (19–39 ft). Holding and protection vary.

*Note: Thief Rock is visible only by the debris floating around its peak and the foraging birds at HW. The "Hard to Miss" rocks (named by us) barely dry at HW.*

**B**ecause there are no suitable anchorages in Wakeman Sound and Kingcome Inlet, Moore Bay offers a good base for day trips up the inlets and channels, or to use as a staging point prior to embarking on the next leg of your cruise.

*Dreamspeaker* found a cozy spot to anchor below the steep cliffs, tucked in behind the "Hard to Miss" rocks. The Forestry Service dinghy dock at the head of the bay provides a chance to stretch your legs, dip your toes in the icy stream and picnic beneath Mount Plumridge. Four campsites are also available.

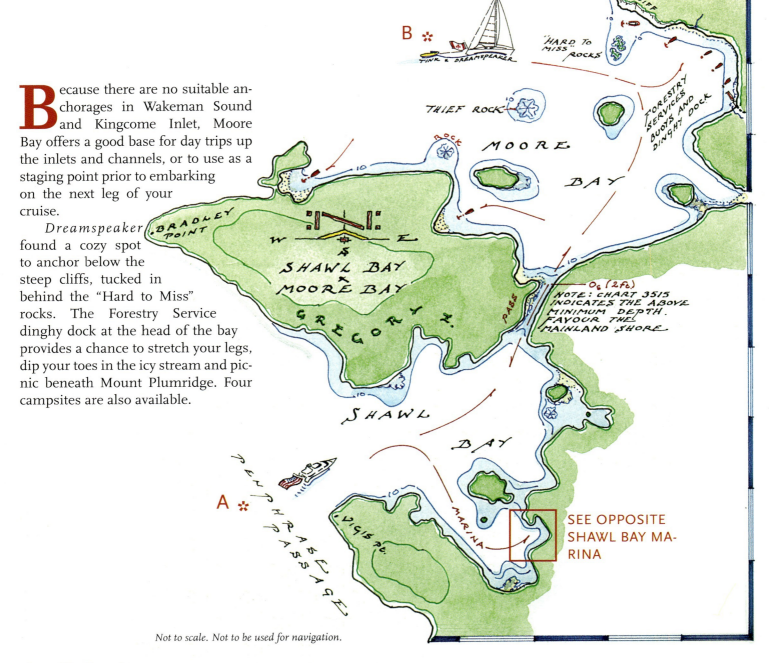

*Not to scale. Not to be used for navigation.*

# SHAWL BAY MARINA

**CHARTS**   3515, inset Knight Inlet.

**APPROACH**   The marina is tucked into the NE corner of the southern portion of the bay.

**MARINA**   SHAWL BAY MARINA monitors VHF Channel 66A, or call 250-483-4022. For updated information, visit www.shawlbaymarina.com or email shawlbaymarina@gmail.com. Water, Wi-Fi and up to 30-amp power are available on the docks. Payment by cash only – no credit cards. Floatplane and water taxi service to Port McNeill are also available.

*Look for the blue roof of the picnic tent*

The original docks in Shawl Bay were owned by the Viner Logging Company and became a historic meeting place for loggers and fishermen. Today, boaters meet up at the family-owned marina to share pot-luck suppers under the picnic tent and indulge in the all-you-can-fit-in, complimentary pancake breakfasts (served daily from 8–9 a.m.).

Relaxed and informal, floating SHAWL BAY MARINA is owned by Lorne Brown. It's a fun place to socialize while catching up on laundry and boat tasks. There can be a line out the door of the former store when Lorne's freshly baked bread and sticky buns are delivered hot from the oven. They have a limited lunch menu (from 12–2 p.m.). In July and August, the marina hosts dining events that can include seafood chowder and deep-fried turkey.

The marina also has a doggy-dedicated pocket lawn for cooped-up canines. (Please note that hounds should remain onboard when humans are dining on the picnic dock.)

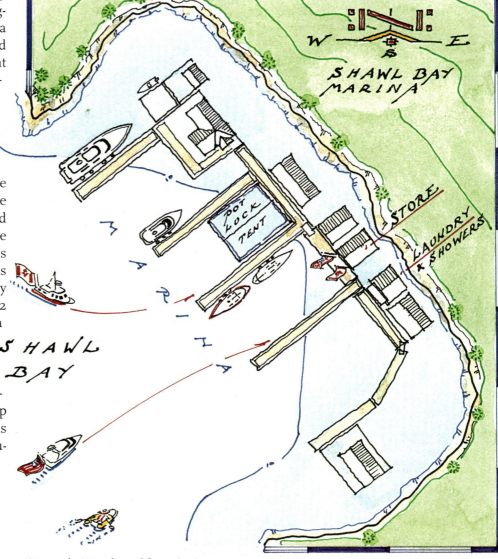

*Not to scale. Not to be used for navigation.*

# 13.3 BELLEISLE SOUND, KINGCOME INLET

✳ 50°54.57'N 126°25.63'W

**CHARTS** 3515, inset Knight Inlet.

**APPROACH** From Kingcome Inlet, between Edmond Islet and the mainland. The entrance channel and run into Belleisle Sound and anchorage is deep and without obstruction.

**ANCHOR** There's space for a few boats S of "Belle Island" (our name), off the creek's gravel shelf. Alternatively, try the one- or two-boat basin SW of "Belle Islet." Good protection from the E and SW in depths of 4–10 m (13–32 ft); the holding varies.

*Note: The anchorage is open to outflow winds from Wakeman Sound.*

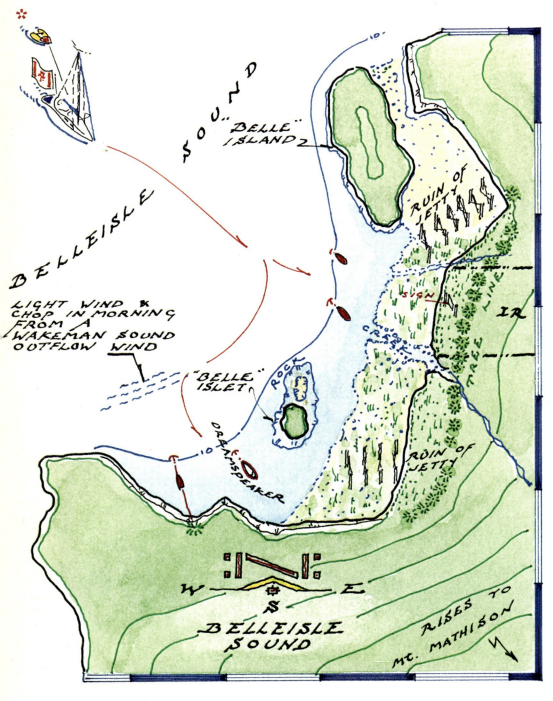

*Ruins of 1960s-era logging operations*

Fed by the glacial waters of Kingcome River six miles (9.6 km) up the inlet, the converging waters at the junction of Wakeman Sound and Kingcome Inlet take on a mystic, milky-green hue. Seeking refuge from the fog and rain, we slipped through the narrow, steep-sided entrance into Belleisle Sound, a mist-shrouded hideaway that turned out to be one of the most spectacular anchorages in the area.

Backed by mighty Mount Mathison, with Mount Prescott to the west and the conical-shaped mounds of Craig Hills to the north, we anchored in a spot behind "Belle Islet" and were lulled to sleep by the soothing sound of a small waterfall at the mouth of the creek. For the true story of "Dad McKay," who lived in a big, hollow cedar stump in Belleisle Sound, read Bill Proctor's *Full Moon, Flood Tide.*

*The steep rock bluffs dive deep into Tribune Channel*

# 13.4 SIMOOM SOUND

✿ 50°51.44'N 126°30.64'W

**CHARTS** 3515, inset Simoom Sound.
**APPROACH** The entrance to Simoom Sound is deep and without obstructions. Bald Mountain dominates the N shore. The approach waypoint is off Hannant Point. The recommended anchorages are to the N and E.

**ANCHOR** As indicated in McIntosh Bay, which appears a little gloomy, and the coves to the E, behind Hannant Point. The islets and rock clusters have deep water all around, and the challenge is to find good anchoring depths while avoiding the unmarked rocks.

Stunning Simoom Sound, with its big features and fantastic scenery, is dominated by the mask-like, black-granite face of Bald Mountain. Although the sound appears calm, strong winds will sometimes find their way in and ruffle its waters.

Cruising through the peaceful waters of the sound today, it's hard to imagine that between the early 1900s and the late 1930s (when the whole camp moved to Little Simoom Sound) this was a well-populated area with scheduled visits from the Union Steamship Company. Boat Day was a big event: the freight/passenger boat visited once a week heading north, then returned two days later on its southbound journey. A store, post office, blacksmith (to take care of the logging horses) and small school provided everything that the loggers and their families needed in the wilderness.

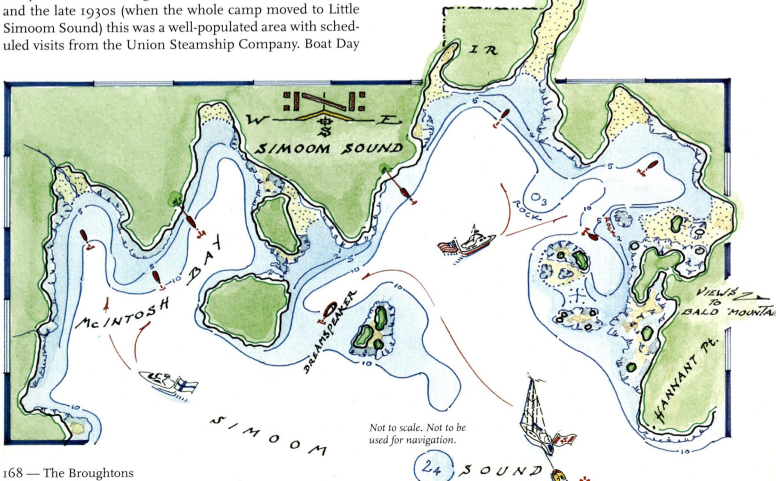

*Not to scale. Not to be used for navigation.*

*Mirror-calm in Simoom Sound*

*East of "Twin Rocks" in the Burdwood Group*

# 13.5 THE BURDWOOD GROUP

✳ (A) 50°47.43'N 126° 30.17'W
✳ (B) 50°47.70'N 126° 27.26'W

**CHARTS** 3515, with caution.

**APPROACH** (A) At LW from Raleigh Passage – favour the W shore at the entrance between the two islets. (B) From Hornet Passage – note the islet omitted on chart 3515. The position as indicated is courtesy of a CHS aerial photograph. The channel lies between the two islets.

**ANCHOR** The main anchorage in a typical southwesterly wind is N of the uncharted islet; however, in an easterly wind it is untenable. We did explore two one-boat spots, "Twin Beaches" and "Twin Islets" (named by us), which provided shelter during an easterly wind.

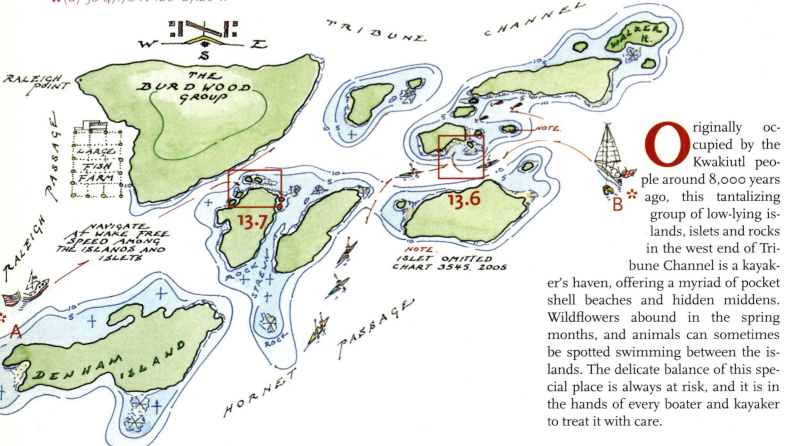

Originally occupied by the Kwakiutl people around 8,000 years ago, this tantalizing group of low-lying islands, islets and rocks in the west end of Tribune Channel is a kayaker's haven, offering a myriad of pocket shell beaches and hidden middens. Wildflowers abound in the spring months, and animals can sometimes be spotted swimming between the islands. The delicate balance of this special place is always at risk, and it is in the hands of every boater and kayaker to treat it with care.

# "TWIN BEACHES," 13.6
# BURDWOOD GROUP

**ANCHOR**  To the W of the rock and shell cluster with a stern line, or anchor ashore. The pool formed by the beach and rocky outcrop gives adequate protection from the E.

The most popular camping spot in the group, "Twin Beaches" has a glorious white-shell beach for swimming and is the site of one of the six or seven First Nations villages in the Burdwood Group. Just across the channel from the west-facing beach is the site of a unique and significant monument to the area's ancient ab-original history. Ably described in Bill Proctor's *Full Moon, Flood Tide* (see page 188), it is worth locating the trail that leads to where a large, culturally modified red cedar stands proudly in the dense forest.

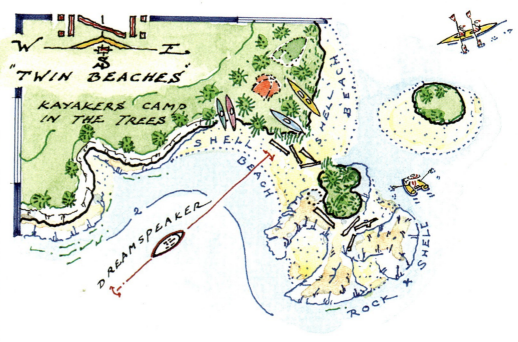

# "TWIN ROCKS," 13.7
# BURDWOOD GROUP

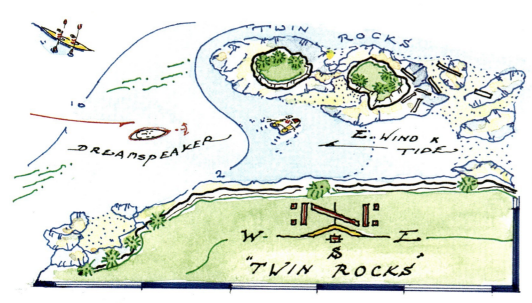

**ANCHOR**  Approach from the W between the two kelp patches. Anchor as indicated – the tide and E wind will keep you steady. In a SW wind take a stern line to the outer rock to keep the boat from swinging.

"Twin Rocks" (named by us) is scattered with small shell beaches, sun-bleached driftwood, grassy knolls, mussel-encrusted rocks and tidal pools – pure heaven for the boat-bound brood and the kid at heart.

✿50°51.69'N 126°14.98'W

**CHARTS** 3515.

**APPROACH** From Tribune Channel, Kwatsi Bay is deep and without obstructions. The run into the inner cove should be made to the E of the islet that lies off the W shore.

**ANCHOR** As indicated; this is a deepwater, stern-to anchoring alternative with swinging room on the 10-m (32-ft) contour in the far E corner.

**MARINA** KWATSI BAY MARINA monitors Channel 66A, or email kwatsibay@kwatsibay.com. You may also leave cellular messages at 250-949-1384. Wi-Fi, shower facilities and treated water are available on the dock. No power. Reservations necessary in July and August.

KWATSI BAY MARINA, tucked into the northwest portion of this dramatic bay, is a successful, family-run business. Owners Max and Anca welcome visitors to share in their peaceful wilderness setting. The bay itself is a deep bowl created by the surrounding, steep-sided mountains interspersed with mini-waterfalls and magnificent views out to the south; you will often be rewarded with a visit from whales.

Wide docks and shaded lounging areas invite interaction with fellow boaters and the owners, as this is their home. The daily five-o'clock happy hour will often turn into a jovial pot-luck supper.

Be sure to visit the 1,000-year-old cedar tree at Watson Cove or dinghy, then hike, to the nearby waterfall.

KWATSI BAY MARINA

A GREAT PLACE TO RENDEZVOUS, GREET OLD FRIENDS AND MAKE NEW ONES

*Note: The gift store carries works by West Coast painters, carvers, potters, authors, and jewellery designers.*

"INNER COVE" KWATSI BAY

MINK WHALES

IMPORETTO

ROCKS

ISLET

TINK & DREAMSPEAKER

KWATSI BAY

*Friendly Kwatsi Bay Marina*

❀50°51.64'N 126°10.46'W

CHARTS  3515.

APPROACH  Without obstruction. The head of Bond Sound is deep with no protected anchorage.

ANCHOR  Temporary. (1) As per sailboat *Shaunsea* (in illustration), tucked in close behind a small outcrop of rocks, which they suggest may give some protection from the S. (2) *Dreamspeaker* explored a rocky promontory in the N, off the Ahta River delta. Reasonable protection from an outflow wind, but no protection from the SW.

*Idyllic sand-and-shell beach, Bond Sound*

A lovely strip of fine-sand beach is etched with sun-bleached shell fragments, where Bond Sound meets the Ahta River mouth. From here you can beach your dinghy and climb along the seaweed-covered rocks to view the abundant wildlife in the shallows of the river delta.

With its headwaters in British Columbia's Coast Mountains, the healthy, nine-mile-long (14.5 km) Ahta River is the only major watershed south of Cape Caution that still remains un-logged. The surrounding old-growth forest provides habitat for endangered animals, including a safe nesting environment for bald eagles, certain owl species and a huge variety of wildlife.

The Ahta River Valley is reputed to be one of the most beautiful settings you could ever wish to visit and encompasses an unspoiled and diverse ecosystem. The area is prime grizzly-bear habitat and is also home to otter, beaver and many species of wildfowl and songbirds.

*Cautionary Note: Be aware of the extremely steep drop-off in both anchorages – a stern line ashore is highly recommended if you plan to overnight or leave your boat at any time.*

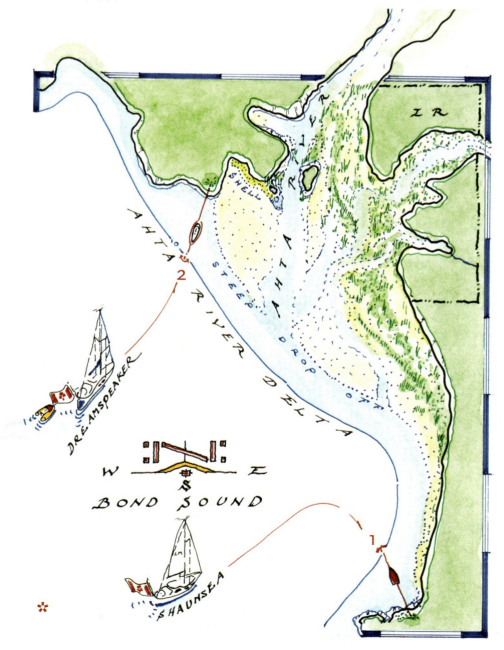

*Dwarfed by the Coast mountain range, a tug and boom head west in Knight Inlet*

Chapter 14

# KNIGHT INLET, LAGOON COVE TO CHATHAM CHANNEL

# Chapter 14

# KNIGHT INLET, LAGOON COVE TO CHATHAM CHANNEL

**TIDES** – *Volume 6, Canadian Tide and Current Tables*
Reference Port – Alert Bay
Secondary Ports – Glendale Cove, Lagoon Cove

**WEATHER**
Weather Station – WX1 162.55 MHZ
Area – Queen Charlotte Strait, Johnstone Strait
Reporting Station – Alert Bay

**CURRENTS**
Reference Station – Seymour Narrows
Secondary Station – Chatham Channel

*An evening potluck feast at Lagoon Cove Marina*

**CAUTIONARY NOTES:** *Knight Inlet may lure the cruising boater with its turquoise waters, however, it has a reputation equal to Johnstone Strait and it's not the place to be when bad weather is forecast.*

*The waters in Chatham Channel may not be turbulent, but even 5 knots of current spells caution. If a log boom or other vessels are in the channel, do not be tempted to overtake – stay back and in line with the range markers.*

There are few good anchorages in this part of Tribune Channel, which makes the protected anchorage off Kumlah Island a pleasant surprise.

Nearing Knight Inlet, the waters of Tribune Channel and Sargeaunt Passage take on a muted turquoise hue and we were enticed into the pass by a group of playful porpoises blowing at the entrance. Although Sargeaunt Passage is deep and steep-sided, it has the best anchorage in the area and provides a staging point for the trip up Knight Inlet to Glendale Cove.

The section of water east of Hoeya Head to Glendale Cove offers no shelter from easterly or westerly winds but with a strong westerly in your favour, you can enjoy an exhilarating sail up Knight Inlet into the cove and small anchorage.

With fuel, water and power available on the docks, a laid-back, easygoing ambience and a legendary happy hour and potluck tradition, LAGOON COVE MARINA is a destination on the Broughtons' social cruising chart. The industrious owners, Jean Barber and the late Bill Barber, have been successful in turning their hospitable marina into an extension of their own pleasant boating experiences. It's a kid-friendly place where cruising families and parties of boaters can tie up for a day or two to hike the old logging roads, catch up with friends and make new acquaintances.

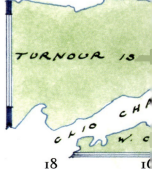

# FEATURED DESTINATIONS

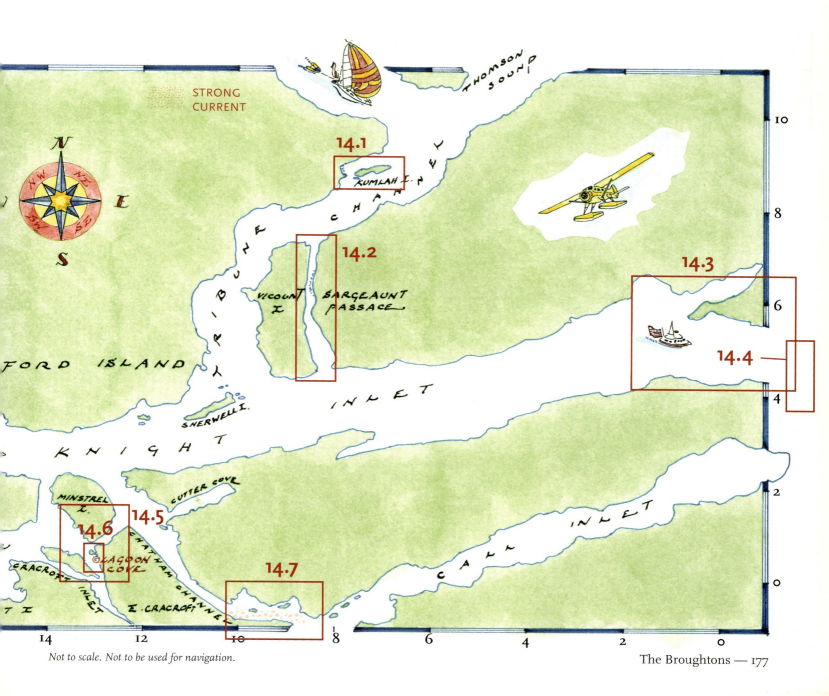

*Not to scale. Not to be used for navigation.*

# 14.1 KUMLAH ISLAND, TRIBUNE CHANNEL

❀ (A) 50°44.69'N 126°09.39'W
❀ (B) 50°44.27'N 126°10.52'W

*Views up Thompson Sound to snow-topped Mount Everard*

**CHARTS**   3515.

**APPROACH**   (A) From the E, the run in from Tribune Channel is free of obstructions. (B) From the S, favour the Kumlah Island shore to clear the reef off the tip of Gilford Island.

**ANCHOR**   In the centre channel within the 5-m contour; there is a charted minimum depth of 4.6 m (15 ft). The holding is good over a gravel rocky bottom, where your boat will swing to the current. An alternative anchorage can be found off the gravel beach, with a stern line ashore. A mussel-encrusted mooring buoy lies on the 10-m (32-ft) contour – use at your own discretion.

*Note: The current flows in a clockwise direction around Kumlah Island, on both the flood and ebb tides.*

*Clouds washed by the evening light*

There are very few good anchorages in this part of Tribune Channel. Kumlah Island appears to be the meeting point of the current around Gilford Island and kept *Dreamspeaker* steady while at anchor. With remarkable views up Thompson Sound to snow-capped Mount Everard, this calm, sunny spot allowed us to dry out the boat and bedding after many days of rain.

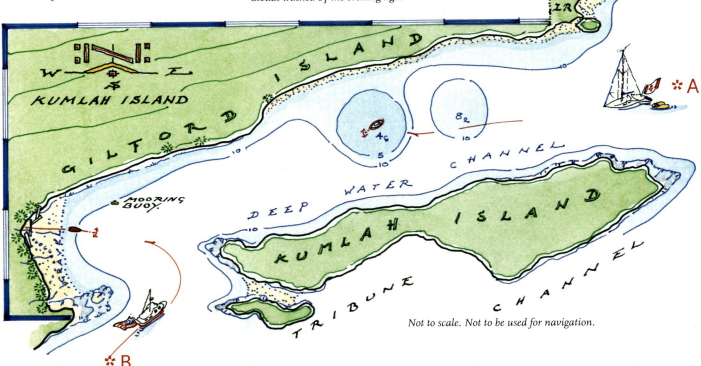

*Not to scale. Not to be used for navigation.*

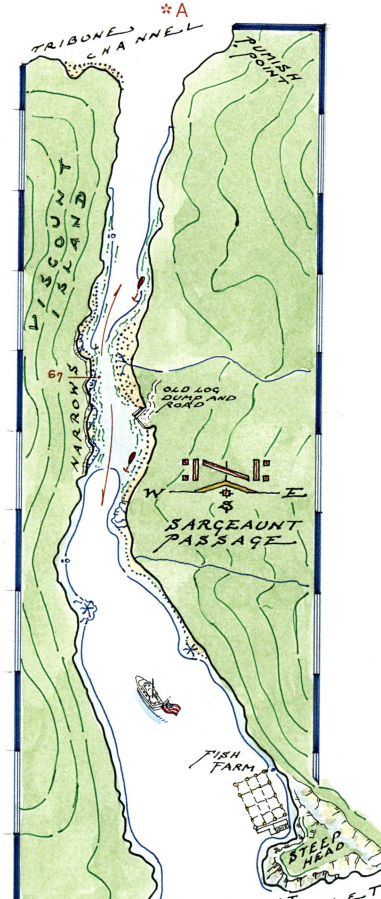

✳ (A) 50°42.89'N 126°11.74'W
✳ (B) 50°40.00'N 126°11.28'W

CHARTS   3515.

APPROACH   The passage between Viscount Island and the mainland is narrow, kelp-fringed and steep-sided – favour the Viscount Island shore; this detour is used frequently by pleasure boats and small commercial craft. The passage is deep, with a minimum charted depth of 6.7 m (22 ft) at the narrows.

ANCHOR   Two small bights with good shelter and anchoring depths of 5–10 m (16–32 ft) can be found N and S of the gravel-beach delta that protrudes W, from the mainland shore.

*A fish-farming operation nestled under Steep Head*

Although Sargeaunt Passage is deep and steep-sided, it has the best anchorage in this area, providing a staging point for a trip up Knight Inlet to Glendale Cove. Once home to a large, early-1900s cannery and – until quite recently – logging operations, all that remains is a float and a logging road. If walking the pooch, let the bears know that you are around.

*Not to scale. Not to be used for navigation.*

# 14.3 KNIGHT INLET, HOEYA HEAD TO GLENDALE COVE

❀(A) 50°40.47'N 126°01.51'W
❀(B) 50°41.42'N 125°44.10'W

CHARTS 3515.

APPROACH  Although this portion of Knight Inlet is deep, straight and without obstruction, it is also notorious for dangerous sea conditions when the wind is against the current. Plan your trip with the wind and current in your favour.

*Note: Shelter from the E can be found in Hoeya Sound, but the portion from E of Hoeya Head to Glendale Cove offers no shelter from either E or W winds.*

With a strong westerly wind in our favour, we enjoyed an exhilarating sail up Knight Inlet, arriving in record time at Macdonald Point. The Knight Inlet Lodge in Glendale Cove is private and has no facilities for visiting boats. If you wish to view bears feeding on the Glendale River estuary, please observe the international protocol and keep all human (and wild-animal) stress levels to a minimum (see page 13).

*Note: If a gale-force westerly or outflow wind is forecast, Glendale Cove is not the place to be! Knight Inlet can be as treacherous as Johnstone Strait in a wind-against-current situation.*

*Not to scale. Not to be used for navigation.*

# GLENDALE COVE, KNIGHT INLET

**CHARTS**  3515.

**APPROACH**  From Knight Inlet, rounding Macdonald Point, head SE. Knight Inlet Lodge is highly conspicuous on the eastern shore.

**ANCHOR**  Glendale Cove is deep and shelves rapidly – the challenge is finding suitable anchoring depths. We anchored *Dreamspeaker* in the one-boat bight off the river's mouth, which shallows rapidly. There is moderate protection from the W and the anchorage is open to outflow winds. Holding is good in sand, on the 10-m (32-ft) contour.

*Rounding Macdonald Point, Glendale Cove opens to the south*

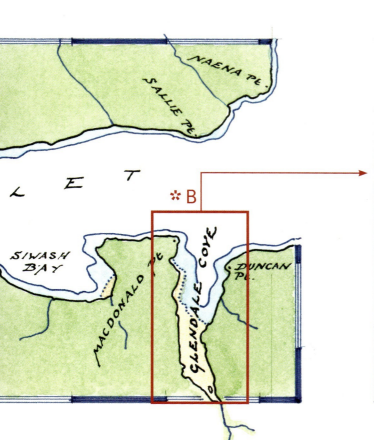

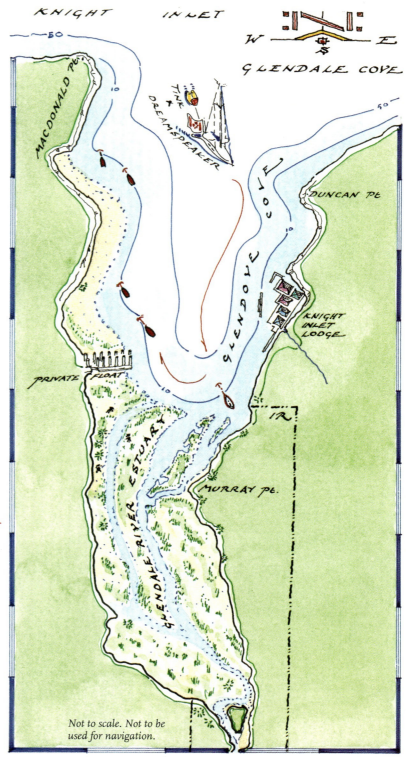

*Not to scale. Not to be used for navigation.*

✻ (A) 50°36.80'N 126°18.15'W
✻ (B) 50°36.66'N 126°18.17'W
✻ (C) 50°36.23'N 126°19.49'W

**CHART**   3545.

**APPROACH**   (A) Sailcone Wilderness Fishing Lodge (next to the former Minstrel Island Public Wharf), from the E. There is no public access or moorage at the lodge. It is reserved for guests only. (B) The Blow Hole (a channel between Minstrel Island and East Cracroft Island). From the E out of Chatham Channel or from the W in Clio Channel. The Blow Hole is kelp-infested but regularly navigated by pleasure craft and small commercial vessels. Favour the Minstrel Island shore and stay N of the rock, as indicated. (C) Lagoon Cove,

East Cracroft Island. From the head of Clio Channel between Perley and Farquharson Island. The run in is clear and free of obstructions.

**ANCHOR**   In "Otters Cove" (our name), SE of The Blow Hole. This anchorage provides moderate protection for one or two boats. Anchorage depths within Lagoon Cove are over 10 m (32 ft) and well protected. In settled weather, moderate protection can be found at the head of the entrance to Cracroft Inlet in 6–8 m (19–26 ft). Both anchorages have good holding in mud.

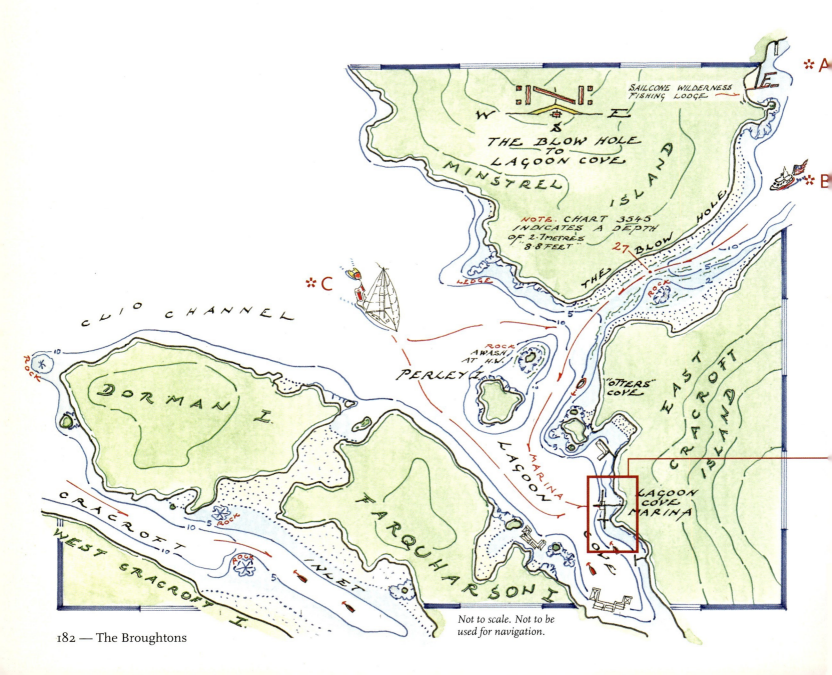

*Not to scale. Not to be used for navigation.*

# LAGOON COVE MARINA

*Extensive moorage at Lagoon Cove Marina*

**CHART** 3545.

**APPROACH** The marina lies on the eastern shore. Groups of float homes are situated across from the marina and at the head of the cove.

**MARINA** This well-maintained marina provides year-round transient moorage, 15- and 30-amp power on the docks, Wi-Fi, showers and washrooms, plus a place to have fun. They don't take reservations, so plan to arrive by early afternoon, as the marina fills up quickly. To ease moorage planning, call on VHF Channel 66A with your estimated arrival time.

**FUEL** At the marina. Diesel, gas and propane are available. Ice, oil, charts, fishing supplies and other small but important essentials can be obtained at the marina office.

The relaxed and good-natured ambience at LAGOON COVE MARINA makes it a destination on the Broughtons' social cruising chart. (Be sure to enjoy the legendary happy-hour bucket of prawns on the deck at the historic toolshed.)

Owners Bill and Jean Barber wanted to create a hospitable marina that was an extension of their own pleasant boating experiences—a kid-friendly place to tie up for a day or so, get off the boat and catch up with old friends or make new ones.

With the historic marina came a marine ways, a workshop filled with marine artifacts and a small cottage surrounded by a variety of fruit trees and flowers. Many years of hard work, together with time and labour given by their loyal clients and friends, has made it possible for boating visitors to enjoy all the Barbers built, including dog-friendly hiking trails through the forest. (Note that owners are responsible for their dogs at all times.) Sadly, Bill Barber passed away in 2013—his fireside stories will be missed.

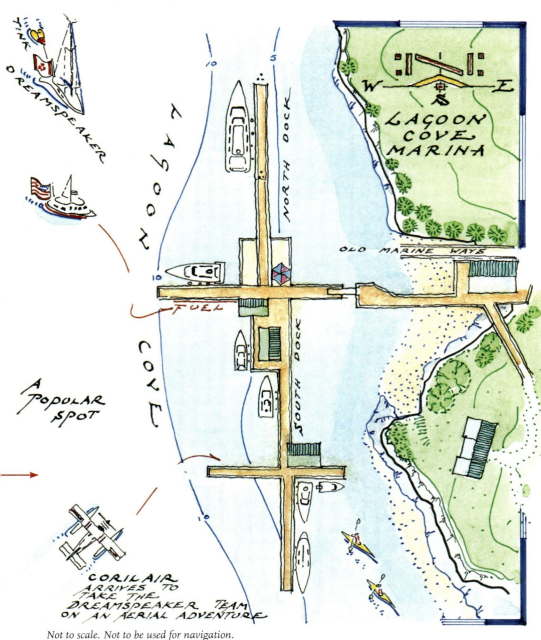

*Not to scale. Not to be used for navigation.*

*Lagoon Cove Marina: Pop over to Vancouver Island or take a Broughtons floatplane adventure with Corilair*

# CHATHAM CHANNEL 14.7

**CHART** 3564 inset detail.

**APPROACH** (A) From the W, aligning the boat to the easterly range (leading mark) off Ray Point. (B) From the E, after rounding Root Point and off the port-hand mark, aligning the boat to the westerly range (leading mark).

*Note:* Be aware that the E end of Chatham Channel is shallow and requires your boat to be kept on a straight and steady course. The strong, swift current of between 5–7 knots runs parallel to the East Cracroft shore on both the flood and the ebb tides. Although the channel is full of kelp, the central pass is easily apparent.

## CURRENTS

Reference Station – Seymour Narrows
Secondary Station – Chatham Channel

*Note:* Do not overtake another boat while in the channel, whatever your speed; concentrate on lining up the markers. We ended our lovely Broughtons cruise at Blind Channel Resort and found that Chatham Channel wasn't as restricted as it was rumoured.

❈ (A) 50°35.00'N 126°14.73'W
❈ (B) 50°34.73'N 126°12.31'W

RANGE

ON

COURSE

IF

ALIGNED

*Looking astern, west. The craft is turning to align the range.*

*Looking forward, east. The craft is on the range*

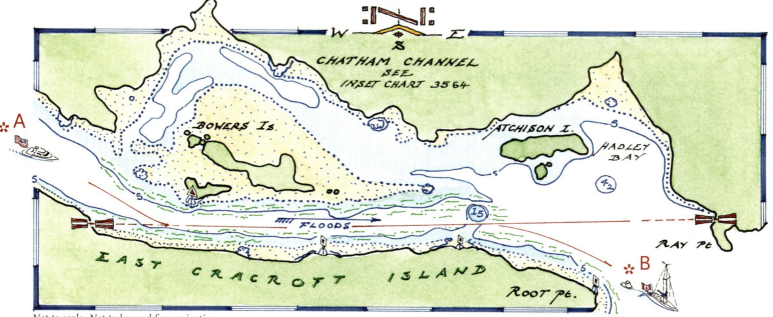

*Not to scale. Not to be used for navigation.*

*Lone sailboat on the last of the evening wind approaches the entrance to Echo Bay*

Chapter 15

# SELECTED READING & INDEX

# SELECTED READING

Barber, Bill and Jean. *Lagoon Cove Marina. A Bit of History and a Book of Recipes.* Kearney, NE: Morris Press Cookbooks, 2004.

Baron, Nancy and John Acorn. *Birds of Coastal British Columbia.* Edmonton: Lone Pine Publishing, 1997.

*BC Marine Parks Guide.* 2nd Edition. Vancouver: OP Publishing, 2005.

Blanchet, M. Wylie. *The Curve of Time.* Sidney, BC: Gray's Publishing Ltd., 1977.

Campbell River Museum Society. *The Raincoast Kitchen: Coastal Cuisine with a Dash of History.* Madeira Park, BC: Harbour Publishing, 1997.

Chappell, John. *Cruising Beyond Desolation Sound. Channels and Anchorages from the Yuculta Rapids to Cape Caution. Revised Edition.* Surrey, BC: Naikoon Marine, 1987 (out of print 2006).

Clark, Lewis. *Wild Flowers of the Sea Coast in the Pacific Northwest.* Madeira Park, BC: Harbour Publishing, 2004.

Day, Beth. *Grizzlies in their Backyard.* Surrey, BC: Heritage House, 1994.

Douglass, Don and Reanne Hemingway-Douglass. *Exploring the South Coast of British Columbia. Gulf Islands and Desolation Sound to Port Hardy and Blunden Harbour.* 2nd Edition. Anacortes, WA: FineEdge, 1999.

Drushka, Ken. *Working in the Woods: A History of Logging on the West Coast.* Madeira Park, BC: Harbour Publishing, 1992.

Hadley, Michael. *God's Little Ships: A History of the Columbia Coast Mission.* Madeira Park, BC: Harbour Publishing, 1995.

Hale, Robert. *Waggoner Cruising Guide.* Bellevue, WA: Weatherly Press. Updated and Published Annually.

Harold, Hughina. *Totem Poles and Tea.* 2nd Edition. Surrey, BC: Heritage House, 2006.

Henry, Tom. *The Good Company: An Affectionate History of the Union Steamships.* Madeira Park, BC: Harbour Publishing, 1994.

Hill, Beth. *Guide to Indian Rock Carvings of the Pacific Northwest Coast.* Surrey, BC: Hancock House Publishers, 1984.

_____. *Upcoast Summers.* Ganges, BC: Nunaga Publishing, 1975.

Hoar, David and Noreen Rudd. *Cooks Afloat! Gourmet Cooking on the Move.* Madeira Park, BC: Harbour Publishing, 2001.

Hume, Stephen. *A Stain Upon the Sea: West Coast Salmon Farming.* Madeira Park, BC: Harbour Publishing, 2004.

Iglauer, Edith. *Fishing with John.* Madeira Park, BC: Harbour Publishing, 1992.

Kennedy, Liv. *Coastal Villages.* Madeira Park, BC: Harbour Publishing, 1991.

Lowman Carey, Betty. *Bijaboji: North to Alaska by Oar.* Madeira Park, BC: Harbour Publishing, 2004.

McAllister, Ian and Karen. *The Great Bear Rainforest: Canada's Forgotten Coast.* Madeira Park, BC: Harbour Publishing, 1997.

McKerville, Hugh. *The Salmon People.* Sidney, BC: Gray's Publishing, 1967.

Maximchuk, Yvonne. *Drawn to Sea: Paintbrush to Chainsaw – Carving out a Life on BC's Rugged Raincoast.* Halfmoon Bay, BC: Caitlin Press, 2013.

Morton, Alexandra. *Beyond the Whales: The Photographs and Passions of Alexandra Morton.* Victoria, BC: Touchwood Editions, 2004.

_____. *Listening to the Whales: What the Orcas Have Taught Us.* New York, NY: Ballantine Books, 2004.

Morton, Alexandra and Bill Proctor. *Heart of the Raincoast: A Life Story.* Victoria, BC: TouchWood Editions, 2005.

Pacific Yachting's *Marina Guide and Boater's Blue Pages: The Complete Guide to BC Marinas and Marine Services.* Magazine Supplement (January Issue), updated and published annually by *Pacific Yachting* Magazine.

Proctor, Bill and Yvonne Maximchuk. *Full Moon, Flood Tide: Bill Proctor's Raincoast.* Madeira Park, BC: Harbour Publishing, 2003.

Proctor, Bill and Yvonne Maximchuk. *Tide Rips and Back Eddies: Bill Proctor's Tales of Blackfish Sound.* Madeira Park, BC: Harbour Publishing, 2015.

Spilsbury, Jim. *Spilsbury's Album: Photographs and Reminiscences of the BC Coast.* Madeira Park, BC: Harbour Publishing, 1990.

Thommasen, Harvey and Kevin Huchings. *Birds of the Raincoast: Habits and Habitat.* Madeira Park, BC: Harbour Publishing, 2004.

Turner, Nancy J. *Food Plants of Coastal First Peoples.* Vancouver: UBC Press, 1995.

van Schyndel, Nikki. *Becoming Wild. Living the Primitive Life on a West Coast Island.* Halfmoon Bay, BC: Caitlin Press, 2012.

Vassilopoulos, Peter. *North of Desolation Sound.* Seagraphic Publications Limited, 2003.

Walbran, John T. *British Columbia Coast Names, 1592–1902.* Vancouver: Douglas & McIntyre, 1971.

Wastell Norris, Pat. *High Boats: A Century of Salmon Remembered.* Madeira Park, BC: Harbour Publishing, 2003.

White, Howard and Jim Spilsbury. *Spilsbury's Coast: Pioneer Years in the Wet West.* Madeira Park, BC: Harbour Publishing, 1991.

_____. *The Accidental Airline.* Spilsbury's QCA. Madeira Park, BC: Harbour Publishing, 1994.

Wild, Paula. *Sointula: Island Utopia.* Madeira Park, BC: Harbour Publishing, 1995.

Williams, Judith. *Two Wolves at the Dawn of Time: Kingcome Inlet Pictographs, 1893–1998.* Vancouver BC: New Star Books, 2001.

_____. *Clam Gardens, Aboriginal Mariculture on Canada's West Coast.* Vancouver, BC: New Star Books, 2006.

Wood, Charles E. *Charlie's Charts – North to Alaska: Victoria BC to Glacier Bay, Alaska.* Surrey, BC: Charlie's Charts, 2003.

# INDEX

# OTHER DREAMSPEAKER PRODUCTS

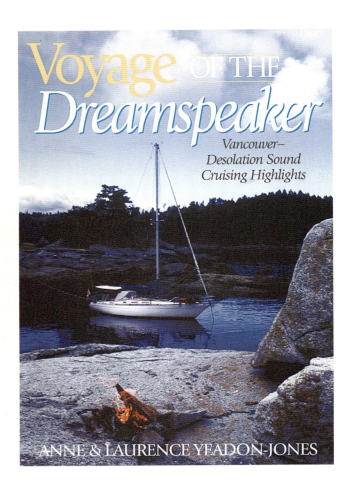

## VOYAGE OF THE DREAMSPEAKER
### Anne & Laurence Yeadon-Jones

**V**oyage of the Dreamspeaker is a personal record of three magical and balmy months from early July to late September when Anne and Laurence cruised the beautiful coast of BC aboard their sailboat *Dreamspeaker*, with *Tink* their faithful dinghy in tow. Their voyage took them from the cosmopolitan city of Vancouver to the laid-back anchorages of Howe Sound, the delights of the Sunshine Coast, warm-water swimming in the lakes of Desolation Sound and the majesty of Toba Inlet. The authors had always dreamed of taking an unhurried journey with their Dreamspeaker guides in hand to revisit favourite haunts that they had discovered during their fifteen years of adventuring and recording. This personal cruising companion will also give readers a special insight into a number of new experiences that Anne has smoothly interwoven with stories and discoveries from earlier journeys among the islands and along a coastline that they have grown to love. This coast has won their hearts.

*Voyage of the Dreamspeaker* is published by Harbour Publishing at www.harbourpublishing.com and distributed in the US by Fine Edge www.fineedge.com. Personalized books and guides are also available from the authors' website at www.dream speaker.ca.

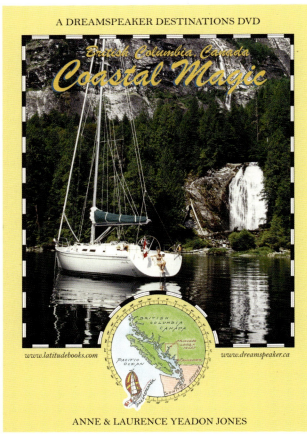

## A DREAMSPEAKER DESTINATIONS DVD
### Anne & Laurence Yeadon-Jones

**D**reamspeaker Cruising Guide authors Anne and Laurence Yeadon-Jones have added *A Dreamspeaker Destinations* DVD titled *Coastal Magic* to their series of colourful and informative guides.

With Anne and Laurence as your hosts, this scenic DVD takes you on a 5-day dream cruise from the city of Vancouver, up the Sunshine Coast to Jervis Inlet and magical Princess Louisa Marine Park, backed by the powerful beauty of Chatterbox Falls.

The 5-day cruising itinerary includes the authors' favourite anchorages and marinas en route to Princess Louisa Inlet: Snug Cove on Bowen Island, colourful Gibsons Landing, Halfmoon Bay, Simson Marine Park and the white sand beaches of Buccaneer Bay, popular Smuggler Cove Marine Park, Secret Cove and historic Pender Harbour.

*A Dreamspeaker Destinations* DVD – *Coastal Magic* – is available worldwide at www.dreamspeaker.ca.

# SIX PLANNING CHARTS
## Hand-drawn and Watercolour by Laurence Yeadon-Jones

Following requests from numerous boaters, Laurence Yeadon-Jones spent over two years developing six handy Passage Planning Charts to complement his and Anne's Dreamspeaker Cruising Guide Series. His practical approach was to build a set of workable charts layered from current chart mapping data that included NOAA, CHS and Admiralty Charts. Initially hand-drawn at a scale of 1:200,000 each chart was reduced equally to ensure that the final product was of equal scale, and when overlapped, created a consistent representation of the Inside Passage from Puget Sound, WA, to the Broughtons, BC.

Sized at 12 x 17 inches and sold individually or as a set of six, these passage planning charts are available online at www.dreamspeaker.ca.

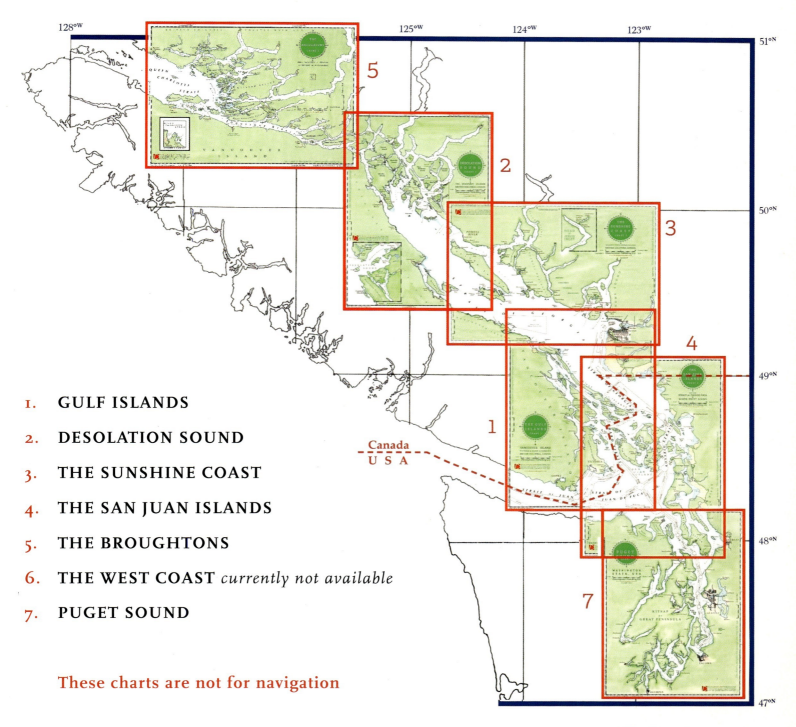

1. **GULF ISLANDS**

2. **DESOLATION SOUND**

3. **THE SUNSHINE COAST**

4. **THE SAN JUAN ISLANDS**

5. **THE BROUGHTONS**

6. **THE WEST COAST** *currently not available*

7. **PUGET SOUND**

**These charts are not for navigation**

# THE DREAMSPEAKER SERIES

## BY ANNE & LAURENCE YEADON-JONES

**A** COMPREHENSIVE SERIES OF CRUISING GUIDES TO THE COASTAL WATERS OF THE PACIFIC NORTHWEST

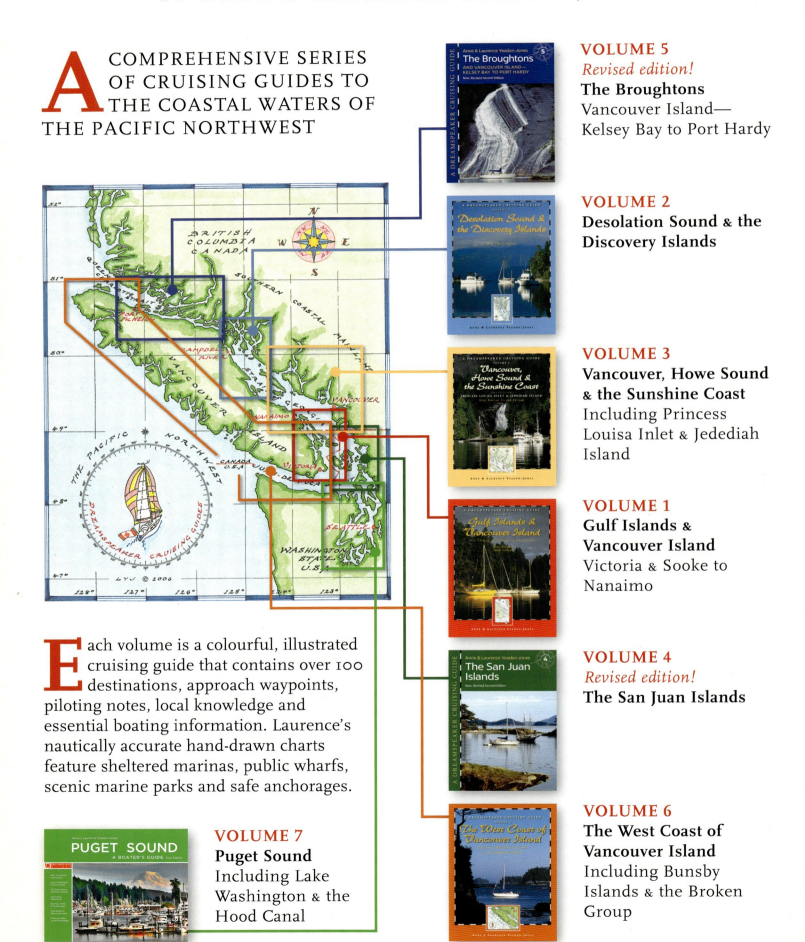

**E**ach volume is a colourful, illustrated cruising guide that contains over 100 destinations, approach waypoints, piloting notes, local knowledge and essential boating information. Laurence's nautically accurate hand-drawn charts feature sheltered marinas, public wharfs, scenic marine parks and safe anchorages.

### VOLUME 5
*Revised edition!*
**The Broughtons**
Vancouver Island—
Kelsey Bay to Port Hardy

### VOLUME 2
**Desolation Sound & the Discovery Islands**

### VOLUME 3
**Vancouver, Howe Sound & the Sunshine Coast**
Including Princess Louisa Inlet & Jedediah Island

### VOLUME 1
**Gulf Islands & Vancouver Island**
Victoria & Sooke to Nanaimo

### VOLUME 4
*Revised edition!*
**The San Juan Islands**

### VOLUME 7
**Puget Sound**
Including Lake Washington & the Hood Canal

### VOLUME 6
**The West Coast of Vancouver Island**
Including Bunsby Islands & the Broken Group